2.65

D0983695

INSTANT ENGLISH HANDBOOK

by

Madeline Semmelmeyer

*Former Supervisor of Languages, Chicago Public Schools,
and Lecturer in Education: Chicago Teachers Review School,
Roosevelt University, and National College of Education.*

and

Donald O. Bolander

Director of Education, Career Institute

An Authoritative Guide and Reference

on GRAMMAR, CORRECT USAGE, and PUNCTUATION

Published by

CAREER INSTITUTE

555 East Lange Street   Mundelein, Illinois 60060

Instant English Handbook

a quick, handy, reference guide
especially prepared for the use of

Secretaries	Businessmen
Authors	Typists
Proofreaders	High School and
Teachers	College Students
Clergymen	Foreign-born
Reporters	Printers
Copywriters	Editors
Executives	Parents
Correspondents	Librarians

and for those in other occupations or activities where
a knowledge of grammar, correct usage, and
punctuation is essential.

ISBN 0-911744-03-7

© Copyright 1968 by
CAREER INSTITUTE, INC.
Library of Congress Catalog Card No. 68-57782
This Handbook is an abridgement of *Practical English*,
copyright 1968, 1965, 1955 by Career Institute, Inc.
Printed in the United States of America

EH-74-2

Purpose of This Book

No matter what your natural abilities or talents, no matter how expert you may be in certain fields, you are judged not only by what you know but how correctly and effectively you speak and write. Either in social life or in business, if you make glaring mistakes in English... if you can't carry on a correctly worded conversation or business discussion... if your writing ability is only poor to average, it's embarrassing both to you and to friends or associates who are exposed to your mistakes.

The main purpose of this *Instant English Handbook* is to provide a quick, easy-to-use guide to grammar, correct usage, and punctuation. It is intended for use in the business office, in the home, and in school. Secretaries, writers, teachers, and students, will find it especially useful.

The *Handbook* is divided into 25 sections or chapters each covering an important aspect or problem in English. The book is designed so that it may be used as a step-by-step text in English courses and by those who need a complete self-study English review. In addition, because of the comprehensive index at the end of the book, it is a complete reference handbook for day-to-day use whenever a question arises concerning English usage or punctuation.

Special Features

Short Table of Contents

Printed on the inside of both the front and back covers, the Short Table of Contents gives fast, quick reference to main sections of the Handbook.

Complete Table of Contents

Starting on page 5, is a detailed table of contents for use in finding subtopics within each chapter.

Comprehensive Index

On page 303, you will find an unusually complete index which enables you to locate easily any point on correct usage, grammar, or punctuation. Look in the index for topics such as *Capitalization, Possessive Pronouns,* or *Active Voice* when you are interested in such items. But the index also enables you to locate explanations on the usage of specific words, such as *among-between, farther-further, lay-lie, should-would, who-whom,* and many, many other troublesome words.

Clear Explanations and Examples

Throughout the book, each explanation is followed by one or more specific examples. The examples clarify the principles and rules of good English usage.

Glossary of Terms

On page 293, is a glossary which gives a brief definition of the meaning of words or terms used in describing or explaining language. Whenever you are in doubt about the meaning of a term, you can quickly find the answer by referring to this glossary.

To order extra copies of this
book, see page 320.

COMPLETE
TABLE OF CONTENTS

7

1

THE PARTS OF SPEECH

Your English is an integral part of your personality, your character, your real self. You can no more get rid of it than of your shadow. A knowledge of good English gives you poise and confidence. Its employment enables you to take your place in all circles confidently—without fear of ridicule.

A. CHARLES BABENROTH

LANGUAGE is the expression of ideas by means of words. The grammar of a language is primarily the study of the forms of words and their relationship to each other. You need to know grammar and usage if you are to speak and write correctly and if the words you use are to express our ideas most clearly and effectively.

When you put words together in a sentence, you are working in much the same way as a mechanic works when he is trying to put together a piece of machinery. Like the mechanic, you must be familiar with the parts that are needed and with the use or purpose of each part.

In dealing with language, *words* are the parts that are used to build sentences. The English language has thousands of words, but all of them fall into eight groups or classes known as the *parts of speech*. The following names have been given to the parts of speech:

Nouns   Pronouns   Verbs   Adjectives   Adverbs

Prepositions   Conjunctions   Interjections

Each group has its special work to do. *Nouns* are the names of persons, places, and things. *Pronouns* take the place of nouns. *Adjectives* and *adverbs* help express the ideas that give color and more definite meanings to nouns, verbs, and other words. *Conjunctions* are joining or connecting words.

Words, then, are the tools of communication. Like any other tool, a word may be used for different purposes at different times. For example, a word might be used as a noun in one sentence and as a verb in another sentence. Another word might be used as a preposition in one sentence and as an adverb in another sentence. All words do not have more than one use, but many words do.

The most important fact concerning any word is its *function* or use in a particular sentence. If you keep this fact in mind, you will have no difficulty in understanding the simple principles that govern the relationships of words in sentences.

NOUNS

WORDS USED AS NAMES

A noun is one of the most important words that you use when either speaking or writing. It is the word that tells what you are talking about. *A noun is a word that names something.* You have a name. I have a name. Everything that we see, or examine, or talk about must have a name. There are names for *persons, animals, places,* and *objects* that can be pointed out and recognized. There are also names for *substances, qualities, actions,* and *measures* of time or quantity. The following list includes examples of different kinds of nouns.

Persons:	soldier—Jane—friend—Englishman
Animals:	elephant—mouse—zebra—panda
Places:	home—Chicago—camp—factory
Objects:	desk—picture—typewriter—hammer
Substances:	iron—air—water—food
Qualities:	kindness—heroism—beauty—faith
Actions:	climbing—cooking—batting—reading
Measures:	year—pound—inch—bushel—day

Nouns Used in Sentences

The *soldier* is wearing his new *uniform*.

noun   noun

Chicago is a great industrial *city*.

noun   noun

Iron is a useful *metal*.

noun   noun

**A noun is a word
used as a name.**

10

PRONOUNS

SUBSTITUTES FOR NOUNS

You will often find it necessary to refer to a *name* a number of times in a single sentence. This repetition usually results in a sentence that is very awkward or monotonous. You can readily see what might happen from the following illustration:

> *Jack* went to *Jack's* closet and took out *Jack's* new suit because *Jack* was going to a dance given by *Jack's* company.

In this sentence the word *Jack* is stated five times. This awkward repetition of the word *Jack* and *Jack's* could be avoided by substituting another part of speech for these words.

> Jack went to *his* closet and took out *his* new suit because *he* was going to a dance given by *his* company.

The words *his* and *he* used in the revision of the sentence are called **pronouns.** They are substitutes for the noun *Jack.* The prefix **pro** in the word pronoun means *for.* The word **pronoun** simply means *for a noun,* or *in place of a noun.*

The underlined words in the following illustrations are pronouns. The words to which they refer are underlined twice.

Mary came to America when she was five years old.

The men forgot their tickets.

The officer blew his whistle.

A pronoun is a word used in place of a noun or a name.

Commonly Used Pronouns

You should be familiar with the pronouns in common use. For that reason a list of pronouns is a handy reference guide. Whenever you are not certain whether a word is a pronoun, refer to the following list. In a short time you will be familiar with most of them.

I	you	hers	what	all	none	somebody
my	yours	it	who	any	some	no one
mine	your	its	whose	both	several	someone
me	he	they	whom	each	other	everyone
we	his	their	this	either	another	one
our	him	theirs	that	neither	anybody	whoever
ours	she	them	these	few	everybody	whosoever
us	her	which	those	many	nobody	anyone

VERBS

ACTION AND LINKING VERBS

The **verb** is the most important part of speech. *It is the only part of speech that can make a statement about the subject.* The subject is the part of a sentence that names the person, place, or thing that is talked about. If you wanted to write or say something about *a hunter*, you could not complete your statement without the use of a verb. You must have a verb in every sentence. The following illustration will make this clear.

The hunter *shot* the deer. (The verb is the word *shot*.)

If you take the verb *shot* out of the sentence, you have left the words, *the hunter, the deer,* but you do not have a complete thought. You need a verb to state what the hunter did to the deer. When you supply a verb, you have a complete statement.

Most of the verbs in common use express **action.** The action is not always physical action like the action expressed in the sentence, *The hunter shot the deer.* In the sentence, *I solved the problem,* the meaning of the verb *solved* implies both mental and physical activity.

In the sentence, *The engineer built a bridge,* all the types of activity that went on until the bridge was completed are implied in the verb *built.* The same would be true of the verb *made* in the sentence, *The chef made a cake.* All the verbs in the following sentences express action of some kind:

The painter *decorated* the hall.

I *pricked* my finger.

The stenographer *wrote* a letter.

The president *called* a meeting.

The officer *handed* a ticket to the driver.

A small, but very important group of verbs, do not express action. The verb **to be** is the most important verb in this group. The most common forms of the verb *to be* include *is, are, was* and *were.* Since the verb *to be* does not express action, it must have another function in the sentence. With the help of some other word or words, it makes a statement about the *condition* of the subject, or the person, place, or thing that is talked about.

In the sentence, *Henry is ill,* the verb *is* does not express action of any kind, but it serves two purposes in the sentence. With the help of the word *ill* it makes a statement about the subject, *Henry.* It also serves to connect the word *ill* with *Henry.* The sentence really means *ill Henry,* but you need the verb *is* to make the statement a complete sentence. Because the verb has this connecting function, it is called a **linking verb.**

From the following illustrations, you will see that the verb *to be* with the help of some other word describes or explains the condition of the subject in some way. The verb *is* is a form of the verb *to be.*

My uncle *is* a famous surgeon. (classifies uncle as surgeon)

Mother *is* very happy. (describes the condition of mother)

This cabinet *is* a television set. (identifies the cabinet)

Her dress *is* beautiful. (describes dress)

A number of other verbs are often used in the same way as the verb *to be* is used in the preceding illustrations. The point to remember is that not all verbs express action. Some verbs have a *linking* function. In defining a verb you must include both functions.

**A verb is a word which expresses
action, condition, or state of being.**

VERB PHRASES
PRINCIPAL AND AUXILIARY VERBS

A *verb* is not always a single word. *When the verb is composed of two or more words, it is called a* **verb phrase.** The verb form at the end of the verb phrase is always the *principal verb.* It is the verb form that indicates the nature of the action, if the verb expresses action. The other verb forms in the verb phrase are called *auxiliary verbs* or *helping verbs.*

The men *work* in the fields.

The men *are working* in the fields.

The men *have been working* in the fields.

The men *must have been working* in the fields.

In the first sentence the verb consists of one word, the verb *work.* The verb *work* tells the kind of action that is going on. The verb in the second sentence consists of two words. The principal verb is *working.* The auxiliary, or helping verb is *are.* The verb phrase is *are working.* The verb phrase in the third sentence is *have been working.* The principal verb is *working,* and the two helping verbs are *have been.* The verb phrase in the fourth sentence is *must have been working.* The principal verb is *working* and the three helping verbs are *must have been.*

Some persons have trouble in deciding what words belong in the verb phrase. You will never encounter this difficulty if you become familiar with the commonly used auxiliary verbs. A list of these auxiliary verbs follows. You should refer to this list constantly until you become familiar with the verbs that help make verb phrases.

A verb phrase is a group of words consisting of two or more verb forms.

Commonly Used Auxiliary Verbs

am	have	do	should
is	has	did	must
are	had	does	should have
was	have been	may	would have
were	had been	can	must have
will be	has been	might	should have been
shall be	shall	could	could have been
could be	will	would	must have been

Verb Phrases Used in Sentences

She <u>has said</u> that you <u>will receive</u> the money.
   verb phrase   verb phrase

He <u>was talking</u> with the manager when you came in.
   verb phrase

The new office building <u>was destroyed</u> by fire.
                         verb phrase

The books <u>were inspected</u> by the librarian.
          verb phrase

SUMMARY

Words are classified into eight groups according to the work that they do in sentences. These eight groups are called the **parts of speech.** The parts of speech are known as *nouns, pronouns, verbs, adjectives, adverbs, prepositions, conjunctions,* and *interjections.*

A **noun** is a word that is used to **name** something. Nouns name *persons, places, animals, objects* of various kinds, *substances, qualities, actions,* and *measures,* such as year, pound, quart, etc.

A **pronoun** is a word that is used *in place of a noun* or a name. Pronouns are commonly used to avoid the awkward repetition of nouns.

A **verb** is usually regarded as the most important part of speech because it is impossible to make a statement without using a verb. A verb is a word that expresses *action, condition,* or *state of being.*

Most verbs express **action.** There is a small, but very important group of verbs that do not express action. With the help of some other word, these verbs usually describe the condition of the person, place, or thing that is being talked about. They are called **linking** verbs to distinguish them from action verbs. The verb *to be* is the most important linking verb. The forms *is, are, was,* and *were* belong to the verb *to be.*

A verb is not always a single word. Sometimes it is made up of two, three, and even four verb forms. When the verb is made up of more than one form, it is called a **verb phrase.** The verb form at the end of the phrase is called the *principal verb.* The other verbs forms are called *auxiliary verbs,* or *helping verbs.*

2

THE PARTS OF SPEECH—II

WITH the three parts of speech, *nouns*, *pronouns*, and *verbs*, or *verb phrases*, you can build the framework of any sentence. But it is only a framework. The sentence that contains only a noun or a pronoun and a verb is not a very interesting sentence. It does not give very specific information, or present a very interesting picture. Such sentences become very monotonous if repeated often, as you will readily see from the following illustrations:

Birds fly.	Dogs bark.
Men work.	She knits.
He swims.	They sing.

ADJECTIVES—Modifiers

You will generally find it necessary to add other parts of speech to a skeleton sentence to make the meaning clearer and more exact. You can add words to nouns and pronouns that tell *what kind, what color, which one*, etc. If you wanted to tell about the hat a woman was wearing, you would describe the hat in some way. You might say that it was a *large* hat, an *atrocious* hat, or a *red* hat, depending upon the meaning which you intended to convey.

When you add one or more of these *describing words* to hat, you give a clearer picture of what the hat is like. *Words which add new ideas to nouns and pronouns are called* **adjectives**.

The adjective not only describes by telling what kind or what color, but it may limit the meaning by telling *which* hat, *whose* hat, or the

18

number of hats. For example, you might limit the meaning by saying *that* hat, *Fred's* hat, *two* hats, or *several* hats.

In grammar, we say that the adjective *modifies* the meaning of the noun or pronoun. The word **modify** means *to change the meaning slightly* by *describing* or *limiting* the meaning to a certain kind or to a certain number.

When we speak of a hat as an *attractive* hat, we are limiting the meaning because we are leaving out all the hats that are not attractive. If a word describes, limits, or restricts the meaning in any way, it is called a **modifier.** This is an important term that is frequently used in grammar.

The words *a, an,* and *the* are adjectives although in grammar they are called **articles.** The word *the* is called the *definite* article. The words *a* and *an* are called the *indefinite articles.* When we say, *the* book on *the* table, we are pointing out a particular book on a particular table. When we say, *I have a book,* no specific or particular book is indicated.

Adjectives Modifying Nouns

The following examples show how adjectives modify nouns and how their use makes the meaning clearer or more explicit.

long road	*good* friend	*rainy* day
rusty nail	*beautiful* dress	*accurate* accountant
old piano	*worthy* cause	*rapid* typist
five dollars	*steep* hill	*essential* parts
intelligent answer	*difficult* task	*juicy* orange

An adjective is a word used to modify
a noun or a pronoun.

ADVERBS—Modifiers

Another interesting group of words that serve as modifiers are **adverbs.** The prefix *ad* in the word adverb means *to, toward,* or *in addition to.* An adverb is a word that you *add to a verb to modify or expand the meaning of the verb.* Adverbs may also modify adjectives or other adverbs. In this unit we shall consider the adverb as a modifier of the verb. A later unit will give you the other uses of an adverb.

Adverbs are easy to identify because they usually answer the questions *when, where, how, in what manner,* or *to what extent* or *degree.* The following illustrations will make this clear:

You must set up the copy *now. (Now* tells when to set it up.)

We put the desk *there. (There* tells where to put it.)

Mary walks *gracefully. (Gracefully* tells how she walks.)

The old man traveled *far. (Far* tells the extent of traveling.)

When we say, *The paper is issued weekly,* the adverb *weekly* introduces an additional idea of *time.* The adverb *weekly* makes the meaning explicit because we know *how often* or *when* the paper is issued. When we say, *Dandelions grow everywhere,* we have introduced the idea of *place,* or we tell *where* the dandelions grow. In the sentence, *We walked farther into the forest,* we have added the idea of *extent* or the *degree to which.* The adverbs in the preceding sentences are called adverbs of *time, place, manner,* or *degree.*

---

*An adverb is a word used to modify a verb,
an adjective, or another adverb.*

POSITION OF THE ADVERB

Although an adverb often modifies the verb in the sentence, it is not always placed directly after the verb. Sometimes the adverb introduces the sentence. In this position it gives more emphasis. At times the adverb is placed between the parts of the verb phrase. Study the following sentences carefully. Note the position of the adverb.

Sometimes I take a walk in the woods.

Jack *always* leaves the house at seven.

We added a room to our house *recently.*

Tom studies *diligently.*

I have *always* admired him.

In the first sentence, the adverb *sometimes* introduces the sentence. It modifies the verb *take.* In the second sentence, the adverb *always* modifies the verb *leaves.* Instead of following the verb, it is placed before the verb. This is done for emphasis.

In the third sentence, the adverb *recently* appears at the end of the sentence. It modifies the verb *added.* In the fourth sentence, the adverb *diligently* follows the verb *studies,* which it modifies. In the last sentence, the adverb *always* comes between the parts of the verb phrase *have admired.*

PREPOSITIONS

Words That Show a Relationship

Another important part of speech is the **preposition.** A preposition is not a modifier. The only parts of speech that are modifiers are adjectives and adverbs. The preposition has a different function to perform in the sentence. *A preposition shows the relationship that exists between certain words in a sentence.*

The word *preposition* comes from two Latin words which mean *placed before.* A preposition is a word that is *placed before some noun or pronoun.* It shows the relationship that exists between that noun or pronoun and some other word in the sentence. When we say "a bag *for* the mail," the word *for* is a preposition. It shows a relationship between *bag* and *mail.* The word *mail* which follows the preposition is called the **object** of the *preposition.*

In the sentence, *The accident occurred on the bridge,* the word *on* is a preposition. The preposition *on* is followed by the word *bridge* which is called its object. The entire group of words, *on the bridge,* is called a **prepositional phrase.** The preposition *on* shows the relation between the noun *bridge* and the verb *occurred.* The entire phrase *on the bridge* tells where the accident occurred.

We might use a number of prepositions to show the relationship between the noun *bridge* and the verb *occurred.* Each preposition would show a slightly different type of relationship, as you will readily see from the following illustrations:

The accident occurred <u>under</u> the bridge.
preposition

The accident occurred <u>near</u> the bridge.
preposition

The accident occurred <u>above</u> the bridge.
preposition

The accident occurred <u>behind</u> the bridge.
preposition

The accident occurred <u>beneath</u> the bridge.
preposition

You should become acquainted with the words that are commonly used as prepositions. A list of these prepositions is given here for your reference. Refer to this list repeatedly until you are able to identify the prepositions that are in common use. The fact that a word is in this list does not mean that it is always used as a preposition. Some of these words often function as other parts of speech. The test of its use as a preposition is to determine whether it shows the *relationship* between its object and some other word in the sentence.

A List of Commonly Used Prepositions

above	at	by	into	toward
about	before	down	like	through
across	behind	during	near	under
after	below	except	of	until
against	beneath	for	off	up
along	beside	from	on	upon
among	between	in	since	with
around	beyond	inside	to	within

A preposition shows the relationship that exists between certain words in a sentence.

23

CONJUNCTIONS—Connecting Words

In many of your sentences you need words that serve to join words or groups of words. In grammar, words that have this connecting function are called **conjunctions**.

The word *conjunction* comes from two Latin words which mean to *join with* or to *join together*. In the sentence, *Jane and Alice are stenographers*, the word *and* connects the two nouns, *Jane* and *Alice*. The word *and* in this sentence is a conjunction. In the sentence, *The manager or his secretary will see you*, the word *or* connects the words *manager* and *secretary*. The word *or* in this sentence is a conjunction. In the sentence, *Her small but attractive apartment is for rent*, the word *but* joins the words *small* and *attractive*.

The conjunctions that were used in the preceding illustrations were *and, but,* and *or.* These conjunctions always connect words or groups of words of equal rank. For the present, we shall limit our discussion to the use of these three conjunctions.

Mark drives too fast *and* too recklessly. (joins two adverbs)
          adverb   adverb

He   *or*   I will audit the account. (joins two pronouns)
pronoun   pronoun

I fell *and* broke my arm. (joins two verbs)
  verb   verb

He will give the book to Mary *or* Jane. (joins two nouns)
                 noun   noun

They bought a large *but* attractive home. (joins two adjectives)
           adjective   adjective

A conjunction is a word used to connect words or a group of words.

INTERJECTIONS—Exclamatory Words

In English we have a number of words that are used to express strong feeling or sudden emotion. Words that serve this purpose are called **interjections.** The word *interjection* comes from two Latin words which mean *to throw between.* Interjections are really thrown into the sentence to express some type of emotion such as disgust, joy, excitement, enthusiasm, etc.

Interjections have no grammatical relation to any word or group of words in the sentence. In grammar we call words of this type *independent elements.* Sometimes words which are independent elements stand for an entire sentence. The following illustrations show the kinds of words that are commonly used as interjections:

Alas! This is the end of everything! (Interjection is *Alas.*)

Hey! Do you know where you're going? (Interjection is *Hey.*)

Bah! That's humbug. (Interjection is *Bah.*)

Oh! I can't believe that. (Interjection is *Oh.*)

Pshaw! Why did I do that? (Interjection is *Pshaw.*)

The words classified as interjections in the preceding illustrations *are always interjections.* In addition to such words, nouns, pronouns, adjectives, and other parts of speech *are often used* as interjections.

Heavens! I cut my finger instead of the cloth!

Good! I'm glad to hear that.

Horrors! Look at that hat!

Well! When are you going to pay that bill?

Some of the interjections that you use or hear in speech are not even words, although it is possible to represent the sounds expressed. A careful speaker or writer does not use interjections very often, especially expressions like the following:

Whew! What a day!

Um! This soup tastes good.

Humph! I knew that ages ago.

FUNCTION OF WORDS

One of the most important things to learn about the English language is the fact that *the same words are often used as different parts of speech.* A word may perform a certain function in one sentence and an entirely different function in another sentence. This will become more apparent to you as you progress further in the course.

Adjectives are commonly used as nouns, and nouns are frequently used as adjectives. The same word may function both as an adverb and as a preposition. Almost any type of word may be used as an interjection. The following sentences show how words function as different parts of speech:

The *light* in my study is very poor. (*Light* is a noun.)

Please *light* the candles. (*Light* is a verb.)

Her hat is a *light* shade of blue. (*Light* is an adjective.)

Father is a *fast* driver. (*Fast* is an adjective.)

Father drives too *fast.* (*Fast* is an adverb.)

I *fast* one day every week. (*Fast* is a verb.)

**The same words are often used as
different parts of speech.**

SUMMARY

It is possible to have a sentence with only a noun or a pronoun and a verb. This is the essential framework or skeleton of a sentence. But it is often desirable and necessary to add other parts of speech to make our meaning clearer, or to make our sentences more interesting. *Adjectives* and *adverbs* are used for this purpose.

Adjectives and **adverbs** are *modifiers*; that is, their chief purpose is to modify or change the meaning in some way. Adjectives modify *nouns* and *pronouns*. Adverbs modify *verbs, adjectives,* and *other adverbs.*

The words *a, an,* and *the* are called **articles** although they function just like adjectives. The word *the* is called the *definite article,* and the words *a* and *an* are called the *indefinite articles.*

Another important part of speech is the **preposition.** A preposition has an entirely different function in the sentence. It is used to show the *relationship* between certain words. One of these words is the noun or pronoun which follows the preposition. This noun or pronoun is called the **object** *of the preposition.*

We often need to use words that serve to connect words and groups of words. The part of speech that performs this function is the **conjunction.** The most commonly used conjunctions are *and, but, or.*

There are a number of words whose purpose is to express strong feeling or sudden emotion. Such words are called **interjections.** An interjection is usually independent of the rest of the sentence.

Keep in mind that *the same words are often used as different parts of speech.* Adjectives are commonly used as nouns, and nouns are commonly used as adjectives. A word might be a preposition in one sentence, and an adverb in another sentence. The only way to tell the part of speech of a word is to study its *function* in a particular sentence.

3

THE SENTENCE

WHEN A NUMBER of words (parts of speech) are put together in such a way that they express a **complete thought,** you have a *sentence.* The sentence may consist of one word, or it may consist of as many as three hundred words. The tendency in modern writing is to use short, effective sentences. Twenty words is about the average length in present-day writing.

Often those who are beginning the study of language find it difficult to understand what is meant by a *complete thought.* Some students punctuate parts of sentences as if they were sentences because they do not realize that some essential element is missing. The following groups of words are not sentences, although they are punctuated as if they were complete.

The officers of our company. (*not a sentence*)

Enjoyed the banquet. (*not a sentence*)

On the top of the hill. (*not a sentence*)

These groups of words are not sentences because they lack something that is necessary in order to express a complete thought. When you examine the first group of words, you will readily see that you know what the writer is talking about. However, the writer did not complete the sentence by telling you what the officers did. The second group of words tells you that somebody enjoyed a banquet. But the author neglected to tell you who it was. The third group of words tells you very little. You have no way of knowing what the writer is talking about.

SUBJECT AND PREDICATE

In order to express a complete thought, a sentence must have both a *subject* and a *predicate.* These are two important grammatical terms used to describe the essential elements of a sentence.

The **subject** is the word or group of words that tells us *what or whom the speaker or writer is talking about.* The **predicate** is the part of the sentence *that makes a statement about the subject.* The *predicate* usually tells what the subject is doing, or what is happening to the subject.

Study the following sentences carefully. Note that the subjects have been separated from the predicates so that you will be able to see the relationship between the two parts more easily.

Subjects	Predicates
My friend	lives in New York.
The letter	contained exciting news.
The men in our office	are experienced salesmen.

In the first sentence, I am talking about *my friend.* Therefore, *my friend* is the subject of the sentence. I complete the sentence by making a statement about my friend. I say that my friend *lives in New York.* The predicate is *lives in New York.* This group of words, *My friend lives in New York,* is a sentence because it expresses a complete thought. It has both a subject and a predicate.

The second group of words, *The letter contained exciting news,* expresses a complete thought. It has a subject, *The letter,* and a predicate, *contained exciting news.*

The third group of words, *The men in our office are experienced salesmen,* is also a sentence. It expresses a complete thought. The subject is *The men in our office,* and the predicate is *are experienced salesmen.*

COMPLETE SUBJECT AND COMPLETE PREDICATE

In many sentences the subject or the predicate is only a single word. But more often, the subject consists of two or more words. In grammar, we call the entire subject, regardless of the number of words, the **complete subject.** We call the entire predicate the **complete predicate.**

If the subject of a sentence is a single word, that word is the *complete subject.* If the predicate of the sentence is a single word, that word is the *complete predicate.* In the sentence, *Birds fly,* the word *birds* is the complete subject, and the word *fly* is the complete predicate.

SIMPLE SUBJECT AND SIMPLE PREDICATE

After you have learned how to identify the complete subject and the complete predicate, you can easily find the **simple subject** and the **simple predicate.**

Somewhere in the complete subject you will find the *particular word* about which something is said. That word is the *simple subject.* It is usually either a noun or a pronoun.

Somewhere in the predicate you will find a word that serves as the *key* to the predicate. That word is the *verb,* the most important word in any sentence. If the verb consists of more than one word, it is called a *verb phrase,* as you learned in Unit One. In the following examples the simple subject is underlined once and the simple predicate is underlined twice:

The American <u>ambassador</u> <u>attended</u> a conference.

The <u>hero</u> of the story <u>had</u> many thrilling adventures.

My <u>friend</u> in Boston <u>has bought</u> a new television set.

The simple subject of the first sentence is *ambassador*. The simple predicate, or the predicate verb, is *attended*. The simple subject of the second sentence is *hero*. The simple predicate is *had*. The simple subject of the third sentence is *friend,* and the simple predicate is the verb phrase *has bought*.

Sometimes you will find only one word in the subject or one word in the predicate. In that case, the single word in the subject is the simple subject. It is also the complete subject. The single word in the predicate is the simple predicate and also the complete predicate.

Pronouns are often used as the simple subject and the complete subject. In the sentence, *We are buying a new home,* the pronoun *we* is the simple subject. It is also the complete subject since there are no other words in the subject.

In the sentence, *The building collapsed,* the verb *collapsed* is the simple predicate. It is also the complete predicate since it is the only word in the predicate.

In the following illustrations, the abbreviations **s.s.** and **s.p.** are used to indicate the simple subject and the simple predicate:

Fast <u>driving</u> <u>is</u> often dangerous.
    s.s.   **s.p.**

The <u>detectives</u> on the case <u>found</u> the jewels.
    s.s.   **s.p.**

The <u>people</u> of the village <u>were listening</u> to the bell.
    s.s.   **s.p.**

The <u>cashier</u> immediately <u>reported</u> the shortage.
    s.s.   **s.p.**

<u>Children</u> <u>play</u>.
  s.s.   **s.p.**

A verb phrase is regarded as a unit. It is the simple predicate and the predicate verb.

COMPOUND SUBJECT AND COMPOUND PREDICATE

A sentence may have two or more simple subjects and two or more simple predicates. In the sentence, *Harry and Fred joined a lodge,* there are two simple subjects, *Harry* and *Fred.* The connecting word is *and.* In grammar we say that the sentence has a **compound subject.**

In the sentence, *The stenographer wrote the letter and mailed it,* there are two predicate verbs, *wrote* and *mailed.* The connecting word is *and.* This sentence has a **compound predicate.**

Some sentences have a compound subject and a compound predicate. In the sentence, *Alice and Jane washed the curtains and ironed them,* there are two simple subjects and two simple predicates. The subject nouns are *Alice* and *Jane.* The two predicate verbs are *washed* and *ironed.* In both cases, the connecting word is *and.*

The following sentences contain either a compound subject, a compound predicate, or both.

Corn and beans | are grown in the valley. (*compound subject*)

I | attended the lecture and took notes. (*compound predicate*)

The boys and girls | sang and danced at the club. (*compound subject and compound predicate*)

SENTENCE FRAGMENTS

If you have studied this unit carefully, you will have a thorough understanding of the essential elements of a sentence. But even persons who have this knowledge often punctuate groups of words as sentences when one or both of the essential elements are missing .

Any incomplete group of words punctuated as if it were a sentence is called a *sentence fragment* or a *fragmentary sentence.* As you know, a fragment is only a piece or a part of the whole. A fragment always refers to something that is incomplete.

A fragmentary sentence always lacks one or both of the essential elements of a sentence. That is, either the subject or the predicate, or both the subject and predicate are missing. Whenever you are in doubt about a particular sentence, apply this test: Does the group of words contain both a subject and a predicate? Does it express a complete thought?

Very often the subject of the sentence is missing. The following group of words is *not* a sentence because it does not tell who it is that the writer is talking about:

Interviewed the candidate. (This is not a sentence.)

The president interviewed the candidate. (This is a complete sentence.)

The sentence was completed by supplying a subject, *The president.*

Sometimes the predicate is missing. The following group of words is *not* a sentence because the entire predicate is missing:

The sound of footsteps. (This is not a sentence.)

The sound of footsteps *alarmed us.* (This is a complete sentence.)

The use of fragmentary or incomplete sentences is an unsatisfactory way of communicating your ideas. Surprising as it may seem, sentence fragments similiar to the following examples can be found repeatedly in letters sent out by reputable business firms. Check the letters of your company. You may be amazed at what you find. Be sure you do not use fragments in your own personal writing.

Received your letter this morning. (*Subject* is missing.)

Will send order at once. (*Subject* is missing.)

Have shipped your order. (*Subject* is missing.)

Hoping this meets with your approval. (*No subject or predicate.*)

With kind personal regards. (No *subject* or *predicate.*)

SUMMARY

A **sentence** is a group of words that expresses a complete thought. A sentence must have both a *subject* and a *predicate*.

The **subject** of a sentence is the part that tells what the speaker or writer is talking about.

The **predicate** of a sentence is the part that makes a statement about the subject.

The *simple subject* names the person, place, or thing that is talked about. It is usually a noun or a pronoun.

The *simple predicate* is the verb or verb phrase in the sentence.

The *complete subject* is the simple subject with all its modifiers.

The *complete predicate* is the verb or verb phrase with its modifiers and any other words used to complete the predicate.

A *compound subject* consists of two or more simple subjects.

A *compound predicate* consists of two or more simple predicates.

A **fragmentary sentence** is a group of words that lacks one or both of the essential parts of a sentence, but is punctuated as if it were a complete sentence.

4

SENTENCE PATTERNS

A SENTENCE must express a complete thought. It must also have both a subject and a predicate. However, it is possible to express a complete thought in a variety of ways. You should become familiar with the different ways of arranging words in sentences and the different sentence patterns that are the result of these arrangements.

KINDS OF SENTENCES

Sentences fall into four groups according to the purpose the sentence serves and the manner in which the thought is expressed. Some sentences simply *make statements*. Some sentences *ask questions*. Another type of sentence *gives a command* or *makes a request*. The last group is the kind of sentence that *expresses strong feeling* or *sudden emotion*.

In grammar, the sentence that makes a statement is called a **declarative sentence.** The sentence that asks a question is called an **interrogative sentence.** The sentence that gives a command or makes a request is called an **imperative sentence,** and the sentence that expresses strong feeling is called an **exclamatory sentence.** The following are examples of the four types of sentences:

My friend is a business executive. (*declarative sentence*)

Have you entered the contest? (*interrogative sentence*)

Clear the road at once! (*imperative sentence*—command)

Please shut the door. (*imperative sentence*—request)

What a tragedy this is! (*exclamatory sentence*)

If you examine the preceding illustrations carefully, you will notice that the *declarative sentence* ends with a *period*. The *interrogative sen-*

tence ends with a *question mark* (?). Sometimes the *imperative sentence* ends with an *exclamation mark* (!) and sometimes it ends with a *period*. If the command is given in a very emphatic or decisive manner, an exclamation mark is placed at the end. A mild request always ends with a period. An *exclamatory sentence* usually ends with an *exclamation mark*.

If you have any difficulty in determining the types of sentences in Exercise 1, refer to this brief summary:

A **declarative** sentence *makes a statement.*

An **interrogative** sentence *asks a question.*

An **imperative** sentence gives a *command* or makes a *request.*

An **exclamatory** sentence expresses *strong feeling* or *sudden emotion.*

INVERTED ORDER

You have probably observed that these four types of sentences follow certain patterns of word arrangement. These patterns will now be discussed in more detail.

Every sentence has a basic structure or framework. This is true of all four types of sentences—*declarative, interrogative, imperative,* and *exclamatory.* This framework, as you already know, consists of the subject noun or pronoun and the predicate verb.

There are a number of ways of introducing the subject in a declarative sentence. The **normal order,** or the grammatical order, is *subject first,* followed by the predicate. If you always followed this pattern, your sentences would soon become monotonous and uninteresting. The following illustration will make this clear. The sentences in this paragraph sound very much like the sentences in a primer or in a first reader.

I like this book. It is a book about Mexico. My friend sent this book to me. My friend lives in New York. She speaks Spanish.

In this short paragraph, all the sentences follow the same pattern—subject first, followed by the predicate. You can give more variety to your sentence patterns by placing words in unusual positions.

You can put the subject after the verb or throw it to the very end of the sentence. Varying the position of the subject gives you an opportunity to place other words at the beginning of the sentence to give them more emphasis. This also makes our sentences more interesting.

On my desk I found an interesting book about Mexico.

In this sentence, the subject is placed after the group of words, or the phrase, *on my desk.* This arrangement throws the phrase to the front of the sentence and gives it more emphasis.

When the subject of the sentence does not appear in its normal position, we say that the order of the sentence is inverted, or turned around. Always remember that *normal* or grammatical order *means subject first,* followed by the predicate. Examine the following sentences carefully. Note the position of the subject in the two sentences.

The *band* marched down the street.

Down the street marched the *band.*

The first sentence is in normal, or grammatical order. The subject noun *band* appears at the beginning of the sentence. The verb *marched* follows the subject.

The second sentence is the same sentence in **inverted order.** The subject noun *band* now appears at the end of the sentence. The verb *marched* comes before the subject. A phrase, *Down the street,* appears at the beginning of the sentence.

An adverb often introduces a sentence. The following sentence begins with an adverb, and not with the subject.

Suddenly the train stopped. (*inverted order*)

The train stopped *suddenly.* (*normal order*)

Some students find it difficult to determine the true subject when a

37

sentence is not in grammatical order. This difficulty can be avoided by *transposing* the sentence and putting it back in normal order. The only purpose in transposing a sentence is to see the grammatical relations more clearly.

Sometimes when you put a sentence back in grammatical order by transposing it, you will find that the transposed sentence is not so smooth as the original sentence. However, the following sentence is just as effective in either order.

Along the road we passed a number of army trucks.

We passed a number of army trucks *along the road.*

Whenever you are dealing with a sentence in inverted order, you should transpose it before you attempt to analyze the sentence from the grammatical point of view.

INTERROGATIVE SENTENCE PATTERNS

In asking a question, you seldom start with the subject first, as you do in a declarative sentence. For that reason, *the interrogative sentence is generally in inverted order.* Sometimes the interrogative sentence starts with the *verb.* Often it begins with an *adverb,* which is used to ask the question.

Did you bring your camera? (introduced by the *verb*)

Where did you buy your watch? (introduced by an *adverb*)

In order to see the grammatical constructions in an interrogative sentence that is inverted, you must transpose the sentence and put it in normal order. Sometimes the interrogative sentence becomes a statement when it is transposed.

You did bring your camera.

You did buy your watch where?

IMPERATIVE AND EXCLAMATORY SENTENCE PATTERNS

The imperative sentence presents a different problem. The *subject* of the sentence that gives a command or makes a request *is seldom expressed*. If the subject is not expressed, it is the word *you* understood.

Sound the alarm at once! (Subject is not expressed.)

(You) Sound the alarm at once! (Subject *you* is understood.)

Please read the announcement. (Subject is not expressed.)

(You) Please read the announcement. (Subject *you* is understood.)

Sometimes an imperative sentence begins with a noun that indicates the name of the person to whom the command or the request is given.

An interrogative sentence may also begin in this way. The point to keep in mind is that such a noun *is not the subject* of the sentence. In fact, it has no grammatical connection with the rest of the sentence. It is an independent element. For that reason, it is separated from the rest of the sentence by a comma. Study the following illustrations carefully:

Imperative Sentence

Fred, please close the door. (*Fred* is the person addressed.)

Fred, (you) please close the door. (Subject is *you* understood.)

Interrogative Sentence

Alice, did you lock the door? (*Alice* is a noun in direct address.)

Alice, you did lock the door. (Subject is *you* expressed.)

In the first sentence, the word *Fred* is a noun in **direct address** because it names the person spoken to directly. It is not the subject of the sentence. The subject of an imperative sentence is *you* understood. The word *Fred* is set off from the rest of the sentence by a comma to show that it is used *independently*.

In the second sentence, the word *Alice* is a noun in direct address because it names the person spoken to directly. Since this is an interrogative sentence, the subject is expressed. When the sentence is placed in normal order, you can easily see that the subject is *you*, and not Alice.

A noun in *direct address* may appear at the beginning or at the end of the sentence. It may even appear within the sentence.

Fred, please close the door. (beginning of the sentence)

Please close the door, *Fred.* (end of the sentence)

Come here, *Fred,* and look at this book. (within the sentence)

The exclamatory sentence is often expressed in inverted order. In the sentence, *What a feast she spread!,* the subject and the verb appear at the end of the sentence. When the sentence is transposed, the subject appears at the beginning of the sentence and is followed by the verb.

What a feast she spread! (*inverted order*)

She spread what a feast! (*normal order*)
<u>s.s. s.p.</u>

How beautiful the sunset is tonight! (*inverted order*)

The sunset is how beautiful tonight! (*normal order*)
<u>s.s. s.p.</u>

What a tragedy that would be! (*inverted order*)

That would be what a tragedy! (*normal order*)
<u>s.s. s.p.</u>

SENTENCES THAT BEGIN WITH "THERE"

Another sentence pattern that we use frequently is the sentence that begins with the word *there*. We have a very good reason for beginning some of our sentences in this way.

When the word *there* is used to introduce the sentence, it is possible to place the subject after the verb. In many cases this results in a much smoother sentence, as you will see from the following illustration:

A heavy frost was last night.

There was a heavy frost last night.

Although the first sentence is in grammatical order, it is a very awkward sentence. The second arrangement results in a much smoother style, but it presents a grammatical problem. In dealing with a sentence that begins with *there,* you must always remember that the word *there* is neither the subject of the sentence, nor an adverbial modifier. It is merely an introductory word which has a special function, that of introducing the sentence.

When the word *there* functions in this way, it is called an **expletive**. The word **expletive** comes from the Latin and means *"added merely to fill up."* This is a very suitable term because it explains exactly what takes place.

The word *there* merely "fills up" the place normally occupied by the subject. It has no other function in the sentence. Like the noun in direct address, it is an independent construction. When the sentence is transposed, and placed in grammatical order, you should enclose the word *there* in parentheses to show that it is used independently.

There are twelve candidates for the position.

(There) twelve candidates are for the position.

It is important to transpose the sentence beginning with *there* in order to determine the true subject of the sentence. It is also important to

41

determine whether the word *there* is used as an introductory word or whether it is used as an adverb.

> *There* they are. (*There* is an adverb of place.)

> They are *there*. (*There* is an adverb of place.)

> *There* were ten men in the band. (*there*—expletive)

> (*There*) ten men were in the band. (*there*—expletive)

> The coach stood *there* watching the game. (*there*—adverb of place)

> *There* is a telephone directory on the table. (*there*—expletive)

> We met *there* last year. (*there*—adverb of place)

> *There* will be some objection to the plan. (*there*—expletive)

The word *it* is also used as an expletive in certain sentence patterns. The use of *it* as an expletive will be discussed in later units.

SUMMARY

1. A **declarative sentence** makes a statement and may be written in several different ways. The *normal order* is for the subject to appear at the beginning of the sentence. However, for variety, emphasis, or clearness, the subject may appear at other places in the sentence. The declarative sentence ends with a period.

2. An **interrogative sentence** asks a question and is usually in inverted order. To determine the subject and the predicate, the interrogative sentence should be transposed or placed in normal order. The interrogative sentence ends with a question mark.

3. An **imperative sentence** gives a command or makes a request, and its subject is seldom expressed. When the subject is not expressed, it is always the word *you* understood. An imperative sentence sometimes ends with a period and sometimes with an exclamation mark.

4. An **exclamatory sentence** expresses strong feeling or sudden emotion, and is often not in normal order. When it is not in normal order the sentence should be transposed to determine the subject and predicate. Exclamatory sentences usually end with an exclamation mark, but may end with a period.

5. The word *there* is often used as an **expletive** to introduce a sentence. When *there* performs this function, it is not used as an adverb. It is used independently merely to "fill up" the place normally occupied by the subject. The subject appears later in the sentence.

6. Imperative or interrogative sentences are often introduced by a noun in **direct address.** A noun in direct address is not the subject of the sentence but is used independently.

7. When you want to determine the subject and predicate of a sentence that is not in normal order, you should transpose the sentence. You are then able to see grammatical relations more clearly.

5

NOUNS-CAPITALIZATION

KINDS OF NOUNS

A NOUN is a word used as a name. Some nouns begin with capital letters, and others begin with small letters. The subject of *capitalization* is important because it is closely concerned with the division of nouns into groups or classes.

In English, nouns are divided into two main classes called **common nouns** and **proper nouns.** A *common noun* names any one of a class of persons, places, or things. We have a name for all the chairs in the world when we use the common noun *chair*. We have a name for all the lakes in the world when we use the common noun *lake*.

But when we want to name a particular lake, we must give it a special name. The name of a particular lake might be *Lake Louise, Lake George,* or *Lake Michigan*. These particular names are called proper nouns. *A proper noun always begins with a capital letter.*

We have particular names for persons, such as *John Adams, General Eisenhower, Queen Elizabeth,* and *Governor Stevenson*. We also have particular names for certain objects, such as buildings, hotels, theaters, and clubs: *Conway Building, Congress Hotel, Harris Theater,* and *Union League Club*.

Sometimes a common noun names a collection of objects or a group of persons. When we use the word *band* in music, we include under one name all the musicians who play the different instruments. When we use the word *jury,* we include all the members who make up the jury. Nouns that name a group of persons or a collection of objects are called *collective nouns*.

A **common noun** is the name of *any one* of a class of *persons, places,* or *things*.

aviator	ocean	tiger	meat
city	book	lily	desk

A **proper noun** is the name of a *particular person, place,* or *thing.*

Pacific Ocean	Thomas Edison
Chicago	Amazon River
England	Wrigley Building
State Street	Bay of Fundy

A **collective noun** is a common noun whose singular form names a *group* of persons, objects, or acts.

herd	company	team	crowd
army	corps	audience	faculty

Some nouns are *common nouns* in one sentence and *proper nouns* in another sentence.

Common Nouns	Proper Nouns
Roy is studying to be a doctor.	The family called in Dr. Allen.
John's uncle is an engineer.	Uncle John is a colonel in the army.
I went to the theater with May.	The play was given at the Grand Theater.
We spent the summer at the lake.	Did you ever cross Lake Erie?

CAPITALIZATION OF PROPER NOUNS

A student of language should be familiar with the accepted rules regarding the capitalization of *proper nouns* and *proper adjectives*. **Proper adjectives** *are adjectives derived from proper nouns.*

Proper Nouns	Proper Adjectives
America	an *American* soldier
Spain	a *Spanish* house
a Baptist	a *Baptist* minister
China	a *Chinese* vase

The following list of rules for the capitalization of proper nouns follows accepted, present-day usage:

1. Capitalize names of *particular persons* and *places*.

Mr. Smith	Yankee Stadium
Eleanor Roosevelt	Radio City
Helen Hayes	Cuba
Senator Clark	Ellis Island
Miss Hamilton	Soldier Field

2. Capitalize *geographic names:* continents, countries, states, cities, rivers, mountains, lakes, falls, harbors, valleys, bays, etc.

Africa	Pikes Peak	Cape Horn
Brazil	Rocky Mountains	Gulf of Mexico
Montana	Victoria Falls	New York Harbor
Cleveland	Hudson Bay	Long Island

3. Capitalize names of *definite regions, localities,* and *political divisions.*

the Orient	Third Precinct
the Wheat Belt	First Ward (of a city)
the Bad Lands	Wheeling Township
the Arctic Circle	French Republic
the North Pole	the Badger State

4. Capitalize names of *bridges, buildings, monuments, parks, ships, automobiles, hotels, forts, dams, railroads, streets,* etc.

Brooklyn Bridge	Plymouth Court
Fine Arts Building	Michigan Avenue
Statue of Liberty	New York Central (railroad)
Central Park	Plaza Hotel
Dodge (car)	Eiffel Tower
Queen Mary (ship)	Missouri (battleship)
Fort Knox	Alton Railroad
Rush Street	Boulder Dam

5. Capitalize names of *historical events, historical periods,* and *historical documents.*

the Middle Ages	Battle of Gettysburg
World War II	Louisiana Purchase
the Crusades	Treaty of Paris
Atlantic Charter	Fourteenth Amendment
Magna Charta	the Civil War (American)

6. Capitalize names of *governmental bodies* and *departments*.

Bureau of Mines	Civil Service Commission
the Federal Government	Federal Trade Commission
United States Senate	Eighty-ninth Congress
Federal Courts	the President's Cabinet
Bureau of the Census	Supreme Court of the United States

7. Capitalize names of *political parties, business* and *fraternal organizations, clubs* and *societies, companies,* and *institutions.*

Republicans	County Hospital
Democratic Party (or party)	John Crerar Library
Gold Star Mothers	Chapman Chemical Company
Odd Fellows	Career Institute
a Shriner	Chicago Athletic Club
the Elks	Ford Motor Company
Volunteers of America	Northwestern University

8. Capitalize *titles of rank* when they are joined to a person's name.

Lord Beaverbrook	Professor Thomas
President Johnson	Doctor Hayden
Senator Lodge	Judge Harmon
Bishop Dudley Stark	Dean Mary Allison
Dr. Allen Reed	Pope Paul VI
Chancellor Hutchins	Cardinal Wolsey
Prime Minister Wilson	Queen Elizabeth II
Secretary U Thant	His Honor the Mayor

9. Capitalize *days* of the *week, months* of the *year, holidays,* and *days* of *special observance,* such as feast and fast days.

Monday	Feast of the Passover
September	Saint Valentine's Day
Labor Day	Mother's Day
Easter Sunday	Good Friday

10. You should not capitalize names of the seasons unless they are personified. When something is personified it is represented or considered as if it were a person. Personification is frequently used in poetry.

spring	winter
Spring's warm touch	Winter's icy breath

11. The words *north, east, south,* and *west* are capitalized when they refer to *sections* of the country. They are not capitalized when they refer to *directions.*

Sections of Countries	Directions
the Midwest	I travel north on my way home.
the Far West	The sun rises in the east.
the Near East	The southern part of Idaho is beautiful.
the Middle West	The colonists moved west to obtain more land.

12. The *special names* given to planets and stars are capitalized. The words *sun, moon, star,* and *planet* are not capitalized.

Jupiter	The *sun* rose at six that morning.
Venus	Scientists have discovered a new *star.*
Mars	The *moon* is a heavenly body.
Milky Way	A *planet* shines by reflected light.
Big Dipper	A *constellation* is a group of stars.

49

SPECIAL USES OF CAPITAL LETTERS

1. Words derived from proper nouns are usually capitalized. If the word has acquired a special meaning, it is not capitalized.

Capitalized	Not Capitalized
a Pullman car	navy blue
Mongolian race	china cabinet
Venetian blinds	morocco leather
Swiss cheese	chinaware
Manila hemp	paris green
English tweeds	panama hat or Panama hat
Turkish bath	turkish towel or Turkish towel

2. The principal words in *titles of books, magazines, pictures, songs, articles,* etc., are capitalized. Prepositions, conjunctions, and the articles *a, an,* and *the* are not capitalized unless the title begins with one of these words.

The Last of the Mohicans (book)

The Saturday Evening Post (magazine)

"Outside Our World" (article)

Battle Hymn of the Republic (song)

The Angelus (picture)

"The Northerners" (radio program)

"Forum of the Air" (television program)

3. The definite article *the* is not capitalized unless it is the first word of a title. Many titles do not begin with *the*. If the word *the* is within the title, it is written with a small letter. The only way to be sure about

the correct form of a title is to check the official form, or the form adopted by the company, publication, etc.

Chicago Daily News

The Christian Science Monitor

Book Review Digest

The John C. Winston Company

National Geographic Magazine

Pinnacle Oil Company

4. All words referring to the Deity, the Bible, books of the Bible, and other *sacred books* are capitalized.

God, the Father	the Koran
Saviour	Genesis
the Trinity	Supreme Being
Talmud	Bible
Book of Job	New Testament

5. The pronoun *I* and the interjection *O* are capitalized. The word *oh* is not capitalized unless it is the first word of a sentence.

"O say! can you see, by the dawn's early light, . . ."

" 'Tis the Star Spangled Banner, oh, long may it wave . . ."

6. Names of school subjects are not capitalized unless they are names of the languages. Subjects listed in school catalogs as names of special courses are capitalized.

mathematics	History 101 (title of course)
French	Advanced Chemistry II (title of course)
economics	Economics 345 (title of course)
English	Physics II (title of course)

51

7. Capitalize words which show family relationships when they are used with a person's name. The words *father* and *mother* are not capitalized when they are preceded by a pronoun. When used without a pronoun, they are usually capitalized.

Aunt Martha	her cousin
Cousin John	their uncle
Sister Sue	his grandmother
Uncle Jack	my father

8. Capitalize the first word in a *compound word that is used as a proper noun.* If the second word in the compound word is a proper noun, it should also be capitalized. Capitalize both parts of *compound titles of distinction.*

Eighty-ninth Congress	un-American activities
Forty-third Street	ex-President Eisenhower
Army-Navy game	Rear Admiral Simpson
The Honorable John Willis	Vice-President Humphrey
	or
Chief Justice Warren	Vice President Humphrey

9. The names of special departments of business firms may be written with small or with capital letters. In business writing, it is considered good practice to capitalize titles such as *president, secretary, office manager, general superintendent,* etc. They may also be written with small letters.

claim department *or* Claim Department

advertising department *or* Advertising Department

The Company will reimburse you for your loss. (or company)

Our President will grant you an interview. (or president)

The Court will grant you a hearing. (or court)

PLURAL FORMS OF NOUNS

When a noun refers to one person or thing, it is singular in number. When a noun refers to more than one person or thing, it is plural in number. Nouns have special forms to show these distinctions, as you will see from the following illustrations:

Singular	Plural
boy	boys
box	boxes
leaf	leaves
tomato	tomatoes

The plurals of nouns are formed in a number of different ways. Since there are exceptions to almost every one of these methods, you should consult a reliable dictionary whenever you are in doubt regarding a correct plural form. You should also be familiar with the following methods of forming the plurals of nouns:

1. Most nouns add the letter *s* to the singular to form the plural.

kite	kites	college	colleges
lamp	lamps	chimney	chimneys
dance	dances	manager	managers
zebra	zebras	dynamo	dynamos
chief	chiefs	orange	oranges
radio	radios	island	islands

2. Nouns ending in *s*, *sh*, *ch*, *x*, or *z* form the plural by adding *es*. The plural adds another syllable in the pronunciation.

dress	dresses	ax	axes	couch	couches
match	matches	tax	taxes	waltz	waltzes
bush	bushes	loss	losses	marsh	marshes

3. Nouns ending in *o* preceded by a vowel add *s*. Musical terms ending in *o* add *s*.

Vowel Preceding "o"		Musical Terms	
cam*e*o	cameos	pian*o*	pianos
pat*i*o	patios	alt*o*	altos
rod*e*o	rodeos	cell*o*	cellos

Some nouns ending in *o* preceded by a consonant add *s*. Others add *es*. Some form the plural either way.

Add "s"		Add "es"		Add "s" or "es"		
kimo*n*o	kimonos	Neg*r*o	Negroes	car*g*o	cargos	cargoes
ze*r*o	zeros	he*r*o	heroes	mot*t*o	mottos	mottoes
dyna*m*o	dynamos	pota*t*o	potatoes	torna*d*o	tornados	tornadoes

4. Nouns ending in *y* preceded by a consonant, change the *y* to *i* and add *es*.

par*t*y	parties	coun*tr*y	countries
ci*t*y	cities	foun*dr*y	foundries
f*l*y	flies	ene*m*y	enemies
la*d*y	ladies	ber*r*y	berries

5. Nouns ending in *y* preceded by a vowel, usually add *s*. In many cases the vowel before the final *y* is *e*.

all*e*y	alleys	journ*e*y	journeys
bo*y*	boys	vall*e*y	valleys
ke*y*	keys	da*y*	days

6. Some nouns ending in *f* or *fe* change the *f* or the *fe* to *v* and add *es*. Some nouns ending in *f* have two plurals, one in *s* and one in *ves*. Some simply add *s*.

Changes to "ves"		Add "s" or Change to "ves"		
wife	wives	scarf	scarfs	scarves
shelf	shelves	wharf	wharfs	wharves
thief	thieves	beef	beefs	beeves
wolf	wolves	hoof	hoofs	hooves
half	halves	chief	chiefs	(no second plural)

7. Some nouns form the plural by a change in the vowel.

man	men	mouse	mice
foot	feet	goose	geese
tooth	teeth	louse	lice

8. Some nouns have the same form for both singular and plural.

Singular and Plural		Singular and Plural	
fish	fish	species	species
sheep	sheep	series	series
gross	gross	salmon	salmon
Chinese	Chinese	deer	deer

55

9. The plurals of compound nouns are generally formed by adding *s* to the *principal word* in the compound.

mother-in-law	*mothers*-in-law
board of education	*boards* of education
attorney general	*attorneys* general or attorney *generals*
brigadier general	brigadier *generals*
court-martial	*courts*-martial
editor-in-chief	*editors*-in-chief

Sometimes *both parts* of the compound are made plural.

manservant	menservants
woman doctor	women doctors
Knight Templar	Knights Templars or Knights Templar

Sometimes an *s* is added to the end of the compound. In that case, there is no important word in the compound.

Jack-in-the-pulpit	Jack-in-the-pulpits
forget-me-not	forget-me-nots
toothbrush	toothbrushes

Compounds ending in *ful* are made plural by adding *s* to the end of the compound. This rule applies when the same container is filled a number of times.

spoonful	spoonfuls	handful	handfuls
bucketful	bucketfuls	cupful	cupfuls

Six cups full of flour means that there are six separate cups, and that each one is filled with flour.

10. The plurals of proper names are formed by adding *s* or *es*.

There are three *Ruths* in this class.

The two *Burnses* left the hall.

The *Joneses* and the *Smiths* attended the banquet.

The two *Marys* are friends.

The spelling of proper names must not be changed. If we followed the rule for words ending in *y* in the case of *Mary*, we would change the *y* to *i* and add *es*. The name would then be changed to *Marie*, for the plural would be *Maries*. The correct plural of *Mary* is *Marys*.

Titles are made plural in several ways. The plural of *Miss* is *Misses;* the plural of *Mr.* is *Messrs*. *Mrs.* has no plural. The plural of *Madam* is *Mesdames*, which is sometimes used for the plural of *Mrs. Misses* should not be followed by a period. It is not an abbreviation. In the first column of the following examples, the title is made plural. In the second column the name is made plural. Either form is correct.

the *Misses* Thomas   *or*   the Miss *Thomases*

the *Messrs.* Churchill   *or*   the Mr. *Churchills*

Mesdames Greene   *or*   the Mrs. *Greenes*

Foreign Plurals

Words taken from foreign languages usually retain their foreign plurals. Some of these words are used so commonly that they have acquired an English plural which is formed in the regular way; that is, by adding *s* or *es* to the singular.

The following list gives the foreign and English plurals for some commonly used foreign words. If no English plural is given, the foreign plural is used.

Foreign Word	Foreign Plural	English Plural
alumna *(feminine)*	alumnae	_____
alumnus *(masculine)*	alumni	_____
analysis	analyses	_____
appendix	appendices	appendixes
axis	axes	_____
bacterium	bacteria	_____
basis	bases	_____
cactus	cacti	cactuses
candelabrum	candelabra	candelabrums
crisis	crises	_____
criterion	criteria	criterions
curriculum	curricula	curriculums
datum	data	_____
focus	foci	focuses
formula	formulae	formulas
genus *(kind, class)*	genera	genuses
gymnasium	gymnasia	gymnasiums
hippopotamus	hippopotami	hippopotamuses
hypothesis	hypotheses	_____
index	indices	indexes
madam	mesdames	_____
medium	media	mediums
memorandum	memoranda	memorandums
parenthesis	parentheses	_____
phenomenon	phenomena	_____
radius	radii	radiuses
synopsis	synopses	_____

58

12. The plural of numbers, letters, signs, and symbols is formed by adding the apostrophe and *s*.

Your *2's* look like your *3's*.

You use too many *ands* in your writing. (correct)

or

You use too many *and's* in your writing. (correct)

You must always cross your *t's*.

He received three *A's* and two *B's* last semester.

13. The following nouns are used only in the plural. You may find some of them used in the singular, but the general practice is to regard them as plural. When you are in doubt, consult the dictionary.

trousers	shears	contents
pants	pliers	riches
breeches	pincers	links (golf)
scissors	scales (weighing)	alms
tongs	forceps	remains
billiards	nuptials	suds
clothes	gallows	victuals

SUMMARY

A **noun** is a word used as the name of a person, place, thing, idea, or action.

A **proper noun** is the name of a particular person, place, or thing. A proper noun is written with a capital letter.

A **common noun** is the name of any one of a class of persons, places, or things. A common noun is written with a small letter unless it is the first word of a sentence.

A **collective noun** is a common noun whose singular form names a group of persons, objects, or acts.

Proper adjectives are usually written with capital letters. If the adjective has acquired a special meaning it is not capitalized.

When a noun refers to one person or thing, it is *singular* in number. When a noun refers to more than one person or thing, it is *plural* in number.

The plurals of nouns are formed in various ways. Since there are exceptions to almost every one of these ways of forming the plural, you should consult a reliable, up-to-date dictionary when you are in doubt regarding a correct plural form. You should also be familiar with the methods that are outlined in this unit.

Words taken from foreign languages usually retain their foreign plurals. A number of commonly used foreign words have acquired English plurals.

6

PRONOUNS

A PRONOUN is a word used in place of a noun. Because pronouns can be used in place of nouns, they avoid the monotonous repetition of nouns. The following illustration shows what happens when we repeat the same noun too often in a sentence.

> **Alice** went to **Alice's** room to dress because **Alice** was going to a reception given by **Alice's** club in **Alice's** honor.

This sentence is very awkward and monotonous because of the tiresome repetition of *Alice* and *Alice's*. When we rewrite the sentence and substitute pronouns for *Alice* and *Alice's,* we have a much better sentence.

> Alice went to **her** room to dress because **she** was going to a reception given by **her** club in **her** honor.

You should not only learn how to use pronouns effectively, but you should also learn how to use them correctly. Many of the language errors that are commonly made are errors in the use of pronouns. These mistakes occur because some of the pronouns that we use constantly have a number of different forms.

As a student of English you should know how and when to use the different forms of pronouns. In order to do this, you must be familiar with the changes in form that certain pronouns undergo. To illustrate: The pronoun *I* is used as the subject of a sentence. When this same pronoun is used as the object of a preposition, the form changes to *me*. It is incorrect to say, "between *you* and *I*." The correct form of the pronoun to use in this phrase is *me*.

Illustrations of Changes in the Forms of Pronouns

I saw the accident. (The pronoun *I* is the subject.)

Jane saw **me** at the game. (The pronoun *me* is the object of *saw*.)

61

He *won* the first prize. (The pronoun *he* is the subject.)

We met **him** in the lobby. (The pronoun *him* is the object of *met*.)

In the first sentence, the pronoun *I* is used as the **subject** of the sentence. When this same pronoun is used as the **object of a verb,** the form changes to *me*. In the third sentence, the pronoun *he* is the subject of the sentence. When this same pronoun is used as the object of the verb *met,* the form changes to *him*.

KINDS OF PRONOUNS

There are five groups or classes of pronouns in English: **personal** pronouns, **interrogative** pronouns, **demonstrative** pronouns, **indefinite** pronouns, and **relative** pronouns. The personal pronouns include the *compound personal* pronouns, and the relative pronouns include the *compound relative* pronouns.

PERSONAL PRONOUNS

The personal pronouns are the most important group of pronouns. They are also the pronouns that will give you the most trouble unless you are familiar with the various forms that belong to each pronoun.

A **personal pronoun** is a pronoun that shows by its form whether it refers to the *person speaking,* the *person spoken to,* or the *person or thing spoken of*. All the personal pronouns, with the exception of the pronoun *it,* refer to persons. The following sentences show the use of personal pronouns in the first, second, and third person:

I shall spend the winter in Texas. (*I* is the *person speaking.*)

You are working too hard. (*You* is the *person spoken to.*)

He bought a new Ford. *(He* is the *person spoken about).*

We built the garage. (*We* refers to the *persons speaking.*)

They operate two farms. (*They* refers to the *persons spoken about.*)

Ted has a new radio. **It** is a Zenith. (*It* refers to the *thing spoken about.*)

Jan has two fur coats. **They** are both mink coats. (*They* refers to the *things spoken about.*)

The pronoun of the **first person** is the pronoun *I* with its plural form *we*. The pronoun of the **second person** is *you*. The plural form is also *you*. The pronouns of the **third person** are *he, she,* and *it* with the common plural *they* for all three pronouns.

The personal pronouns also have different forms to indicate case. You will learn more about the case of pronouns in Unit Nine. For the present, you should be familiar with all the forms of the personal pronouns and the pronoun *who* so that you will be able to identify them.

Forms of the Personal Pronouns

1. **First person**—personal pronouns referring to the *speaker*:

   I, my, mine, me (singular)
   we, our, ours, us (plural)

2. **Second person**—personal pronouns referring to the *person spoken to*:

   you, your, yours (same forms in both singular and plural)

3. **Third person**—personal pronouns referring to the *persons* or *things spoken about*:

   he, his, him, she, her, hers, it, its (singular)
   they, their, theirs, them (plural)

4. Forms of the pronoun **who**:

   who, whose, whom

63

COMPOUND PERSONAL PRONOUNS

Sometimes the word *self* or *selves* is added to certain forms of the personal pronouns. Pronouns formed in this way are called **compound personal pronouns**.

List of Compound Personal Pronouns

myself	herself
yourself	ourselves
himself	yourselves
itself	themselves

Compound personal pronouns are used in two ways: (1) as *reflexive pronouns* and (2) as *intensive pronouns*.

A compound personal pronoun is used *reflexively* when the pronoun is the object of the verb. It tells *who* or *what* received *the* action expressed by the verb. In this case the pronoun *always refers back* to the same person or thing as the subject. The following illustration will help to make this clear.

The <u>chef</u> burned <u>himself</u> yesterday.

In this sentence the word *himself* is a compound personal pronoun used as the object of the verb *burned*. *Himself* refers to the same person as the subject, which is the word *chef*. In other words, *chef* and *himself* are the same person. This is called the **reflexive** use of the compound personal pronoun. It means that the pronoun *refers* or *reflects back* to the subject.

Sometimes the compound personal pronoun is used to give added emphasis to a noun or pronoun in the sentence. This is called the **emphatic** or **intensive** use of the compound personal pronoun.

When a compound personal pronoun is used in this way, it must give emphasis to some noun or pronoun that is already in the sentence. Observe the following sentences carefully. In each sentence you will find that there is a *noun* or a *pronoun* to which the compound personal pronoun refers.

I made the dress myself. (*Myself* intensifies the pronoun *I*.)

John himself built the canoe. (*Himself* intensifies the noun *John*.)

Incorrect Use of Compound Personal Pronouns

One of the mistakes commonly made in English is to use the compound personal pronoun when there is no word in the sentence to which it refers. These pronouns should never be used as a substitute for a personal pronoun. They should never be used as the subject of the sentence.

My wife and *myself* appreciate your courtesy. (incorrect)

My wife and **I** appreciate your courtesy. (correct)

The manager and *myself* checked the accounts. (incorrect)

The manager and **I** checked the accounts. (correct)

He sent the book to John and *myself*. (incorrect)

He sent the book to John and **me.** (correct)

The first sentence is incorrect because there is no noun or pronoun in the sentence which the pronoun *myself* refers to or gives emphasis to. The second sentence is correct because a *personal pronoun* is used.

Whenever you use a compound personal pronoun in a sentence, always remember that such a pronoun must have an *antecedent,* or a word in the sentence which refers to the same person or thing as the pronoun does. In other words, it must have its own antecedent in the sentence. Do not make mistakes like the following:

Alice and *yourself* were appointed on the committee. (incorrect)

Alice and **you** were appointed on the committee. (correct)

The owner gave Tom and *myself* his old lawn mower. (incorrect)

The owner gave Tom and **me** his old lawn mower. (correct)

Everyone in the club has a car as well as *myself*. (incorrect)

Everyone in the club has a car as well as **I**. (correct)

They sent an invitation to the Smiths and *ourselves*. (incorrect)

They sent an invitation to the Smiths and **us**. (correct)

INTERROGATIVE PRONOUNS

Interrogative pronouns are pronouns that are used in asking questions. The interrogative pronouns are *who (whose, whom), which,* and *what.* An interrogative pronoun also has another function to perform in the sentence, just as any other pronoun has. It may be the *subject* of the sentence, or it may be the *object* of the verb or of a preposition.

Who is the director of the band?

For **whom** are you waiting?

What did they say about his speech?

Which is your car?

Whose car did you borrow?

DEMONSTRATIVE PRONOUNS

Demonstrative pronouns are pronouns that point out definite persons, places, or things. There are only two demonstrative pronouns: *this* with its plural *these,* and *that* with its plural *those.*

This is my hat. (A definite hat is pointed out.)

That is your book. (A definite book is pointed out.)

These are the theater tickets. (Definite tickets are pointed out.)

Those are John's shoes. (Definite shoes are pointed out.)

INDEFINITE PRONOUNS

A large group of pronouns are called **indefinite pronouns** because they do not point out particular places, persons, or things.

Somebody took my coat. (*Somebody* is an indefinite pronoun.)

A **few** left the hall early. (*Few* is an indefinite pronoun.)

The following list contains the commonly used indefinite pronouns. Refer to this list, and to the other lists in this unit, whenever you are not sure of the classification of a pronoun.

Commonly Used Indefinite Pronouns

all	everybody	one
any	everyone	one another
anybody	everything	ones
anyone	few	other
anything	many	others
both	neither	several
each	nobody	some
each one	none	somebody
each other	no one	someone
either	nothing	something

RELATIVE PRONOUNS

A **relative pronoun** is a pronoun that joins the clause which it introduces to its own antecedent. The *antecedent* of a pronoun is the noun or pronoun to which it refers.

The relative pronouns are *who, which, that,* and *what.* The pronoun *who* has two other forms, *whose* and *whom.* When the relative pronoun is combined with *ever* or *soever,* it is called a **compound relative pronoun.**

List of Compound Relative Pronouns

whoever	whosoever	whichsoever
whomever	whatsoever	whomsoever
whatever	whosesoever	whichever

68

The *relative pronoun* is always found in a clause which it introduces. For that reason, we shall postpone further study of relative pronouns until we take up the study of subordinate clauses.

Use of Relative Pronouns

The following distinctions are generally observed in the use of relative pronouns. A careful writer or speaker always observes these distinctions:

Who is used when the antecedent is a *person.*

That is used to refer to either *persons* or *things.*

Which is used to refer to anything *except persons.*

The book **which** (or **that**) I was reading has disappeared. (correct)

(*Which* or *that* refers to things.)

She is the girl **who** won the award. (correct)

(*Who* refers only to persons.)

This is the dog **that** (or **which**) was lost. (correct)

(*That* or *which* refers to things.)

She is the girl **that** won the award. (correct)

(*That* may refer to persons.)

Margaret is the girl **which** entered the contest. (incorrect)

(*Which* should not be used to refer to persons.)

69

PRONOUNS USED AS ADJECTIVES

The *possessive forms* of the personal pronouns are often used with nouns in much the same way as adjectives are used to modify nouns. Although they function as adjectives when they are placed before the noun, they still retain the idea of possession. For that reason, they are sometimes called **possessive adjectives** to distinguish them from other types of adjectives.

In the sentence, *Herbert forgot his coat,* the possessive form of the pronoun *he,* which is *his,* is used as an adjective modifying the noun *coat.* It also shows that the coat belongs to Herbert. Therefore, it is called a possessive adjective. All the adjectives in the following sentences show possession. They are called possessive adjectives.

Possessive Forms of Personal Pronouns Used as Adjectives

These are **her** gloves. (modifies *gloves*)

I bought **their** home. (modifies *home*)

Did you bring **your** violin? (modifies *violin*)

The dog lost **its** collar. (modifies *collar*)

We like **our** new radio. (modifies *radio*)

Do you like **my** new coat? (modifies *coat*)

The manager has **his** report. (modifies *report*)

Demonstrative and *indefinite pronouns* are also used as adjectives. Demonstrative pronouns that function as adjectives are often called **demonstrative adjectives** because they have not lost their pointing out function. In the following sentences the demonstrative pronouns are used as adjectives:

This camera belongs to Jane. (modifies *camera*)

Those apples are delicious. (modifies *apples*)

That man is an army officer. (modifies *man*)

These cards are Easter cards. (modifies *cards*)

Indefinite pronouns used as adjectives are generally regarded as pure adjectives, although they may be called **indefinite adjectives.** They have no special function. The following examples illustrate their use as adjectives:

Each girl carried a flag. (modifies *girl*)

Both men received a promotion. (modifies *men*)

Neither answer is correct. (modifies *answer*)

Many soldiers were on that ship. (modifies *soldiers*)

Any mechanic could do that job. (modifies *mechanic*)

Several tables were ruined. (modifies *tables*)

Interrogative pronouns are also often used as adjectives. Since the adjective is the word that asks the question, these adjectives are called **interrogative adjectives.** In the sentence, *Which house did you buy?* the word *which* asks the question. It is also an adjective modifying the noun *house*. Note how the pronouns are used to ask questions in the following sentences:

What newspapers does he read? (modifies *newspapers*)

Whose name did he call? (modifies *name*)

Which play do you like best? (modifies *play*)

POSSESSIVE FORMS OF PRONOUNS

The possessive forms of the *personal pronouns* and the possessive form of the pronoun *who* are never written with an apostrophe. These pronouns have a special form to show possession and do not require an apostrophe. The correct forms to use in order to show possession are the following: *my, mine, yours, his, hers, its, ours, theirs, whose.* Do not place an apostrophe either before or after the **s** in any of these words.

The word *it's* is a contraction of *it is.* It is not a form of the pronoun, and should never be used to show possession. The word *who's* is a contraction of *who is* or *who has,* and should not be confused with the possessive form *whose.*

Contractions

It's on my desk. (*It is* on my desk.)

Who's speaking tonight? (*Who is* speaking tonight?)

Who's finished the test? (*Who has* finished the test?)

Indefinite pronouns do not have special forms to show possession. Therefore, it is necessary to use the apostrophe to show the possessive forms of these pronouns. Since most of these pronouns are used only in the singular, the possessive is formed by adding the *apostrophe* and **s** (**'s**). The plural of the indefinite pronoun *other* is *others.* In the case of this plural form, the apostrophe is placed after the **s**. Study these forms carefully:

Possessive Forms of Indefinite Pronouns

everybody's job	*anyone's* opinions
somebody's hat	*someone's* car
one's relatives	*each one's* duty
another's problems	*others'* affairs (plural)

When *else* is added to an indefinite pronoun, it is regarded as part of the pronoun. In this case, the apostrophe and **s** are added to *else* to form the possessive.

I came home with *somebody else's* coat.

Someone else's book was substituted for mine.

SUMMARY

1. There are five kinds or classes of pronouns in English: *personal* pronouns, *interrogative* pronouns, *demonstrative* pronouns, *indefinite* pronouns, and *relative* pronouns.

2. **Personal pronouns** indicate by the form whether they refer to the *speaker*, the *person spoken to*, or the *person* or *thing spoken of*.

3. **Interrogative pronouns** ask questions.

4. **Demonstrative pronouns** point out definite persons, places, or things.

5. **Indefinite pronouns** do not refer to definite persons, places, or things.

6. **Relative pronouns** join subordinate clauses to their *antecedents*.

7. Pronouns often function as adjectives. When the personal pronoun functions as an adjective, it is called a **possessive adjective** because it still shows possession. When the demonstrative pronoun functions as an adjective, it is called a **demonstrative adjective** because it still retains the pointing out function.

8. When the interrogative pronoun functions as an adjective, it is still the word that asks the question. For that reason, it is called an **Interrogative adjective.** When the indefinite pronoun is used as an adjective, it is generally regarded as a pure adjective, although it may be called an **indefinite adjective.**

9. The *personal pronouns* and the pronoun *who* have special forms to show possession. The following forms, which show possession, are never written with an apostrophe: *yours, theirs, ours, whose, hers, its.* The possessive forms of the indefinite pronouns are formed by adding the apostrophe and **s** (**'s**) in the singular: *anybody's, another's, each one's, everybody's, someone's,* etc.

10. **Contractions** should not be confused with the possessive forms of pronouns. *It's* is a contraction of *it is,* and *who's* is a contraction of *who is* or *who has.* These forms (contractions) should never be used as the possessive forms of pronouns.

73

7

AGREEMENT OF PRONOUN WITH ANTECEDENT

A PRONOUN usually refers to a noun or pronoun which precedes it in the sentence. The word to which the pronoun refers is called its antecedent. The word *antecedent* comes from two Latin words which mean "*going before.*" The antecedent of a pronoun is the word which "*goes before*" the pronoun. It is the word to which the pronoun refers.

In the sentence, *Robert lost his fishing tackle,* the pronoun *his* refers to *Robert.* The word *Robert* precedes the pronoun *his* or "goes before" it. *Robert* is the antecedent of *his.* It is the word to which the pronoun *his* refers.

Antecedents of Pronouns

Margaret attended her class reunion. (*Margaret* — antecedent of *her*)

Every day brings its duties. (*day*—antecedent of *its*)

The men brought their golf clubs. (*men*—antecedent of *their*)

Only a few brought their equipment. (*few*—antecedent of *their*)

The professor himself did not know the answer. (*professor*—antecedent of *himself*)

AGREEMENT OF PRONOUN AND ANTECEDENT IN GENDER

Since a pronoun stands for, or replaces a noun, it must agree with that noun in person, number, and gender. We have already considered the problems of number and person in Grammar Units Five and Six. In this unit we shall take up the problem of gender, and show its connection with the agreement of pronoun and antecedent.

In grammar **gender** means the classification of nouns and pronouns according to distinctions in sex. There are four genders: *masculine gender, feminine gender, common gender,* and *neuter gender.*

Masculine gender denotes the male sex. **Feminine gender** denotes the female sex. **Common gender** denotes either sex. **Neuter gender** denotes absence of sex. The following are examples of nouns and pronouns in the four genders:

Masculine gender—he, him, father, king

Feminine gender—sister, she, her, princess

Common gender—child, adult, cousin, neighbor

Neuter gender—table, book, dress, radio, it

Some nouns and a few pronouns have special forms to show gender. The following list shows the changes that occur in some words to indicate a change in the gender. Some of the distinctions formerly used to show gender are passing out of use. The words *authoress* and *poetess,* for example, are seldom used.

SPECIAL FORMS TO SHOW GENDER

Masculine	Feminine	Masculine	Feminine
uncle	aunt	god	goddess
bull	cow	aviator	aviatrix
waiter	waitress	hero	heroine

SPECIAL FORMS TO SHOW GENDER (continued)

Masculine	Feminine	Masculine	Feminine
alumnus	alumna	count (title)	countess
emperor	empress	gander	goose
host	hostess	sir	madam
peacock	peahen	ram	ewe
bridegroom	bride	lion	lioness
monk	nun	duke	duchess
actor	actress	nephew	niece
bachelor	spinster	prince	princess
executor	executrix	lord (title)	lady
baron	baroness	stallion	mare
he	she	father	mother
lad	lass	him	her
man	woman	boy	girl
rooster	hen	husband	wife
master	mistress	buck (stag)	doe
brother	sister	landlord	landlady
drake	duck	son	daughter
man-servant	maid-servant	male	female
fiancé	fiancée	salesman	saleswoman

GENDER AND NUMBER OF INDEFINITE PRONOUNS

Indefinite pronouns present a problem in gender. These pronouns often refer to both sexes, masculine and feminine. When we say, *Everybody went to the game,* the indefinite pronoun *everybody* includes individuals of both genders, masculine and feminine.

The problem arises when the indefinite pronoun is the antecedent of another pronoun. In that case, the accepted practice is to *use the masculine gender for the pronoun that is used in place of the indefinite pronoun.*

In the sentence, *Everyone received his income tax form,* the indefinite pronoun *everyone* is the antecedent of the pronoun *his.* It is the word to which the pronoun *his* refers. Although *everyone* includes persons of both genders, the masculine pronoun *his* is used instead of saying *his or her* income tax form.

If the sentence shows clearly that the indefinite pronoun refers to members of only one sex, the pronoun that refers to that sex should be used.

Everyone attending the meeting of the Women's Athletic Club presented **her** membership card.

In this sentence the members are women, and the pronoun *her* is used correctly. In cases where it is not clear whether the antecedent is masculine or feminine, use the pronoun *his.*

Anyone may have **his** money refunded.

Somebody left **his** pen on my desk.

Indefinite pronouns also present a problem in number. Some of them are always singular. Some are always plural, and some may be either singular or plural.

Pronouns That Are Always Singular

The following pronouns are always singular. A pronoun that is used in place of one of these indefinite pronouns must also be singular.

anybody	everybody	neither
anyone	everyone	one
another	many a one	other
each	nobody	someone
either	no one	somebody

Study the following illustrations carefully. These sentences show the proper agreement between pronoun and antecedent when the antecedent is singular.

Neither of the men had **his** tools. (not *their*)

If **anyone** wants a pen, **he** can obtain one here. (not *they*)

One likes to do what **he** can do well. (not *they*)

Someone left **his** coat in **his** locker. (not *their*)

Pronouns That Are Always Plural

The following pronouns are always plural. A pronoun that is used in place of one of them must also be plural.

many   both   few   several   others

Notice that *many a one* is included in the list of pronouns that are always singular, whereas *many* is included in this plural list. When singular expressions, such as *a man, a one, a person*, etc., are added to *many*, the *pronoun* is singular, not plural.

Several found **their** cars unlocked. (*Several*—plural)

Only a **few** would sacrifice **their** savings. (*few*—plural)

Many brought **their** lunches with them. (*Many*—plural)

Others found **their** friends in the balcony. (*Others*—plural)

Pronouns That May Be Either Singular or Plural

The pronouns *all, any, some,* and *none* are singular or plural according to the meaning of the sentence. When these pronouns refer to **number,** they are generally regarded as plural. When they refer to **quantity** or to a **mass,** they are regarded as singular.

The pronoun *none* is singular when it clearly means *no one,* or *not one.* It is often difficult to determine the number of this pronoun since there are sentences in which it carries a plural idea. If you want to express the singular idea use *no one,* or *not one.*

Some found **their** children in the park. (*Some* is plural.)

Some of the candy has lost **its** flavor. (*Some* is singular.)

All were waiting for **their** salary checks. (*All* is plural.)

There is no candy in the box. **All** of **it** has been eaten. (*All* is singular.)

Did **any** of the men have **their** membership cards? (*Any* is plural.)

None have arrived. (*None*—plural in use)

None of these is a typical example. (*None*—singular in use)

AGREEMENT OF THE PRONOUN
WITH A COMPOUND ANTECEDENT

Sometimes the pronoun refers to two antecedents connected by *and*. If both of these antecedents are singular and refer to *different persons or things,* the antecedent is plural. The pronoun that refers to these antecedents must also be plural.

The <u>president</u> and the <u>manager</u> have outlined <u>their</u> plans.
    plural   *plural*

If the antecedent refers to *one* person who fulfills *two* functions, the pronoun that takes the place of the antecedent is singular. In the following sentence *cook* and *housekeeper* are the same person.

The <u>cook and housekeeper</u> did not like <u>her</u> duties.
       singular   *singular*

If the housekeeper were another individual, the word *the* would be placed before the word *housekeeper*.

The <u>cook</u> and the <u>housekeeper</u> did not like <u>their</u> duties.
      plural   *plural*

When the connectives, *either—or* and *neither—nor* join singular nouns, the antecedent is singular. When they join plural nouns, the antecedent is plural. When they join nouns that differ in number, the pronoun should agree with the antecedent that is nearer to it.

Either *Jane* or *Alice* left **her** book on **her** desk.
    (Both nouns are singular—pronoun is singular)

Either the *boys* or the *girls* left **their** books on the table.
    (Both nouns are plural—pronoun is plural)

Neither *Harvey* nor his *cousins* wore **their** dress suits.
    (Pronoun is plural—agrees with *cousins*)

Neither the *men* nor the *boy* could find **his** place in the line.
(Pronoun agrees with *boy* which is nearer to it.)

In sentences like the last one, it is better to place the plural noun nearer to the pronoun. By doing so, you make the antecedent plural, and the sentence sounds better.

AGREEMENT OF PRONOUN WITH COLLECTIVE NOUNS

Collective nouns are singular when they designate a group *acting as a unit*. They are plural when the members who make up the group are *acting independently*. The pronoun that takes the place of the collective noun must agree with it in number. If the collective noun expresses a singular idea, the pronoun is singular. If the collective noun expresses a plural idea, the pronoun is plural.

The band played its fifth concert. (*acting as a unit*)
 singular   singular

The band were tuning up their instruments. (*as individuals*)
 plural   plural

You can readily see that the second sentence could not refer to the band as a unit. That would mean that the members of the band were all working on the same instrument.

AGREEMENT OF PRONOUN AND ANTECEDENT IN PERSON

A pronoun must agree with its antecedent in **person.** If the antecedent of the pronoun is in the *third person,* the pronoun that refers to it must also be in the *third person.* If the antecedent is in the *second person,* the pronoun should be in the *second person.*

One of the most common mistakes in English is to start the sentence in the *third person* and then put the pronoun that refers to the antecedent in the *second person.*

If anybody wants an education, you can get it. (*incorrect*)
 third person '   second person

If anybody wants an education, he can get it. (*correct*)
 third person   third person

81

VAGUE ANTECEDENTS

A pronoun should not have two possible antecedents in the same sentence. If it is not clear which of two nouns a pronoun refers to, there will be two possible interpretations of the sentence. Observe the two possible interpretations in the following illustration:

James told his friend that **he** had been elected president.

In this sentence, does the pronoun *he* refer to *James* or to *friend?* If the antecedent of the pronoun *he* is *friend,* the sentence means that *James told his friend that he (the friend) had been elected president.* If the antecedent of the pronoun *he* is *James,* the sentence means that *James told his friend that he (James) had been elected president.*

The sentence might be rewritten in either of the two following ways, since we do not know which meaning the author intended:

James said to his friend, "You have been elected president."

James said to his friend, "I have been elected president."

Many of the errors that are made in the use of pronouns are caused by a lack of agreement between pronoun and antecedent. The pronoun should refer definitely to the noun which it represents. In the following sentence, to what does the pronoun *it* refer?

Your letter and your check arrived promptly, but we cannot ship **it** at present.

There is no antecedent for the pronoun *it* in the sentence. Neither the word *letter* nor the word *check* could be the antecedent. *It* probably refers to an order for goods which was included in the letter. If the word *it* refers to an order for goods, the sentence might be written as follows:

Your letter and your check arrived promptly, but at present we cannot ship the goods ordered.

ADJECTIVE—PRONOUN AGREEMENT

Demonstrative adjectives should agree in *number* with the nouns they modify. The adjectives *this, that, these,* and *those* sometimes cause agreement trouble when they modify such nouns as *kind, sort, type,* and *variety.*

Keep in mind that the demonstrative adjectives *this* and *that* are singular and should be used only with singular nouns. *These* and *those* are plural and should be used only with the plural nouns.

Incorrect	**Correct**
these kind of apples plural singular	**this kind** of apples (or apple) or **these kinds** of apples (plural)
those sort of roses plural singular	**that sort** of roses (or rose) or **those sorts** of roses (plural)
these variety of fruits plural singular	**this variety** of fruits (or fruit) or **these varieties** of fruits (plural)

The forms on the left are incorrect because the adjective does not agree with the noun in number. In the first illustration, the adjective *these* is plural and the noun *kind* is singular. In the second illustration, the adjective *those* is plural and the noun *sort* is singular.

The forms on the right are correct because the adjective agrees with the noun in number. In the first illustration, *this* is singular and *kind* is singular; *these* is plural and *kinds* is plural. The other illustrations on the right are correct for the same reasons.

SUMMARY

1. The **antecedent** of a pronoun is the noun or the pronoun to which it refers.

2. A pronoun must agree with its antecedent in **gender, person,** and **number.**

3. If the antecedent of a pronoun is **masculine gender,** the pronoun that refers to it must be masculine gender. If the antecedent is the **feminine gender,** the pronoun must be the feminine gender.

4. **Indefinite pronouns** usually refer to individuals of both genders, masculine and feminine. In such cases, the general practice is to use the *masculine form* of the pronoun that refers to the antecedent.

5. Some *indefinite pronouns* are always singular in number, others are always plural, and some are either singular or plural according to the meaning of the sentence. The pronoun that is used to refer to the antecedent must agree with it in **number.** If the indefinite pronoun is singular, the pronoun that refers to it must be singular. If the indefinite pronoun is plural, the pronoun that refers to it must be plural.

6. The pronoun must agree with its antecedent in **person.** If the antecedent is in the *third person,* the pronoun that refers to it must also be in the *third person.* If the antecedent is in the *second person,* the pronoun that refers to it must be in the *second person.*

7. A pronoun should not have two possible antecedents in the same sentence. If it is not clear which of the two antecedents the pronoun refers to, the sentence should be recast.

8. **Demonstrative adjectives** should agree in number with the nouns they modify. *This* and *that* are singular and should be used only with singular nouns. *These* and *those* are plural and should be used with plural nouns.

8

COMPLEMENTS OF VERBS

THE DIRECT OBJECT

EVERY sentence must have a basic structure in order to express a complete thought. This basic structure may consist of only two parts, a subject noun or pronoun and a predicate verb or verb phrase. Many sentences require a third part or an additional word in order to express a complete thought. This additional word or group of words is necessary to complete the idea expressed by the verb.

The group of words, *The men lifted*, contains a subject noun *men* and a predicate verb *lifted*. Still it does not express a complete thought. A word is needed to tell **what** the men lifted. The sentence might be completed by adding the word *beam*. The completed sentence, *The men lifted the beam*, expresses a complete thought.

The word *beam* completes the meaning expressed by the verb *lifted*. For that reason it is called a **complement** or a completing word. The three essential parts of this sentence are the **subject**, the **verb**, and the **complement**. The complement is *beam*.

A complement completes the meaning expressed by a verb. The *complement* of a verb that expresses *action* is called the **direct object** of the verb. A direct object usually answers the questions *what?* or *whom?* In the preceding sentence the verb *lifted* expresses action. The complement *beam* tells *what* the men lifted. Notice how the complements in the following sentences complete the meaning of the verb.

I saw Evelyn at the convention. (*Evelyn* tells whom I saw.)
<u>direct object</u>

The engineer stopped the train. (*Train* tells what he stopped.)
<u>direct object</u>

The sailors saluted the captain. (tells *whom* they saluted)
<u>direct object</u>

She refused the invitation. (tells *what* she refused)
<u>direct object</u>

Some verbs that express action are complete without the addition of a complement. When such verbs are used in sentences, only two parts are essential—the *subject* and the *verb*. Study the following illustrations. You will readily see that the thought is complete without the addition of a complement.

Jane is singing. (*complete thought*)

The whistles are blowing. (*complete thought*)

We have been studying. (*complete thought*)

The boys are playing. (*complete thought*)

Although the verbs in the preceding sentences do not require a complement or a completing word, a complement might be added to some of them to make the meaning more explicit.

Jane is singing a ballad. (tells *what* Jane is singing)
direct object

We have been studying Spanish. (tells *what* we have been
studying)   direct object

The boys are playing games. (tells *what* the boys are playing)
direct object

A complement completes the meaning of the verb.

The **direct object** of a verb names the *receiver* of the action. It completes the meaning of the verb. A direct object is usually a noun or a pronoun. Adjectives and adverbs are never used as direct objects. Adjectives and adverbs are always used as modifiers. If you have any difficulty in deciding which word is the direct object, apply this test: Find the word that answers the question *what?* or *whom?* Apply the test in the following sentences:

The farmer planted the **seeds** in rows.

What did the farmer plant? The answer is, "He planted the *seeds.*" The word *seeds* is the direct object of the verb planted. It tells **what** he planted.

I met **Uncle Henry** in the bank.

Whom did I meet? The answer is, "I met Uncle Henry." The direct object is *Uncle Henry.* It tells **whom** I met.

A verb may take two or more direct objects. In this case, the verb or verb phrase has a compound object.

He grows orchids and lilies in his garden.
          compound object

I met Jerry and Jane at the stadium.
     compound object

TRANSITIVE AND INTRANSITIVE VERBS

When an action verb takes a direct object, it is called a **transitive verb.** The word *transitive* comes from two Latin words which mean *"passing across."* When the verb is transitive, the action passes across from a **doer** (the subject) to a **receiver** of the action (the direct object). When we say that a verb is *transitive*, it is the same as saying that it has a *direct object*.

Any verb that does not take a direct object is **intransitive.** That is, the verb does *not* express action that passes over to a receiver.

A verb may be transitive in one sentence and intransitive in another sentence. The verb may express action, but the action may not pass over to a receiver. In that case the verb is intransitive. When the verb is transitive, it always takes a direct object—the receiver of the action.

The following sentences show the same verb used as a *transitive* verb and as an *intransitive* verb:

Transitive	Intransitive
The sexton rang the <u>bell.</u> direct object	The bell rang loudly. (*no object*)
The ship sailed the <u>seas.</u> direct object	The ship sails at noon. (*no object*)
I met my <u>friend</u> at the airport. direct object	The delegates met yesterday. (*no object*)
The soldier saluted the <u>colonel.</u> direct object	The soldier saluted. (*no object*)

A transitive verb is a verb that takes an object.

An intransitive verb is a verb that does not take an object.

THE INDIRECT OBJECT

Some verbs that express action take two objects, a direct object and an indirect object. The **indirect object** tells *to whom* the action is directed or *for whom* the action is performed.

The indirect object is used after certain verbs: *get, give, lend, offer, read, tell, buy, send, show, make, pay,* etc.

In the sentence, *Mother bought Ellen a coat,* there are two objects, a direct object and an indirect object. The word *coat* is the direct *object.* It tells *what* Mother bought. The word *Ellen* is the indirect object. It tells *for whom* Mother bought a coat. The indirect object always precedes or comes before the direct object.

The librarian read the <u>children</u> a <u>story</u>.
                             indirect   direct

Give <u>him</u> five <u>dollars</u> for his services.
     indirect   direct

The tailor made <u>Edward</u> a brown <u>suit</u>.
                 indirect   direct

There are two tests that you can apply in order to identify an indirect object. One test is to determine the position of the object. The indirect object always precedes the direct object. The other test is to determine whether the indirect object seems to be the object of the preposition *to* or *for* understood. The following sentences illustrate this point:

The librarian read (**to**) the children a story.

Give (**to**) him five dollars for his services.

The tailor made (**for**) Edward a brown suit.

The words *to* and *for* are never expressed when a word functions as an indirect object. If we change the order of the sentence and supply the preposition, our sentence would read as follows: *The librarian read a story to the children.* In this sentence the word *children* is no longer the indirect object but is the object of the preposition *to.*

LINKING VERBS

Most verbs describe or express action. However, there are a small group that do not. The verb **to be** is the most important verb in this group. Since it is the most irregular verb in our language, you should be familiar with its various forms. The following verbs and verb phrases are forms of the verb *to be*:

Forms of the Verb "To Be"

am	were	has been	could have been
are	will be	had been	would have been
is	shall be	shall have been	might have been
was	have been	will have been	should have been

Although the verb *to be,* as well as the other verbs belonging in this group, does not express action, it has another function in the sentence. The chief purpose of this verb is to serve as a link which joins the subject to some word in the predicate that gives the meaning to the sentence. For that reason, it is called a **linking verb.**

Linking verbs have very little meaning of their own. With the help of another word, they express various ideas in regard to the subject. In the sentence, *Mary is ill,* the verb *is* (a form of *to be*) is used with the adjective *ill* to describe the condition of the subject, *Mary.* The sentence really means *ill Mary,* but you need a verb in order to make a complete statement.

In the sentence, *The young man was an aviator,* the verb *was* is a linking verb. With the help of the noun *aviator,* it identifies or classifies the young man. The noun *aviator* means the same as the subject. In the sentence, *The actress is very beautiful,* the verb *is,* with the help of the adjective *beautiful,* describes the appearance of the actress.

Verbs like *to be* are sometimes called **copulative verbs.** This is a term that comes from the Latin and means exactly the same as **linking.**

The verbs *become* and *seem,* like the verb *to be,* are almost always used as linking verbs. The following verbs are used both as linking verbs and as action verbs. The meaning of the sentence will show to which classification they belong:

Linking and Action Verbs

grow	look	smell	remain
turn	feel	taste	keep
prove	sound	appear	stay

This group of words is important because a great many mistakes in English are made when a speaker or writer does not understand their linking function.

When these words have a linking function, they have practically the same meaning as the verb *to be* would have in the same sentence. By supplying the verb *to be* mentally after one of these verbs, you can readily tell whether the verb has a linking function or whether it is used as an action verb. Every one of the verbs in the following sentences is a linking verb. The verb *to be* has been supplied to show you how to interpret the sentence when the verbs have a linking function.

The cookies **are** wonderful. (wonderful cookies)

The cookies **look** (to be) delicious. (delicious cookies)

The cookies **smell** (to be) good. (good cookies)

The cookies **taste** (to be) sweet. (sweet cookies)

The cookies **seem** (to be) brittle. (brittle cookies)

The cookies **became** (to be) stale. (stale cookies)

The cookies **proved** (to be) sweet. (sweet cookies)

The cookies **feel** (to be) hard. (hard cookies)

The cookies **stayed** (to be) fresh. (fresh cookies)

The cookies **appear** (to be) tempting. (tempting cookies)

The cookies **remained** (to be) soft. (soft cookies)

The cookies **kept** (to be) fresh. (fresh cookies)

Some of the same verbs that were used in the preceding illustrations may also be used to express action. Note the differences in meaning when these verbs function as action verbs and not as linking verbs.

John **appeared** promptly. (made his appearance)

The horticulturist **grows** orchids. (produces by cultivation)

I **turned** the key in the lock.

We **proved** a theorem in geometry.

The doctor **felt** the broken bone.

The warden **sounded** the gong.

The chef **tasted** the sauce.

We **kept** a record of our journey.

The dog **smelled** the meat.

The judge **will stay** the trial. (postpone)

The committee **looked** at the pictures.

COMPLEMENTS OF LINKING VERBS

A *linking verb* cannot make a complete predicate. It always requires a *complement*. The group of words, *My friend is,* does not make a complete statement. The verb *is* requires some additional word to complete the meaning of the sentence. That word may be a noun, a pronoun, or an adjective.

My friend is an <u>executive</u>.
<small>noun</small>

My friend is very <u>ambitious</u>.
<small>adjective</small>

That is <u>he</u>.
<small>pronoun</small>

The noun that completes the meaning of a linking verb is called a *predicate noun* because it is found in the predicate. A **predicate noun** completes the verb and renames or explains the subject. In the preceding illustration, *executive* is a predicate noun. It renames the subject *friend*

92

and classifies *friend* as an *executive*. The noun *friend* and the noun *executive* refer to the same person.

A pronoun that follows a linking verb functions in the same way as the noun. It completes the verb and means the same person or thing as the subject. It is called a **predicate pronoun.**

An adjective that follows a linking verb is called a **predicate adjective** because it is found in the predicate. A predicate adjective always modifies the subject.

The following sentences illustrate the use of the predicate noun, predicate pronoun, and predicate adjective:

Our <u>manager</u> was a former army <u>colonel.</u> (*manager* and *colonel*—
    subject   predicate noun
same person)

Our <u>manager</u> is very efficient. (*efficient* modifies *manager*)
    subject   predicate adjective

The <u>candidate</u> for the position is <u>he.</u> (*he* and *candidate* — same
    subject   predicate pronoun
person)

In the first sentence, *colonel* is a **predicate noun.** It completes the meaning of the verb *was* and refers to the same person as the subject. In the second sentence *efficient* is a **predicate adjective.** It modifies the subject noun *manager*. In the third sentence, *he* is a **predicate pronoun.** It means the same person as the subject *candidate*.

1. Every sentence must have two main parts—a subject and a verb. Some sentences require a third part, which is called the complement. A **complement** is a completing word. Some verbs require this completing word in order to express a complete predicate.

2. Verbs that express action often require a complement. The complement of a verb that expresses action is called the **direct object.** It names the *receiver* of the action.

3. Some **action verbs** do not require a complement. They express a complete predicate without the addition of a direct object.

4. A verb that takes an object is called a **transitive verb.** A verb that does not take an object is called an **intransitive verb.** An action verb may be transitive in one sentence and intransitive in another sentence.

5. Some action verbs take two complements—a *direct object* and an *indirect object.* The **indirect object** always precedes the direct object. The indirect object tells to whom the action is directed or for whom the action is performed.

6. All **linking verbs** require complements. The complement of a linking verb may be a noun, a pronoun, or an adjective.

7. A noun used as the complement of a linking verb is called a **predicate noun.** A pronoun used as the complement of a linking verb is called a **predicate pronoun.** An adjective used as the complement of a linking verb is called a **predicate adjective.**

8. A **predicate noun** or **pronoun** refers to the same person or thing as the subject. A **predicate adjective** modifies the subject.

9

CASE OF NOUNS AND PRONOUNS

NOUNS AND PRONOUNS have certain relationships to other words in a sentence. We call attention to these relationships by indicating the case of the noun or pronoun. The word *case* is used in grammar to indicate the *relationship* a noun or a pronoun has to other words in the sentence. The case of a noun or a pronoun is determined by the particular use of that noun or pronoun in the sentence.

There are only three cases in English: the *nominative case,* the *objective case,* and the *possessive* case. The **nominative case** is the case of the *subject.* The **objective case** is the case of the *object.* The **possessive case** is the case that shows *ownership.*

CASE OF NOUNS

Nouns present very few problems in case because the same form is used for the nominative case and the objective case. The only way to determine whether a noun is in the nominative case or in the objective case is to determine its relationship to other words in the sentence. If the noun is used as the *subject* of the sentence, it is in the *nominative case.* If the noun is used as the *object* of a verb or a preposition, it is in the *objective case.*

The **door** is open. (*nominative case*—subject)

I closed the **door.** (*objective case*—direct object)

In the first sentence, the noun *door* is used as the subject of the sentence. It is in the nominative case. In the second sentence, the same form *door* is used as the direct object of the verb *closed. Door* is in the objective case in this sentence.

Like nouns, *indefinite pronouns* have the same form for the nominative case and the objective case.

Everyone contributed five dollars. (*nominative case*-subject)

I saw **everyone** at the game. (*objective case*-direct object)

NOMINATIVE CASE

The word *nominative* comes from a Latin word which means *name*. The **nominative case** names the case of the subject of the sentence. It also names the case of a predicate noun. A predicate noun is in the nominative case. For this reason, it is often called a **predicate nominative.**

A *predicate noun* must agree in case with the *subject* because it refers to the same person or thing as the subject. It also follows a verb which cannot take an object. Predicate nouns are always used after linking verbs.

My friend is a naval officer. (*nominative case*)

  subject   predicate noun

       same person

The leading lady was Mary Martin. (*nominative case*)

      same person

In the first sentence, *officer* is a predicate noun. It is used after the linking verb *is* and refers to the same person as the subject. It is in the nominative case to agree with the case of the subject *friend*.

In the second sentence, *Mary Martin* is a predicate noun. It is in the nominative case to agree with the subject *lady*. *Mary Martin* and *lady* refer to the same person.

OBJECTIVE CASE

The **objective case** is the case of the *object*. The *direct object* of a verb, the *indirect object,* and the *object* of a *preposition* are in the objective case.

Lester writes **articles** for the paper. (*articles*—direct object)

Arthur sent the **manager** a detailed report. (*manager*—indirect object)

In the first sentence, *articles* is the direct object of the verb *writes*. It tells **what** Lester writes. *Articles* is in the objective case. In the second sentence, *manager* is the indirect object. It tells **to whom** Arthur sent his report. *Manager* is in the objective case.

In Grammar Unit Two you learned that a preposition is always followed by some noun or pronoun which is called the *object* of the *preposition*. The object of a preposition is always in the objective case.

Edward met his lawyer at the **bank.** (object of preposition *at*)
objective case

We met Marvin in the **lobby.** (object of preposition *in*)
objective case

In the first sentence, the preposition *at* is followed by the noun *bank*. The object of the preposition is *bank*, which is in the objective case. In the second sentence, *lobby* is the object of the preposition *in*. *Lobby* is in the objective case.

It is easy to remember that direct objects of verbs, indirect objects of verbs, and objects of prepositions are in the objective case because they are all called **objects** of some type. The fact that they are objects indicates that they are in the **objective case.**

CASE OF PRONOUNS

Nouns do not present any problems in case because the form of the noun is the same for the nominative case and the objective case. Pronouns do present problems in case. The *personal pronouns* and the pronoun *who* have different forms to indicate the different cases.

There are only *six pronouns* in English that have these special forms to show *case*, but the changes that occur to indicate case are very important. They are responsible for many of the errors that frequently occur in the use of pronouns. You should become familiar with the different forms of these pronouns, and you should learn how to use them correctly. The six pronouns are *I, you, he, she, it, who.*

The following table gives the nominative case forms and the objective case forms of each of the six pronouns:

Nominative Case		Objective Case	
Singular	**Plural**	**Singular**	**Plural**
I	we	me	us
you	you	you	you
he	they	him	them
she	they	her	them
it	they	it	them
who	who	whom	whom

The pronouns *he, she,* and *it* all have the same plural form. *They* is the pronoun used in the nominative case in the plural for each of the three pronouns. *Them* is the pronoun used in the objective case in the plural for each of the three pronouns.

NOMINATIVE CASE OF PRONOUNS

Like nouns, pronouns are in the nominative case when they are used as the subjects of sentences, or as predicate pronouns after one of the linking verbs. Mistakes are seldom made in selecting the correct form of the pronoun to use as the subject of the sentence. Mistakes are frequently made, however, when a pronoun is used as a *predicate nominative.* The following sentences illustrate the correct use of the six pronouns in the nominative case:

Subject of the Sentence	Predicate Pronoun
I saw the accident.	It is *I.*
You have been elected.	It was *you.*
He attended the lecture.	It might be *he.*
She gave me her notebook.	It could be *she.*
It is my overcoat.	Could this be *it?.*
We are great friends. (plural)	It is *we.* (plural)
They arrived early. (plural)	It was *they.* (plural)
Who came in?	*Who* was it? (It was *who?*)

The pronoun *you* does not present any problem in the plural, because the forms for the plural are the same as the forms for the singular. The form of the pronoun *you* is also the same for the nominative case and the objective case.

Interrogative sentences should always be transposed and put in normal order. When this is done, it is easy to determine the case of the pronoun.

OBJECTIVE CASE OF PRONOUNS

Pronouns are in the objective case when they are used as direct objects of verbs, indirect objects of verbs, or as objects of prepositions. The correct forms to use in the objective case are *me, you, him, her, it,* and *whom* in the singular, and *us, you, them, whom* in the plural. The following sentences illustrate the correct use of these pronouns in the objective case:

Object of the Verb	Indirect Object of the Verb
Mother called **me**.	Ethel gave **me** her pen.
Jack saw **him** yesterday.	I sent **him** a notice.
I met **you** in Paris.	David sent **you** a ticket.
The firm sent **her** to Texas.	Jack offered **her** a seat.
My friend invited **us** to the game.	The tailor made **us** new uniforms.
Sue drove **them** to the station.	The teacher read **them** a story.

Whom did you call? (You did call **whom?**)

Object of a Preposition

The telegram was sent to **me**. (object of the preposition *to*)

The manager created the position for **him**. (object of *for*)

The author wrote an article about **her**. (object of *about*)

The waiter placed their table near **us**. (object of *near*)

We distributed the gifts among **them**. (object of *among*)

For **whom** did you vote? (object of the preposition *for*)
(You did vote for **whom?**)

THE POSSESSIVE CASE OF NOUNS

The **possessive case** shows *ownership* or *possession*. The use of the possessive case does not present much of a problem in speaking, but it does present a problem in writing and spelling. Although the rule for forming the possessive case of nouns is very simple, many students have considerable difficulty in spelling and writing the forms correctly.

One simple rule applies to all cases: If the singular form of the noun does not end in **s**, add the *apostrophe* and **s** (**'s**). If the singular ends in **s**, add the *apostrophe* (**'**).

The same rule applies to the plural: If the plural does not end in **s**, add the *apostrophe* and **s** (**'s**). If the plural ends in **s**, add the apostrophe (**'**). Study the following examples carefully and try to apply the rule:

Singular	Singular Possessive	Plural	Plural Possessive
boy	boy's	boys	boys'
lady	lady's	ladies	ladies'
hero	hero's	heroes	heroes'
man	man's	men	men's
Charles	Charles'	Charleses	Charleses'
horse	horse's	horses	horses'
child	child's	children	children's
mouse	mouse's	mice	mice's

There is one fact that you must always keep in mind in order to form the possessive case correctly; that is, the sign of the possessive is something that is *added* to the word. It is not something that is inserted within the word. You must be absolutely sure of the correct form for the singular and the correct form for the plural before you add the sign of the possessive.

Take the proper name, *Dickens,* for example. This is a proper noun in the singular which ends in **s**. The sign of the possessive must be added to the complete word and not inserted within the word. The possessive form is often incorrectly written as *Dicken's.* That would be the possessive form of the name *Dicken,* and not the possessive form of the name *Dickens.* The singular possessive form of *Dickens* is *Dickens'.*

> *Oliver Twist* is one of **Dicken's** novels. (incorrect)

> *Oliver Twist* is one of **Dickens'** novels. (correct)

The possessive forms of proper nouns are formed according to the rule. If the singular form of the name does not end in **s**, add the *apostrophe* and **s**. If the singular ends in **s**, add the *apostrophe.* The same rule applies to the plural.

Name	Singular Possessive	Plural	Plural Possessive
Mary	Mary's	Marys	Marys'
Jones	Jones'	Joneses	Joneses'
Henry	Henry's	Henrys	Henrys'
Burns	Burns'	Burnses	Burnses'

There is one slight modification of the rule which may be followed in the case of the possessive singular of nouns that end in **s**. If you want the sound of the additional **s**, the *apostrophe* and **s** may be added:

This is **Charles'** fishing rod. (correct)

This is **Charles's** fishing rod. (correct)

I saw **Doris'** picture at the studio. (correct)

I saw **Doris's** picture at the studio. (correct)

In modern practice, the first form (*Charles' fishing rod*) is the form that is generally used. It follows the rule given, and is the simpler form to use both in writing and in pronunciation. This rule also applies to nouns ending in **x** and **z**.

I bought a jar of **Heinz'** pickles. (correct)

She has always worn **Knox'** hats. (correct)

I bought a jar of **Heinz's** pickles. (correct)

She has always worn **Knox's** hats. (correct)

USE OF THE POSSESSIVE—SPECIAL FORMS

As a rule, it is better practice not to use the possessive forms for inanimate objects. Inanimate objects cannot possess anything in the sense that animate objects can. Avoid expressions such as *the table's top, the book's ending, the lake's shore,* and *the shop's window.* It is much better to use the phrase with *of* in such cases.

the top **of the table**   the shore **of the lake**

the ending **of the book**   the window **of the shop**

There are certain exceptions to this rule. Usage has established authority for using expressions such as the following:

the earth's surface   the sun's rays

the world's progress   today's edition

the law's delay   time's flight

the season's greetings   the water's edge

Certain expressions relating to *time, distance,* and *value* are also written with the sign of the possessive case. The apostrophe is generally used in expressions like the following:

a moment's delay   a stone's throw

two weeks' salary   a week's journey

a month's vacation   ten cents' worth

a few minutes' quiet   thirty days' notice

The singular possessive and the plural possessive of compound nouns are formed by adding the sign of the possessive to the end of the compound word.

Singular	Plural
sister-in-law's	sisters-in-law's
editor-in-chief's	editors-in-chief's
maid of honor's	maids of honor's

Joint ownership is shown by making the last word in the series possessive. Individual ownership is shown by making both parts possessive.

Baker and Johnson's factory. (joint ownership)

Baker's and Johnson's factories. (individual ownership)

Asia and China's problems. (common to both)

Asia's and China's problems. (separate problems)

Some trade names and names of organizations and institutions are written with the sign of the possessive case, and some are not. In writing letters, one should follow the form established by the organization.

When the apostrophe and **s** (**'s**) are not used, the word which would ordinarily be written as a possessive is regarded as an adjective modifier. In the name of an institution, such as *Teachers College,* the apostrophe is not used. The word *Teachers* is regarded as an adjective modifying *College.* It tells the type of college. It does not mean that the teachers possess the college.

The following illustrations show the methods used in writing place names, institutional names, and titles of publications:

With the Apostrophe	Without the Apostrophe
Woman's Home Companion	Womens Athletic Club
Collier's	Bricklayers Union
Harper's Magazine	Executives Club
Hansen's Pharmacy	Governors Island
Queen's College (Oxford)	All Souls Church
Charles Scribner's Sons	Flanders Fields
Young Men's Christian Association	Pikes Peak
Stelter's Music House	Downers Grove
Working Girl's Club	Harris Brothers Company
Illinois Children's Home and Aid Society	Good Neighbors Service
Nowak's Optical Service	Citizens League
Ladies' Home Journal	American Bankers Association
Martha's Vineyard Island	Buzzards Bay
Christensen's Service Station	Peoples Finance Company

THE POSSESSIVE CASE OF PRONOUNS

The indefinite pronouns do not have special forms to show case. The possessive case of indefinite pronouns is formed in the same way as the possessive case of nouns. Indefinite pronouns are seldom used in the plural. Two of the indefinite pronouns, *one* and *other*, have the plural forms *ones* and *others*. The following are illustrations of the possessive case form of indefinite pronouns:

everyone's opinion   *one's* relatives (singular)

someone's hat   *somebody's* car

anybody's guess   *another's* choice

The *personal pronouns* and the pronoun *who* have special forms to show the possessive case: *my, mine, our, ours, your, yours, her, hers, his, its, their, theirs,* and *whose.* These forms are never written with an apostrophe. To add an apostrophe would be adding a possessive sign to a word that is already possessive.

Whose report did you check? (not *Who's*)

The automobile was **theirs.** (not *their's*)

I did not know that book was **yours.** (not *your's*)

The ship lost **its** anchor in the storm. (not *it's*)

That ranch type house is **ours.** (not *our's*)

PERSONAL PRONOUNS

First Person

Singular				Plural
Nominative	I			we
Possessive	my, mine			our, ours
Objective	me			us

Second Person

Singular				Plural
Nominative	you			you
Possessive	your, yours			your, yours
Objective	you			you

Third Person

Singular				Plural
Nominative	he	she	it	they
Possessive	his	her, hers	its	their, theirs
Objective	him	her	it	them

RELATIVE AND INTERROGATIVE PRONOUN "WHO"

Singular		Plural
Nominative	who	who
Possessive	whose	whose
Objective	whom	whom

Nouns and pronouns have certain relationships to other words in a sentence. We show these relationships by indicating the *case* of the noun or the pronoun. The word **case** is used to show the particular *relationship* that a noun or pronoun has to other words in the sentence.

There are three cases in English: the **nominative case**, the **objective case**, and the **possessive case**. The *nominative case* is the case of the *subject*. A **predicate noun** is also in the nominative case because it refers to the same person or thing as the subject.

The *objective case* is the case of the *object*. The *direct object* of a verb, the *indirect object* of a verb, and the *object* of a *preposition* are in the objective case.

Nouns present very few problems in case because the same form is used for the nominative case and the objective case. The only way to tell whether a noun is in the *nominative case* or the *objective case* is to study its **function** in the sentence.

Pronouns do present a problem in case. There are only *six pronouns* in the English language that have different forms for the different cases. But these changes are very important because they are responsible for many of the errors that occur in the use of pronouns. The six pronouns are *I, you, he, she, it,* and *who.* Every student of grammar should become familiar with the different forms of these pronouns.

The *possessive case* shows *ownership* or *possession.* The possessive case does not involve a change in the form of a noun, but it does require the use of certain endings to show possession. Although the rule for forming the possessive case of nouns is very simple, many students have difficulty in spelling and writing these forms correctly.

If you keep the following fact in mind, you will have little difficulty in forming the possessive case of nouns correctly: The sign of the possessive is something that is *added* to the word. It is not something that is inserted within the word. You must be sure of the correct form for the singular or the plural before you try to make either form possessive.

The *indefinite pronouns* form the possessive case in the same way that nouns do. The *personal pronouns* and the pronoun *who* have special forms to show the possessive case: *my, mine, our, ours, your, yours, her, hers, his, its, their, theirs, whose.* These forms are never written with an apostrophe.

10

MODIFIERS: ADJECTIVES

A DJECTIVES give life and color to language. They also help us give more exact pictures of what we are telling about, if we know how to select them carefully. As you improve your skill in using these words, your language will become more interesting and more explicit.

Let us assume that you were telling someone about a man whom you had seen. You might start out with a sentence like this: "I met a man walking down the street." This sentence does not give us an interesting description or very accurate information. It tells very little about the man, his manner of walking, or the street down which he walked.

Someone who has skill in selecting words that would give a more definite and colorful description might change the sentence into something like this:

> I met a **weary** and **disheartened old** man hobbling down the **narrow, winding** street.

This sentence has been made more colorful and more accurate by the use of the adjectives *weary, disheartened,* and *old* to describe the man, and by the use of the adjectives *narrow* and *winding* to describe the street.

In order to use adjectives effectively, you must know the exact shade of meaning that you wish to convey. Then you must be able to select the adjective or adjectives that express that shade of meaning.

You might want to use an adjective to describe a certain type of individual, and you are not sure whether to use the adjective *sly* or the adjective *cunning*. Whenever you are in doubt, consult a reliable, up-to-date dictionary. In most dictionaries these differences in meaning are pointed out.

The adjective *sly* always implies that the individual is working or acting secretly, or is using underhand methods. The adjective *cunning* implies the use of intelligence, skill, or ingenuity. The two words do not mean exactly the same thing.

The following exercise will give you excellent practice in learning how to select the adjective that expresses the exact meaning you would like to convey. The adjectives listed below are divided into groups of three. Each adjective in a group of three expresses a different shade of meaning. Try to write sentences using these words. Be sure that your sentences show the differences in meaning. The dictionary will be a great help.

1. small—diminutive—little

2. funny—strange—queer

3. strong—robust—sturdy

4. beautiful—handsome—lovely

5. bright—shining—brilliant

"OVERWORKED" ADJECTIVES

There is a tendency on the part of many people to use the same adjective to apply to a number of different situations. When a person does this, the assumption is that he has a very limited vocabulary. As a result, he is not able to express his meaning precisely. For example, he may use the word *lovely* to describe many different things. In certain cases, the adjective *lovely* is appropriate. In other cases, it is not the most appropriate or the most precise word to use. Study the following illustrations carefully:

a *lovely* time	a *lovely* view
a *lovely* dress	a *lovely* voice
a *lovely* picnic	a *lovely* program
a *lovely* motion picture	a *lovely* day
a *lovely* street	a *lovely* necktie

If you wanted to describe a hat, instead of using the word *lovely*, you might use any one of the following adjectives: *becoming, stylish, fashionable, smart, colorful, modish, dashing, beautiful*, etc. The careful speaker or writer would choose the one that expressed the exact shade of meaning he wished to convey. This requires careful analysis, but it is worth the effort.

Adjectives that are applied in many different types of situations are often called "overworked" or "shopworn" adjectives. The following adjectives belong in this list:

fine	lovely	swell	cute
grand	nice	adorable	perfectly lovely
funny	terrible	keen	simply grand
awful	crazy	sweet	perfectly adorable

Some of these adjectives are called "feminine adjectives" because they are popular with women.

112

KINDS OF ADJECTIVES

There are two kinds of adjectives: *descriptive* adjectives and *limiting* adjectives. **Descriptive adjectives,** as the name implies, give color and vividness to the persons, places, or things we talk or write about. **Limiting adjectives** indicate number or quantity.

Descriptive adjectives tell *what kind, what color, what size, what shape,* etc. Limiting adjectives tell *how many, how much, which one, whose,* etc.

three checks (limiting)	*brilliant* speaker (descriptive)
high mountain (descriptive)	*one* airplane (limiting)
a *new* car (descriptive)	a *few* children (limiting)
two branches (limiting)	a *sympathetic* listener (descriptive)

Adjectives derived from proper nouns are called **proper adjectives.** They are usually written with a capital letter. They are usually descriptive adjectives.

Siberian squirrel	*Turkish* tobacco
Canadian bacon	*Norwegian* sardines
American industries	*Danish* silver
Mexican pottery	*Swedish* crystal
United States flag	*Swiss* watches
English wool	*Brazilian* coffee
Venetian blinds	*Indian* summer
Bunsen burner	*Portland* cement

PREDICATE ADJECTIVES

Adjectives that complete the meaning of the verb and modify the subject are called **predicate adjectives.** If an adjective is found in the predicate and modifies a noun in the predicate, it is not a predicate adjective. The adjective must follow a linking verb and modify the subject in order to be classified as a predicate adjective. The predicate adjective usually *describes* the subject noun or pronoun.

The list of linking verbs which was given in Grammar Unit Eight is repeated here for reference. You should become familiar with this important list of verbs. It will help you identify the predicate adjectives that are used after linking verbs.

Linking Verbs

is	grow	look	smell	remain
become	turn	feel	taste	keep
seem	prove	sound	appear	stay

Illustrations

The cookies are <u>delicious</u>. (*delicious* cookies)
pred. adj.

Corn is <u>plentiful</u> in Illinois. (*plentiful* corn)
pred. adj.

The street has become very <u>muddy</u>. (*muddy* street)
pred. adj.

The airplane is an <u>effective</u> weapon. (*effective* weapon)
not a pred. adj.

Note that the adjective *effective* in the last sentence is not a predicate adjective, although it is found in the predicate. The adjective *effective* does not modify the subject, and it is not used to complete the verb *is*. A predicate noun *weapon* completes the verb *is*. *Effective* modifies the predicate noun (*effective* weapon).

114

Position of the Adjective

An adjective is usually placed directly before the noun it modifies. Sometimes the adjective follows the word it modifies. The predicate adjective is always found in the predicate after the verb it completes.

1. Adjectives placed before the noun.

   An **old, gnarled** tree lay across the stream.

2. Adjectives placed after the noun.

   A tree, **old** and **gnarled,** lay across the stream.

3. Predicate adjectives, placed after the verb.

   The tree was **old** and **gnarled.**

NOUNS USED AS ADJECTIVES

Nouns are also frequently *used as adjectives*. The nouns in the following expressions are used as adjectives:

college credits (modifies *credits*)

dress accessories (modifies *accessories*)

window sash (modifies *sash*)

Fourth of July speech (modifies *speech*)

A noun in the *possessive case* is often placed before another noun which it modifies. In such cases, the noun in the possessive case is used as an adjective although it has not lost the function of showing ownership or possession. Nouns used in this way are sometimes called **possessive adjectives.** Sometimes they are described as nouns in the possessive case used as adjectives. Observe how nouns in the possessive case are used in the following sentences:

John's car was wrecked in the crash. (*John's* modifies *car.*)

I like to shop in **Macy's** store. (*Macy's* modifies *store.*)

COMPARISON OF ADJECTIVES

The form of an adjective is often changed to show the extent or degree to which a certain quality is present. In grammar, this change in form to show a difference in degree is called *comparison*.

There are three degrees of comparison in English: the *positive degree*, the *comparative degree*, and the *superlative degree*.

The **positive degree** is really not a degree of comparison because no comparison is indicated when the positive degree is used. The positive degree is the simple form of the adjective. It shows that the quality is present, but it does not show a comparison with anything else. The adjectives in the following sentences are all positive degree:

That is a **beautiful** rose.   Jane is **studious.**

It was a very **cold** day.   The **old** house was sold.

Peter is very **energetic.**   It was a very **warm** day.

In the preceding illustrations, the adjective simply shows that the quality is present. No comparison is made with any other person or thing.

The **comparative degree** of the adjective is used when a comparison is made between **two** persons or things. The comparative degree shows that the quality (expressed by the adjective) exists to a *greater* or to a *lesser* degree in one of the two persons or things that are being compared.

The comparative degree of almost all adjectives of *one* syllable is formed by adding **er** to the positive degree, or to the simple form of the adjective; for example, *colder, smoother, longer, greater, stronger, firmer, thicker,* etc.

John is **stronger** than Michael. (*two persons* compared)
comparative degree *

This table is **larger** than that table. (*two objects* compared)
comparative degree

In the first sentence, *two persons* are compared as to strength. According to the sentence, John possesses this quality of strength to a greater degree than Michael. The comparative degree of the adjective is used because a comparison is made between *two* persons.

In the second sentence, *two tables* are being compared as to size. The comparative degree of the adjective *large* is used because a comparison is made between *two objects*.

The **superlative degree** of the adjective is used when **more than two** persons or things are compared. The superlative degree indicates that the quality (expressed by the adjective) is possessed to the *greatest* or to the *least* degree by one of the persons or things included in the comparison.

> Our house is the **largest** house in the block. (More than two are compared.) _{superlative degree}

> Louis is the **smallest** boy in his class. (More than two are compared.) _{superlative degree}

In the first sentence, *more than two* houses are being compared. The superlative degree of the adjective *large* is used to show this fact. The house that possesses the quality expressed by the adjective *large* to the greatest degree is *our* house. It is the *largest* house in a block which contains more than two houses.

In the second sentence, more than two boys are being compared as to size. Louis possesses this quality to the *least* degree. The superlative degree of the adjective *small* is used to show this fact.

DEGREES OF COMPARISON
Adjectives of One Syllable

Positive	Comparative	Superlative
neat	neater	neatest
sharp	sharper	sharpest
dark	darker	darkest
keen	keener	keenest
long	longer	longest

Adjectives of *two or more syllables* are usually compared by prefixing the words *more* and *most* to the simple form of the adjective. *More* is used to indicate the comparison between two persons or things. *Most* is used to indicate the comparison between more than two persons or things. *Less* and *least* are used in a similar way.

Positive	Comparative	Superlative
fragrant	*more* fragrant	*most* fragrant
famous	*less* famous	*least* famous
precious	*more* precious	*most* precious
difficult	*less* difficult	*least* difficult

Sometimes adjectives of *one syllable* are compared by prefixing *more* and *most*. Sometimes adjectives of *more than one syllable* are compared by adding **er** and **est.** There is no rule to follow for making these exceptions. It is usually a matter of sound. If one form of comparison sounds better than the other, that is the form of comparison to use. It sounds better to say *crisp, more crisp, most crisp,* than to say *crisp, crisper, crispest.* Therefore, the comparison with *more* and *most* is preferred.

Adjectives of more than one syllable that end in **y** are usually compared by adding **er** and **est.** Notice the change in spelling in the comparative and in the superlative degrees. The **y** changes to **i** before the addition of **er** or **est.**

Positive	Comparative	Superlative
silly	sillier	silliest
dainty	daintier	daintiest
clumsy	clumsier	clumsiest
handy	handier	handiest

IRREGULAR COMPARISON OF ADJECTIVES

Some adjectives are compared *irregularly.* The forms for the comparative degree and for the superlative degree usually show a marked change in the form of the word; for example, *many, more, most.* You should be familiar with these changes in order to use the correct forms for the comparative and superlative degrees.

Adjectives Compared Irregularly

Positive	Comparative	Superlative
bad, evil, ill	worse	worst
far	further	furthest
far	farther	farthest
good, well	better	best
little	less	least
many	more	most
much	more	most
out	outer	outmost or outermost

Farther refers to *distance* or remoteness in space. **Further** refers to remoteness in *time*, to *degree*, *extent*, or *quantity*. It is also used to express the idea of something *more* or *additional*.

The garage is **farther** than I thought. (distance in space)

I shall give you **further** instructions tomorrow. (*additional* instructions)

The distinctions between *farther* and *further* are passing out of use. These words are now used interchangeably. There is also a tendency to use *further* to express all the meanings discussed. (See latest dictionaries.)

ADJECTIVES NOT COMPARED

There are a number of adjectives that should not be compared because the **simple** form of the adjective expresses the quality to the highest possible degree. For example, if an answer to a problem is *correct*, another answer could not possibly be *more correct*. If a circle is absolutely *round*, another circle could not be *more round*. If a bottle is *empty*, another bottle could not be *more empty*.

The following are some of the adjectives that are not compared for the reasons given:

perfect	unique	square	universal
single	supreme	fatal	empty
vertical	full	alone	dead
final	mortal	instantaneous	deadly
straight	blind	everlasting	wrong

The expression, *more nearly round,* is often used when comparing two things, one of which is *more nearly round* than the other. In this case, however, neither of the things compared is round. A line could be *more nearly straight* than another line if neither of the lines was absolutely straight.

Sometimes an adjective such as the word *honest* is used in the comparative and superlative degrees. In such cases, we have no standard of absolute honesty. What the writer or speaker means is that one person approaches the absolute state of honesty to a greater or to a lesser degree than another person. The adjective *perfect* is often used in the same way.

119

SUMMARY

An **adjective** is a word used to modify a noun or a pronoun. A *modifier* limits or qualifies the meaning of another word. Adjectives *limit* or *describe* nouns or pronouns.

There are two main classes of adjectives — *limiting adjectives* and *descriptive adjectives*. **Descriptive adjectives** give color and vividness to the words which they modify. **Limiting adjectives** indicate number or quantity.

Adjectives derived from proper nouns are called **proper adjectives**. A proper adjective is usually written with a capital letter.

Adjectives that complete the meaning of linking verbs and modify the subject are called **predicate adjectives**.

Nouns and pronouns are frequently *used as adjectives*. A noun or a pronoun in the possessive case is often used before another noun which it modifies. Nouns and pronouns used in this way are called **possessive adjectives** because they show possession.

An adjective is usually placed before the word it modifies. It may also follow the word it modifies. An adjective is also found in the predicate following a linking verb although it modifies the subject.

The *form* of an adjective is often changed to show the degree or extent to which a certain quality is present. This change in form to show a change in degree is called *comparison*.

There are three degrees of comparison: the *positive degree*, the *comparative degree*, and the *superlative degree*.

The **positive degree** is the simple form of the adjective. No comparison is indicated when the positive degree is used. The positive degree of the adjective *small* is the word *small*.

The **comparative degree** is used when a comparison is made between **two** persons or things. The comparative degree shows that a quality exists to a *greater* or to a *lesser* degree in one of the two persons or things which are compared.

The **superlative degree** is used when **more than two** persons or things are compared. The superlative degree indicates that the quality is possessed to the *greatest* or to the *least* degree by one of the persons or things included in the comparison.

The *comparative degree* of almost all adjectives of **one** syllable is formed by adding **er** to the form of the positive degree. The comparative degree of the adjective *small* is *smaller*. The *superlative degree* of adjectives of **one** syllable is usually formed by adding **est** to the form of the positive degree. The superlative degree of the adjective *small* is *smallest*.

Adjectives of **two or more** syllables are usually compared by prefixing *more* or *most* to the simple form of the adjective (positive degree). *More* is used to indicate a comparison between **two** persons or things. *Most* is used to indicate a comparison between **more than two** persons or things.

Jane is more studious than her sister.
<u>comparative degree</u>

Alice is the most ambitious girl in the class.
<u>superlative degree</u>

11
MODIFIERS: ADVERBS

O N PAGES 20-21 of this Handbook, it is explained that adverbs are modifiers of verbs, telling *how, when, where,* and *to what degree* the action is performed. Here other uses are explained as well as the relationship of adverbs to adjectives and to other adverbs.

FORMS OF ADVERBS

Students sometimes have the idea that all adverbs end in **ly.** There are a great many adverbs that do end in **ly,** but there are probably just as many that do not end in **ly.** Many adverbs are formed by adding **ly** to the adjective form:

Adjective	Adverb	Adjective	Adverb
strange	strangely	awkward	awkwardly
sudden	suddenly	necessary	necessarily
calm	calmly	strict	strictly
sure	surely	forcible	forcibly
usual	usually	extreme	extremely
swift	swiftly	similar	similarly
rapid	rapidly	slight	slightly

The following are some of the adverbs that do not end in **ly:**

seldom	little	why	fast
again	here	now	twice
soon	there	then	too
very	rather	since	much
almost	often	well	quite
late	when	near	yonder
hard	where	far	how

Many adjectives end in **ly**. They should not be confused with adverbs that end in **ly**. The following words ending in **ly** are commonly used as adjectives. Some of them might also be used as adverbs:

| stately | lovely | saintly | manly |
| lonely | womanly | lively | courtly |

Some adjectives have the same form as the adverb. In such cases, the only way you can tell whether the word is an *adjective* or an *adverb*, is to determine its use in a particular sentence. Study the following illustrations carefully:

That was a **hard** task. (*hard*—adjective, modifies *task*)

Our janitor works **hard**. (*hard*—adverb, modifies *works*)

We arrived at the airport **early**. (*early*—adverb, modifies *arrived*)

We had to make an **early** start. (*early*—adjective, modifies *start*)

That was a **cowardly** act. (*cowardly*—adjective, modifies *act*)

He acted **cowardly** in that situation. (*cowardly*—adverb, modifies *acted*)

Some adverbs have two forms, one ending in **ly** and one that does not end in **ly**. The form that does not end in **ly** is the shorter form and is commonly used in giving commands and directions. The form ending in **ly** is preferred in formal writing.

Drive *slow*. (or *slowly*)

Come *quick!* (or *quickly*)

Buy *cheap*. (or *cheaply*)

Hold *tight!* (or *tightly*)

Don't talk so *loud*. (or *loudly*)

Sleep *sound*. (or *soundly*)

123

INTERROGATIVE ADVERBS

An adverb is often used at the beginning of a sentence to ask a question. When an adverb is used in this way, it is called an **interrogative adverb**. An *interrogative adverb* also modifies some word in the sentence.

When did you arrive? (*When*—interrogative adverb)

Where did you put my hat? (*Where*—interrogative adverb)

How many books have you read? (*How*—interrogative adverb)

In the first sentence, the adverb *When* asks the question. It also modifies the verb *did arrive*. (You *did arrive* when?) In the second sentence, the adverb *Where* asks the question and modifies the verb *did put*. (You *did put* my hat where?) In the third sentence, the adverb *How* asks the question and modifies the adjective *many*. (You have read how *many* books?)

YES, NO, AND NOT

The affirmative adverb *yes* and the negative adverb *no* are used independently. They are usually set off by commas. *Not* is an adverb. It is never used as part of the verb, although it often comes between the parts of a verb phrase. The adverb *not* makes the verb express an idea which is the exact opposite of the regular meaning of the verb.

Yes, I shall take the course.

I did *not* give him the plans. (No plans were given.)

No, we are *not* going to Florida this winter.

ADVERBS OF DEGREE

Adverbs of degree tell *how large, how small, how long, how much, to what extent*, etc. They answer the questions "*How much?*" "*To what extent?*" "*In what degree?*" Adverbs of degree usually modify adjectives or other adverbs. In the following illustrations the adverbs of degree modify *adjectives*:

This apple is very sour. (*very*—modifies the adjective *sour*)
adv. of degree

The play was rather dull. (*rather*—modifies the adjective *dull*)
adv. of degree

The price is too high. (*too*—modifies the adjective *high*)
adv. of degree

In the first sentence, the adverb of degree *very* modifies the predicate adjective *sour*. It tells to what degree the apple is sour, or how sour it is. In the second sentence, the adverb *rather* modifies the predicate adjective *dull*. It tells the extent to which the play was *dull*. In the third sentence, the adverb *too* modifies the predicate adjective *high*. It tells the extent to which the price is *high*. The adverbs *very, too,* and *rather* are commonly used as adverbs of degree.

In the following sentences, the adverbs of degree modify other *adverbs*:

The old man moved too slowly. (*too*—modifies the adverb *slowly*)
adv. of degree

John swims much faster than Ned. (*much*—modifies the adverb *faster*)
adv. of degree

Don't talk so loud. (*so*—modifies the adverb *loud*)
adv. of degree

In the first sentence, the adverb of degree *too* modifies the adverb *slowly*. It tells the extent to which the old man moved *slowly*. In the second sentence, the adverb of degree *much* modifies the adverb *faster*. The adverb of degree tells that John swims fast to a greater degree than Ned. In the third sentence, the adverb of degree *so* modifies the adverb *loud*. The sentence means that you should not talk loud to the extent expressed by the adverb *so*. In this sentence, the short form of the adverb (*loud*) is used instead of the longer form, *loudly*.

NOUNS USED AS ADVERBS

Nouns that express *time, size, place, measurement, degree,* or *number* are often used as adverbs. We identify these nouns by calling them *nouns used as adverbs.* Such nouns are not only used as adverbs, but they retain an important characteristic of nouns; namely, they may take an *adjective modifier.*

I am going *home.* (*home*—noun used as an adverb)

Horace will arrive *Monday.* (*Monday*—noun used as an adverb)

We worked all *day.* (*day*—noun used as an adverb)

The fish weighed five *pounds.* (*pounds*—noun used as an adverb)

In the first sentence, the noun *home* tells **where** I am going. It performs the same function as an **adverb of place.** In the second sentence, the noun *Monday* tells **when** Horace will arrive. It performs the same function as an **adverb of time.** In the third sentence, the noun *day* tells **how long** we worked, or the extent to which we worked. In the last sentence, the noun *pounds* tells the amount, or **how much** the fish weighed.

The noun *pounds* in the last sentence is modified by the adjective *five.* Although the noun *pounds* functions as an adverb, it may take an adjective modifier. It still retains that particular characteristic of a noun. It functions as two parts of speech at the same time—both as a **noun** and as an **adverb.**

Some students have difficulty in understanding the use of a noun as an adverb. A noun used as an adverb is really the equivalent of a phrase. The following illustrations will help make this clear:

I am going home. This sentence really means that I am going *to my home.* The noun *home* is the equivalent of the phrase, *to my home.*

Horace will arrive Monday. This sentence means that Horace will arrive *on Monday.* The noun *Monday* is the equivalent of the phrase, *on Monday.*

We worked all day. This sentence means that we worked for the period or to *the extent of a day.*

The fish weighed five pounds. This sentence means that the fish weighed to the extent or *to the amount of five pounds.*

COMPARISON OF ADVERBS

Adverbs are compared in exactly the same way as adjectives are compared. They have the same three degrees of comparison: the *positive degree,* the *comparative degree,* and the *superlative degree.*

A few adverbs form the comparative degree by adding **er** to the positive degree. They form the superlative degree by adding **est** to the positive degree.

Positive	Comparative	Superlative
late	later	latest
hard	harder	hardest
soon	sooner	soonest
fast	faster	fastest
near	nearer	nearest
quick (*short form*)	quicker	quickest
slow (*short form*)	slower	slowest

Most adverbs are compared by placing *more* (for the comparative degree) and *most* (for the superlative degree) before the positive forms. *Less* and *least* are used in the same way as *more* and *most.*

Positive	Comparative	Superlative
carefully	more carefully	most carefully
discreetly	more discreetly	most discreetly
abruptly	more abruptly	most abruptly
gratefully	more gratefully	most gratefully
efficiently	more efficiently	most efficiently
awkwardly	less awkwardly	least awkwardly
favorably	less favorably	least favorably
gracefully	less gracefully	least gracefully

127

IRREGULAR COMPARISON OF ADVERBS

A few adverbs are compared *irregularly*. In the following list you will find some words that were also in the list of adjectives that are compared irregularly. Such words are used both as *adjectives* and as *adverbs*.

Positive	Comparative	Superlative
far	farther	farthest
far	further	furthest
badly	worse	worst
little	less	least
much	more	most
well	better	best

Some adverbs are not compared. The following adverbs can not be used in the comparative or in the superlative degrees:

before	never	now	there	very	by
ever	no	so	thus	past	back
here	not	then	too	yes	whenever

The comparative degree of adverbs is used when comparing two things. The superlative degree is used when comparing more than two.

We drove <u>more slowly</u> than our guide.
comparative degree

Of the three speakers, the senator spoke <u>most convincingly</u>.
superlative degree

CORRECT USE OF ADJECTIVES AND ADVERBS

Errors are frequently made in the use of adjectives and adverbs. The most common error is the use of an adjective for an adverb, or the use of an adverb when the meaning requires an adjective.

If you keep certain facts in mind regarding these modifiers, you will soon learn how to use them correctly. Note that adjectives never modify *verbs*. They modify *nouns* and *pronouns*. Adverbs modify *verbs, adjectives,* and other *adverbs.*

Never use an adjective after an action verb. An action verb requires an adverb as a modifier. The adverb tells the manner in which the action is performed. You may often hear a sentence like this: *Don't drive so reckless.* The adjective *reckless* is used after the action verb *drive.* The sentence requires an adverb. The correct form would be: *Don't drive so recklessly.* The adverb is *recklessly,* not *reckless. Reckless* is an adjective.

Mistakes are commonly made after linking verbs. These verbs must be watched carefully, for they should be followed by adjectives and not by adverbs. When a modifier follows a linking verb it is used to describe the subject, which is usually a noun or a pronoun. Adverbs do not modify nouns and pronouns.

The problem is also complicated by the fact that some of the linking words are often used as action verbs. In that case, they may take an adverbial modifier. Notice the change in the meaning of the verb *looked* in the following sentences:

Helen <u>looked</u> *sad.*   (not *sadly*)
      _{linking}

Helen <u>looked</u> *sadly* at the burnt cake.   (not *sad*)
      _{action}

In the first sentence, the verb *looked* is a linking verb. The sentence means that Helen looked (to be) *sad.* The predicate adjective *sad,* which follows the linking verb *looked,* modifies the subject, which is *Helen.* The verb *looked,* with the help of the predicate adjective *sad,* describes the condition of the subject, *Helen.*

In the second sentence, *looked* is an action verb. Helen is actually looking at the cake. The adverb *sadly* describes the manner in which she looked at the cake.

SPECIAL FORMS

There are several adjectives and adverbs that require special attention because they are used incorrectly so often. If you study the following distinctions in *meaning* and *use,* you should be able to use these adjectives and adverbs correctly.

1. **Good** and **well.** The word *good* is always an adjective. It should never be used as an adverb. The word *well* is used both as an adjective and as an adverb. When *well* is used as an adjective, it refers to a state of health, or to a satisfactory condition of affairs. When *well* is used as an adverb, it refers to the manner in which some action is performed.

I have a <u>good</u> saddle horse. (*good*—adjective, modifies *horse*)

adj.

The child is <u>well</u>. (*well*—adjective, modifies *child*)

adj.

All is <u>well</u>. (*well*—adjective, modifies *all*)

adj.

Heifetz plays the violin <u>well</u>. (*well*—adverb, modifies *plays*)

adv.

2. **Bad** and **badly.** The word *bad* is an adjective. The word *badly* is an adverb. The adverb *badly* should not be used after a linking verb. You would not say, *I feel illy* or *I feel sickly.* For the same reason you should not say, *I feel badly,* when you refer to your state of health.

Mother feels <u>bad</u> today. (*bad*—adjective, modifies *Mother*)

adj.

Mother managed the affair <u>badly</u>. (*badly*—adverb, modifies *managed*)

adv.

When you say, *Mother feels badly,* you mean that Mother performs the act of feeling something in an imperfect manner. Of course, that is not the meaning that you intend to convey. Do not use *badly* unless the verb expresses action. *Badly* indicates the manner in which the action is performed.

Some writers maintain that the sentence, *Mother feels badly today* is correct. They give two reasons for taking this position. One is that the forms *bad* and *badly* are both used as adjectives. The other reason given is that the expression *feels badly* has become an American idiom.

3. **Sure** and **surely**. *Sure* is an adjective. *Surely* is an adverb.

The hunter's aim was sure. (*sure*—adjective, modifies *aim*)
<small>adj.</small>

That is the only sure way to succeed. (*sure*—adjective, modifies *way*)
<small>adj.</small>

I am surely grateful to you. (*surely*—adverb, modifies *grateful*)
<small>adv.</small>

When you say, *I am sure grateful to you,* the adjective *sure* modifies the adjective *grateful.* Adjectives never modify adjectives. Adverbs modify adjectives. The sentence requires the adverb. The use of the adjective *sure* is incorrect. The correct modifier is *surely:* I am *surely grateful* to you.

4. **Real** and **really**. The adjective is *real.* The adverb is *really.* A common error is the use of the adjective *real* for the adverb *very.* Do not say, *The apple is real good.* In this sentence, *real* is an adjective and modifies another adjective, which is grammatically incorrect. The correct form would be, *The apple is very good.* Note the correct use of *real* and *really* in the following sentences:

This is a real emerald. (*real*—adjective, modifies *emerald*)
<small>adj.</small>

The play was really excellent. (*really*—adverb, modifies *excellent*)
<small>adv.</small>

In the last sentence, the adverb *really* modifies the adjective *excellent.* This is a correct use of the adverb *really.* Do not use the adverb *really* unless you mean *actually.* The sentence means that the play was actually excellent.

5. **Most** and **almost**. Both *most* and *almost* are adverbs. The error is one in meaning. The adverb *most* means to the greatest degree. The adverb *almost* means *nearly.* Do not say, *He is most five years old.* The correct word to use in this sentence is *almost.* (means *nearly*)

Of all the fruits, I like plums most. (*most*—adverb, modifies *like*)
<small>adv.</small>

I am almost ready. (*almost*—adverb, modifies *ready*)
<small>adv.</small>

THE DOUBLE NEGATIVE

Only *one negative word* should be used to express a *negative idea*. A common error in English is to use two negative words to express one negative idea. When you use the adverb *not* with such words as *hardly, scarcely, never, no, barely,* and *but,* you are introducing two negative ideas.

Incorrect

We *haven't barely* paid for our car.
  (*haven't* and *barely*—two negatives)

Nobody can't say that I *don't* work hard.
  (*can't* and *don't*—two negatives)

I *can't hardly* hear the speaker.
  (*can't* and *hardly*—two negatives)

There *isn't but* one woman on the committee.
  (*isn't* and *but*—two negatives)

Correct

We have *barely* paid for our car. (one negative)

Nobody can say that I *don't* work hard. (one negative)

I can *hardly* hear the speaker. (one negative)

There is *but* one woman on the committee. (one negative)

Other words used as negatives are *never, no, nobody, none, no one,* and *nothing.* These words should not be used with another negative.

I *haven't no* money. (incorrect)

I *have no* money. (correct)

No one *never* gave me a book. (incorrect)

No one *ever* gave me a book. (correct)

The word *but* requires careful analysis when it is used with a negative. When *but* means *only,* it should not be preceded by a negative such as the word *not.* This combination results in a double negative.

I haven't but one car. (double negative—incorrect)
  <u>only</u>

I have but one car. (correct)

When the word *but* is used as a preposition, it means *except*. When *but* means *except* it is often preceded by a negative. This does not mean that a double negative idea is suggested as you will readily see if you analyze the following sentences carefully:

It never rains but it pours. (correct)
        except

He does nothing but complain. (correct)
               except

Expressions like *cannot help but*, and *can't help but* are generally regarded as colloquial and should not be used in formal speaking or writing.

I *can't help but* criticize the management. (colloquial)

I *can't help* criticizing the management. (better)

SUMMARY

An **adverb** is a word that is used to modify a verb, an adjective, or another adverb. Adverbs usually express time, place, manner, or degree.

An **interrogative adverb** asks a question and modifies some word in the sentence.

Some adjectives and adverbs have the same form. The only way to tell whether a word is an *adjective* or an *adverb* is to determine its use in the sentence. If it modifies a *noun* or a *pronoun*, it is an adjective. If it modifies a *verb*, an *adjective*, or *another adverb*, it is an adverb.

Adverbs are compared in exactly the same way as adjectives are compared. Some adverbs are compared by adding **er** or **est** to the *positive degree*. Some are compared by prefixing *more* or *most* to the positive degree. A few adverbs are compared irregularly.

Errors are frequently made in the use of adjectives and adverbs. This error is commonly made after the *linking verb*, which requires an *adjective* as a complement, and not an adverb. *Verbs* of *action* should be modified by *adverbs*, and not by adjectives.

Nouns are often used as adverbs to express *time, place, measurement, degree, size, or number.* A noun used as an adverb may be modified by an adjective or an adjective phrase because it retains that noun characteristic.

Some adverbs have two forms, a short form and a form that ends in **ly.** The form ending in **ly** should be used in formal writing.

133

12

PRINCIPAL PARTS OF VERBS

THE BASIC FORMS OF VERBS

STUDIES have shown that more than half of the errors made in English are errors in the use of verbs. Most of this trouble occurs because of confusion in the use of the principal parts of verbs.

Every verb has *three basic forms* which are called the *principal parts* of the verb. These three forms are the **present tense**, the **past tense**, and the **past participle.** They are called the principal parts of the verb because (with a few exceptions) the six tenses of the verb can be built from them.

Tense is a property that belongs to verbs. In grammar, *tense* means *time.* Every verb has certain forms which show the *time* of the *action* or the *time* of the *state of condition.* When we want to indicate that a certain action is going on now, or that a certain state of condition exists at the present time, we use the **present tense.**

Present Tense

I **drive.** (Action occurs at the *present time.*)

He **sings.** (Action occurs at the *present time.*)

Florence **is** ill. (The state of condition exists at the *present time.*)

When we want to indicate that the action occurred yesterday, or in some past time, we use the **past tense** of the verb. With a few exceptions, the past tense of the verb is not the same form as the present tense of the verb.

I **drove.** (The action occurred in the *past.*)

He **sang** at the concert. (The action occurred in the *past.*)

Florence **was** ill yesterday. (The state of condition existed in the *past.*)

In the preceding illustrations, the forms, *drive* and *sings,* are used to show that action is going on at the present time. The forms, *drove* and *sang,* are used to show that action occurred at some time in the past. The forms *drive* and *sings* are the present tense of the verbs *drive* and *sing.* The forms *drove* and *sang* are the past tense of the verbs *drive* and *sing.*

The **past participle** of the verb is a verb form that is used with *have, has,* or *had* to form the perfect tenses. The past participle cannot function as the predicate verb. It is always combined with an auxiliary, such as *have, has,* or *had.* It is a part of the verb phrase.

Past Participles

I <u>have **called**</u> her every day this week. (*called*—past participle)
<u>verb phrase</u>

We <u>have **driven**</u> there often. (*driven*—past participle)
<u>verb phrase</u>

The three forms, the *present tense,* the *past tense,* and the *past participle,* constitute the **principal parts** of a verb. It is necessary for the student of grammar to become familiar with the principal parts of certain verbs so that he will be able to use them correctly. The verbs that cause most of our verb troubles are the verbs that form the principal parts irregularly. We shall make a special study of these verbs.

REGULAR AND IRREGULAR VERBS

Verbs are divided into two classes on the basis of the way in which the past tense and the past participle are formed. Some are called *regular* or weak verbs, and others are called *irregular* or strong verbs.

A **regular verb** is a verb that forms the past tense and the past participle by adding **ed** or **d** to the form of the present tense. Sometimes the **ed** or **d** changes to **t**: *build, built, built.*

Verb	Past Tense	Past Participle
call	called	called
bake	baked	baked
build	built	built

The past tense and the past participle of the verb *call* are formed by adding **ed** to the form of the present tense: *call**ed.*** The past tense and the past participle of the verb *bake* are formed by simply adding **d** to the form of the present tense: *bake**d.*** The past tense and the past participle of the verb *build* are formed by changing the **d** to **t**. The old form of the verb build was *builded* in the past tense. That form is no longer used. The simpler form *built* has taken its place.

An **irregular verb** is a verb that does *not* form the past tense and the past participle in the regular way; that is, by adding **d** or **ed** to the form of the present tense. The past tense and the past participle of irregular verbs are formed in various ways. The most common way is by a change in the vowel; for example, *sing, sang, sung.* In the case of a few verbs, the same form is used for the present tense, the past tense and the past participle: *hurt, hurt, hurt.*

Verb	Past Tense	Past Participle
sing	sang	sung
drive	drove	driven
begin	began	begun
go	went	gone
burst	burst	burst

The past tense and the past participle of the verb *sing* are formed by a change in vowel. The *i* in *sing* changes to *a* in the past tense (*sang*) and to *u* in the past participle (*sung*). The verb *begin* follows a similar change in the vowel. The verb *go* has a different form for the past tense and for the past participle: *go, went, gone.* The verb *burst* has the same form for the present tense, the past tense, and the past participle.

VERBS ADDED TO THE LANGUAGE

New verbs are added to the English language as the need arises. Practically all of these new verbs form the past tense and the past participle by adding **ed** or **d;** that is, they follow the pattern of the regular verbs. The following verbs have been introduced in recent years. To form the past tense or the past participle of these verbs, add **ed** or **d.**

Verb	Past Tense	Past Participle
activate	activated	activated
radio	radioed	radioed
camouflage	camouflaged	camouflaged
audition	auditioned	auditioned
laminate	laminated	laminated

THE TROUBLESOME VERBS

The *regular verbs* cause very little trouble in speaking and writing because the past tense and the past participle usually follow the rule of forming the past tense and the past participle by adding **d** or **ed.** It is the *irregular verbs* that are responsible for most of the verb errors.

Errors are frequently made in using the *past tense* and the *perfect tense* forms of irregular verbs. This is due to the fact that these verbs form the past tense and the perfect tenses irregularly. In order to use these verbs correctly, it is highly important for you to become familiar with the principal parts of the irregular verbs that are in common use. You will learn these forms by checking constantly until you are familiar with the correct forms for the past tense and the past participle.

Mistakes are commonly made in using the wrong form for the **past tense:** *done* for *did; seen* for *saw; come* for *came; swum* for *swam; dove* for *dived; run* for *ran; drunk* for *drank.* Mistakes are also made in using the wrong form for the **past participle:** *went* for *gone; did* for *done; swam* for *swum; tore* for *torn; began* for *begun; came* for *come.* The past participle is used in forming the perfect tenses.

Correct Forms for the Past Tense

I <u>did</u> the work assigned to me. (not *done*)
<u>past tense</u>

We <u>saw</u> the parade yesterday. (not *seen*)
<u>past tense</u>

He <u>came</u> from Ireland two years ago. (not *come*)
<u>past tense</u>

She <u>swam</u> across the English Channel last summer. (not *swum*)
<u>past tense</u>

The swimming teacher <u>dived</u> off the pier. (not *dove*)
<u>past tense</u>

The boy <u>ran</u> through the traffic. (not *run*)
<u>past tense</u>

We <u>drank</u> all the milk in the pitcher. (not *drunk*)
<u>past tense</u>

Correct Forms for the Past Participle

The delegates **have gone** home. (not *have went*)

He **has done** the work well. (not *has did*)

She **has swum** the channel several times. (not *has swam*)

The actress **has torn** her dress. (not *has tore*)

They **have begun** to check the accounts. (not *have began*)

Has the mail **come**? (not *has came*)

In the first sentence, the past participle is *gone*. It is combined with the auxiliary *have* to form the verb phrase *have gone*. The form *went* should never be used with *have, has* or *had*.

In the second sentence, the past participle is *done*. It is the correct form of the verb to combine with *has*. In the third sentence, the past participle is *swum*. It is correctly used with *has*. *Tore* should never be used with *have*, *has*, or *had*. The correct form is *have*, *has*, or *had torn*.

Began is the correct form for the past tense. It should not be used for the past participle. The correct form for the past participle is *begun*. Never use the forms *have began*, *had began*, or *has began*. The correct forms are *have begun*, *had begun*, and *has begun*.

The following table gives the principal parts of the irregular verbs that cause most of the verb errors. You should become familiar with the principal parts of these verbs. Consult this list whenever you are in doubt about the correct form to use. If the verb you want is not in this list, consult a reliable, up-to-date dictionary. The principal parts of verbs are given in most dictionaries.

PRINCIPAL PARTS OF TROUBLESOME VERBS

Present Tense (present time)	Past Tense (past time)	Past Participle (*used with have, has, had*)
awake	awaked, awoke	awaked, awoke
be (am)	was	been
beat	beat	beaten
become	became	become
begin	began	begun
bid (offer to buy)	bid	bid
bid (command)	bade	bidden, bid
blow	blew	blown
break	broke	broken
bring	brought	brought
broadcast	broadcast, broadcasted	broadcast, broadcasted
burst	burst	burst
catch	caught	caught
choose	chose	chosen
climb	climbed	climbed
come	came	come
cut	cut	cut
dive	dived	dived
do	did	done

PRINCIPAL PARTS OF TROUBLESOME VERBS (Continued)

Present Tense (present time)	Past Tense (past time)	Past Participle (used with have, has, had)
drag	dragged	dragged
draw	drew	drawn
drink	drank	drunk
drive	drove	driven
drown	drowned	drowned
eat	ate	eaten
fall	fell	fallen
flow	flowed	flowed
fly	flew	flown
forget	forgot	forgotten, forgot
freeze	froze	frozen
get	got	got, gotten
give	gave	given
go	went	gone
hang (a picture)	hung	hung
hang (a criminal)	hanged	hanged
know	knew	known
lay (to place, to put)	laid	laid
lead	led	led
leave	left	left
lend	lent	lent
let	let	let
lie (to recline)	lay (not laid)	lain (not laid)
lie (tell a falsehood)	lied	lied
lose	lost	lost
prove	proved	proved
ride	rode	ridden
ring	rang	rung
rise	rose	risen (not rose)
run	ran	run
say	said	said
see	saw	seen
send	sent	sent

PRINCIPAL PARTS OF TROUBLESOME VERBS (Continued)

Present Tense (present time)	Past Tense (past time)	Past Participle (used with have, has, had)
set	set	set
shake	shook	shaken
shine (give light)	shone	shone
shine (polish)	shined	shined
show	showed	shown, showed
shrink	shrank	shrunk
sing	sang	sung
sink	sank	sunk
sit	sat	sat
spring	sprang, sprung	sprung
steal	stole	stolen
swear	swore	sworn
swim	swam	swum
swing	swung	swung
take	took	taken
teach	taught	taught
tear	tore	torn
tell	told	told
think	thought	thought
throw	threw	thrown
try	tried	tried
understand	understood	understood
wake	waked, woke	waked
wear	wore	worn
weave	wove	woven
weep	wept	wept
wind	wound	wound
wring	wrung	wrung
write	wrote	written

SIX CONFUSING VERBS

Six of the irregular verbs require special attention and study because they are so frequently confused. As a result, they are used incorrectly more often than any of the other irregular verbs. These verbs fall into three sets or pairs: *lie, lay; sit, set; rise, raise.* The forms of the verbs in each pair are somewhat similar, but the meanings are quite different. We shall make a special study of these verbs so that you will be able to use them correctly.

LIE AND LAY

There are two different verbs that are spelled alike (*lie*). One means to tell a falsehood. This is a regular verb and causes no difficulty, either in speaking or in writing. The verb that is confused with *lay* is the verb *lie*, which means *to recline, to rest,* or *to remain in a reclining position.* This verb is an irregular verb. The principal parts are *lie, lay,* and (*have, has, had*) *lain.* The present participle, the form that ends in *ing,* is *lying.*

There are two important facts regarding the verb *lie* (to recline) that you should always keep in mind: (1) There is no form ending in **d** that belongs to the verb *lie,* meaning *to recline.* The form *laid* should never be used when you mean *to recline, rest,* or *remain in a reclining position.* (2) The verb *lie* never takes an object.

Mother **lies** down every afternoon. (*rests, reclines*)

Mother **lay** on the couch all afternoon. (not *laid*)

Mother **is lying** on the couch. (not *laying*)

Mother **has lain** on that couch often. (not *has laid*)

The verb *lie* is also the verb to use when we speak about inanimate objects that are in a reclining or in a *lying-down* position.

The pen **lies** on my desk. (not *lays*)

The pen **lay** on my desk all day. (not *laid*)

The pen **is lying** on my desk. (not *is laying*)

The pen **has lain** on my desk all week. (not *has laid*)

142

The verb **lay,** that is so often confused with *lie,* means *to put some-thing down, to place something somewhere.* The principal parts of this verb are *lay, laid, (have, has,* or *had) laid.* The present participle is *laying.* The verb *lay* always takes an object.

John **lays** carpets for Macey's store. *(carpets*—object of *lays)*

John **laid** carpets all week. *(carpets*—object of *laid)*

John **has laid** carpets for many years. *(carpets*—object of *has laid)*

In the first sentence, the verb *lays* is the present tense of the verb *lay,* which means to put something down. The word *carpets* is the direct object of the verb *lays.* It tells what John put down. In the second sentence, the verb *laid* is the past tense of the verb *lay.*

When we use the form *laid,* we must supply an object telling what we *laid,* or *what we put down. Carpets* is the direct object of the verb *laid.* It tells what John *laid.* In the last sentence, *laid* is the correct form of the verb *lay* to combine with *has.* It helps form the verb phrase *has laid.*

SIT AND SET

The verb *sit* means *to assume a sitting position* or *to occupy a seat*. The principal parts of the verb *sit* are *sit, sat, (have, has, had) sat*. The present participle is *sitting*. The verb *sit* never takes an object. The form *set* does not belong to this verb.

Joe **sat** very still, watching the game.

The children **were sitting** on the floor.

I always **sit** near the fireplace when I read.

My aunt likes **to sit** in a rocking chair.

She **has sat** in the same chair for many years.

The verb *set* means *to place, to put something in position, to make rigid, solid,* or *stiff*. The principal parts of the verb *set* are *set, set, (have, has, had) set*. The present participle is *setting*. The verb *set* usually takes an object. There are a few idiomatic uses of the verb in which it does *not* take an object. The verb *set* takes an object in the following sentences:

Esther **set** the basket on the table. (*basket*—direct object)

We **set** the clock back yesterday. (*clock*—direct object)

The operator **set** her hair beautifully. (*hair*—direct object)

The buyer **has set** the price too low. (*price*—direct object)

Idiomatic Uses

The verb *set* is used *without an object* in the following sentences. Study the types of situations in which the verb *set* is used without an object. These are idiomatic uses of the verb *set*.

The sun **was setting** when we left the lodge.

The cement **will set** in two hours.

We **set** out on a long journey.

The men **set** to work at once.

Jelly **sets** as it cools.

144

RISE AND RAISE

The verb *rise* means *to ascend, to go up, to extend upward, to swell up,* as bread dough in fermentation, *to increase in value,* force or *intensity.* The principal parts of the verb *rise* are *rise, rose,* and (*have, has, had*) *risen.* The present participle is *rising.* The verb *rise* expresses action, but it does not take an object.

The building **rises** to a height of eighty feet.

This river **rises** in the north.

The tide **was rising.**

Dan **has risen** in his profession.

The plane **rose** steadily.

The sun **will rise** at six o'clock tomorrow.

The cliffs **rise** far above the sea.

The verb *raise* means *to lift up something* or cause it *to go up, to increase the amount or price, to collect a number of things,* etc. The verb *raise* always takes an object. You can't raise without raising something. The verb *raise* is a regular verb. The principal parts are *raise, raised, raised.* The present participle is *raising.*

I **raised** my arm. (to lift up)

Don't **raise** so much dust! (to cause to rise)

The leader **raised** an army. (collected)

We **shall raise** the flag at sunrise. (to cause to go up)

The farmer **raises** wheat. (to cause to grow)

The landlord **raised** the rent. (increased)

Do not **raise** your voice. (to make louder)

Every verb has three basic forms which are called the **principal parts.** These three forms are the *present tense,* the *past tense,* and the *past participle.*

Tense in grammar means *time.* Every verb has certain forms which show the time of the action or of the state of condition (linking verbs). The **present tense** denotes *present time.* The **past tense** denotes *past time.*

The **past participle** of a verb is the form that is combined with the auxiliaries *have, has,* or *had* to form a verb phrase. The past participle cannot function as the predicate verb.

Verbs are divided into two classes on the basis of the way in which the past tense and the past participle are formed. Some are called *regular verbs* and others are called *irregular verbs.*

A **regular verb** is a verb which forms the past tense and the past participle by adding **d** or **ed** to the form used in the present tense. Sometimes the **d** changes to **t**: *build, built, built.*

An **irregular verb** is a verb which does *not* form the past tense and the past participle in the regular way; that is, by adding **d** or **ed** to the present tense. The most common way of forming the past tense and the past participle of irregular verbs is by a change of vowel: *sing, sang, sung; drink, drank, drunk; ring, rang, rung.*

The *irregular verbs* are responsible for most of our verb errors. Six of these verbs require special study because they are so frequently confused. These verbs fall into three sets or pairs: *lie, lay; sit, set; rise, raise.*

13

VERBS: TENSE

THE SIX TENSES

A VERB is the most important word in any sentence because more constructions depend upon the verb than upon any other part of speech. Verbs have a number of properties which other parts of speech do not have. One of the properties that belongs exclusively to verbs and verb forms is tense.

In grammar, *tense* means *time*. Verbs have **six tenses** which show differences in the time of *action* or the time of the *state of being* or *condition* (linking verbs).

I *see* a robin on the fence. (**present** time)

I *saw* a robin on the fence yesterday. (**past** time)

I *shall see* a number of birds when I go to the woods. (**future** time)

These sentences do not mean the same thing. The meaning depends to a large extent upon the verb form that is used; that is, the verb form that is used to show the *time* of the action.

The first sentence means that the action expressed by the verb *see* is going on now. The second sentence means that the action expressed by the verb *saw* happened at some time in the past (yesterday). The third sentence means that the action expressed by the verb *shall see* will occur at some future time.

The verbs used in the three sentences are forms of the verb *see*. The verb *see* in the first sentence is the form used in the present tense. It expresses or denotes *present time*. The verb *saw* in the second sentence is the form used to express *past time*. The verb *shall see* is the form used to express *future time*.

Remember, there are six tenses in English. The three tenses which you have just studied are called the **simple tenses.** The other three tenses are called the **perfect tenses.** The only difference between the simple tenses and the perfect tenses is that the perfect tenses include the idea of completion. In grammar, the word *perfect* refers to an action or state of being that is completed at the time of speaking or writing.

Simple Tenses	Perfect Tenses
1. *present* tense	4. *present perfect* tense
2. *past* tense	5. *past perfect* tense
3. *future* tense	6. *future perfect* tense

THE SIMPLE TENSES

The present tense denotes *present time*. It is also used to express *habitual action,* or to express an idea that is *generally accepted as true*.

I hear the bell. (present time)
present tense

Oscar works in an airplane factory. (habitual action)
present tense

"Honesty is the best policy." (generally accepted truth)
present tense

The present tense is often used to express *future time*. Examine the following sentences carefully. In all of them the present tense expresses a future idea:

If it rains, we shall not go to the woods.
present tense

If the bill passes, the tax will be removed.
present tense

Our lease on the factory expires tomorrow.
present tense

The past tense denotes *past time*. The past tense of **regular verbs** is formed by adding *d* or *ed* to the present tense form: call, call*ed;* dive,

148

di*ved*. Sometimes the *d* at the end of the present tense form changes to *t* in the past tense: build, buil*t*.

> I mailed the letter yesterday. (addition of *ed*)
> <u>past tense</u>

> We dived into the pool. (addition of *d*)
> <u>past tense</u>

> The hunter built a cabin in the woods. (change of *d* to *t*)
> <u>past tense</u>

The past tense of **irregular verbs** is formed in various ways. Sometimes there is a change in the vowel: si*n*g, sa*n*g; swi*m*, swa*m*; beg*i*n, beg*a*n; dr*i*ve, dr*o*ve; br*ea*k, br*o*ke. Sometimes the same form is used in the past tense and in the present tense: bid, bid; hurt, hurt; cut, cut; slit, slit.

The future tense denotes *future time.* The future tense is formed by combining the auxiliary *shall* or *will* with the present tense form of the verb. Use *shall* with the pronouns *I* and *we.* Use *will* with the pronouns *you, he, she, it, they.*

> I *shall see* you tomorrow. (*shall*—first person)

> I am sure that you *will be* late. (*will*—second person)

> The speaker *will arrive* at seven. (*will*—third person)

To express future time, use *shall* in the first person and *will* in the second and third persons.

THE PERFECT TENSES

You can remember the *perfect tenses* easily, if you remember that the word **perfect** is always used in identifying them. The three perfect tenses are the *present perfect tense,* the *past perfect tense,* and the *future perfect tense.*

The present perfect tense denotes *action that is completed* at the time of speaking or writing. It may also indicate action that is *continuing into the present.*

The present perfect tense is formed by combining the auxiliary *have*

149

or *has* with the past participle of the principal verb. The auxiliary *has* is always used in the third person singular: He *has spoken* to the manager.

I have seen three of Shaw's plays. (*have seen*—first person)
present perfect

You have earned a promotion. (*have earned*—second person)
present perfect

John has washed the car. (*has washed*—third person)
present perfect

In the first sentence, the verb phrase is *have seen*. It is in the present perfect tense. The verb phrase is made up of the auxiliary *have* and the past participle of the verb *see,* which is *seen* (*have seen*). In the third sentence, the auxiliary *has* is used instead of *have* (*has washed*).

The past perfect tense denotes *action that was completed* before some definite time in the past. The past perfect tense is formed by combining the auxiliary *had* with the past participle of the principal verb: *had walked, had known, had given, had drunk, had become, had been,* etc.

By the time the officer arrived, the thief had disappeared.
                  past tense   past perfect

I liked the speaker better after I had heard him the second time.
past tense   past perfect

The agent had sold all the tickets before I applied for mine.
      past perfect   past tense

The future perfect tense denotes *action that will be completed* at some definite time in the future. The future perfect tense is seldom used in informal speaking or writing.

The future perfect tense is formed by combining the auxiliaries *shall have* or *will have* with the past participle of the principal verb. *Shall have* is used in the first person, and *will have* in the second and third persons.

My friend will have sailed before I reach the pier.
          future perfect

By January, the committee will have completed the investigation.
                            future perfect

I shall have crossed the river three times before noon.
  future perfect

Many verb errors are made because the writer or speaker is not familiar with the forms for the past tense and the past participle. Whenever you are not sure of one of these forms, consult the tables on page 139. If the verb you are interested in is not listed, consult a reliable, up-to-date dictionary. You will find these forms listed after the verb.

You can also avoid verb errors if you know the auxiliaries that indicate the tense:

shall and *will* for the future tense

have and *has* for the present perfect tense

had for the past perfect tense

shall have or *will have* for the future perfect tense

THE VERB "TO BE"

Every person should be thoroughly familiar with the forms of the verb **to be.** It is the most irregular, and also the most important verb in the English language. The verb *to be* is used as an independent verb, and is also used as an auxiliary verb. The entire passive voice and all the progressive forms of other verbs are formed by using the verb *to be* as an auxiliary or helping verb. You should become familiar with the forms for the six tenses of this important verb.

On the following pages you will find reference tables for the tenses of three verbs; the verb *to be,* the regular verb *call,* and the irregular verb *ring.*

SIX TENSES OF THE VERB "TO BE"

PRESENT TENSE

Singular		Plural
First person:	I am	we are
Second person:	you are	you are
Third person:	he, she, it is	they are

PAST TENSE

First person:	I was	we were
Second person:	you were	you were
Third person:	he, she, it was	they were

FUTURE TENSE

First person:	I *shall* be	we *shall* be
Second person:	you *will* be	you *will* be
Third person:	he, she, it *will* be	they *will* be

PRESENT PERFECT TENSE

First person:	I *have* been	we *have* been
Second person:	you *have* been	you *have* been
Third person:	he, she, it *has* been	they *have* been

PAST PERFECT TENSE

First person:	I *had* been	we *had* been
Second person:	you *had* been	you *had* been
Third person:	he, she, it *had* been	they *had* been

FUTURE PERFECT TENSE

First person:	I *shall have* been	we *shall have* been
Second person:	you *will have* been	you *will have* been
Third person:	he, she, it *will have* been	they *will have* been

THE SIX TENSES OF A REGULAR VERB

VERB "CALL"—ACTIVE VOICE

PRESENT TENSE

Singular		Plural
First person:	I call	we call
Second person:	you call	you call
Third person:	he, she, it *calls*	they call

PAST TENSE

First person:	I call*ed*	we call*ed*
Second person:	you call*ed*	you call*ed*
Third person:	he, she, it call*ed*	they call*ed*

FUTURE TENSE

First person:	I *shall* call	we *shall* call
Second person:	you *will* call	you *will* call
Third person:	he, she, it *will* call	they *will* call

PRESENT PERFECT TENSE

First person:	I *have* called	we *have* called
Second person:	you *have* called	you *have* called
Third person:	he, she, it *has* called	they *have* called

PAST PERFECT TENSE

First person:	I *had* called	we *had* called
Second person:	you *had* called	you *had* called
Third person:	he, she, it *had* called	they *had* called

FUTURE PERFECT TENSE

First person:	I *shall have* called	we *shall have* called
Second person:	you *will have* called	you *will have* called
Third person:	he, she, it, *will have* called	they *will have* called

153

THE SIX TENSES OF AN IRREGULAR VERB

VERB *"RING"*—ACTIVE VOICE

PRESENT TENSE

Singular	**Plural**
First person: I ring	we ring
Second person: you ring	you ring
Third person: he, she, it *rings*	they ring

PAST TENSE

First person: I rang	we rang
Second person: you rang	you rang
Third person: he, she, it rang	they rang

FUTURE TENSE

First person: I *shall* ring	we *shall* ring
Second person: you *will* ring	you *will* ring
Third person: he, she, it *will* ring	they *will* ring

PRESENT PERFECT TENSE

First person: I have rung	we have rung
Second person: you have rung	you have rung
Third person: he, she, it has rung	they have rung

PAST PERFECT TENSE

First person: I had rung	we had rung
Second person: you had rung	you had rung
Third person: he, she, it had rung	they had rung

FUTURE PERFECT TENSE

First person: I shall have rung	we shall have rung
Second person: you will have rung	you will have rung
Third person: he, she, it will have rung	they will have rung

PROGRESSIVE FORMS OF VERBS

In addition to the forms which have already been given to show tense, a verb has special forms to show that the *action is continuing.* These forms are called the **progressive forms** of a verb. The *progressive forms* are used to show that an action is *continuing* or *progressing* at the time indicated by a particular tense.

I am <u>studying</u> English. (The action is continuing.)
<u>progressive form</u>

He is <u>planning</u> a trip to Mexico. (The action is continuing.)
<u>progressive form</u>

The progressive form of a verb is made up by using some form of the verb *to be* with the *ing* form of the principal verb. The form of a verb that ends in *ing* is called the **present participle.**

In the first sentence, the progressive form of the verb is *am studying.* It is made up of a form of the verb *to be,* which is *am,* and the present participle of the principal verb, which is *studying.* In the second sentence, the progressive form of the verb, *is planning,* is made up in a similar way.

The following are the progressive forms of the verb *call* for the six tenses (first person, singular).

I *am calling* you. (present progressive)

I *was calling* you. (past progressive)

I *shall be calling* you. (future progressive)

I *have been calling* you. (present perfect progressive)

I *had been calling* you. (past perfect progressive)

I *shall have been calling* you. (future perfect progressive)

The present tense, progressive form often expresses a future idea. The verb *to go* is commonly used in this way:

I *am going* to New York next week. (in the future)

He *is going* to buy a new home in the suburbs. (in the future)

REFERENCE TABLE

VERB "CALL"

PROGRESSIVE FORMS—ACTIVE VOICE

PRESENT TENSE

Singular   **Plural**

First person: I *am* calling   we *are* calling
Second person: you *are* calling   you *are* calling
Third person: he, she, it *is* calling   they *are* calling

PAST TENSE

First person: I *was* calling   we *were* calling
Second person: you *were* calling   you *were* calling
Third person: he, she, it *was* calling   they *were* calling

FUTURE TENSE

First person: I *shall be* calling   we *shall be* calling
Second person: you *will be* calling   you *will be* calling
Third person: he, she, it *will be* calling they *will be* calling

PRESENT PERFECT TENSE

First person: I *have been* calling   we *have been* calling
Second person: you *have been* calling   you *have been* calling
Third person: he, she, it *has been* calling they *have been* calling

PAST PERFECT TENSE

First person: I *had been* calling   we *had been* calling
Second person: you *had been* calling   you *had been* calling
Third person: he, she, it *had been* calling they *had been* calling

FUTURE PERFECT TENSE

First person: I *shall have been* calling   we *shall have been* calling
Second person: you *will have been* calling you *will have been* calling
Third person: he, she, it *will have been*   they *will have been* calling
                     calling

EMPHATIC FORMS OF THE VERB

The **emphatic forms** of a verb are often used to give greater emphasis to the idea expressed by the verb. The auxiliaries *do, does,* and *did* are used to give this additional emphasis. The emphatic forms are used in only two tenses, the *present tense* and the *past tense*.

I <u>do agree</u> with you. (present tense)
emphatic form

Jane <u>did send</u> the letter. (past tense)
emphatic form

The editor <u>does need</u> to know the facts. (present tense)
emphatic form

EMPHATIC FORMS—*PRESENT TENSE*

Singular		Plural
First person:	I *do* call	we *do* call
Second person:	you *do* call	you *do* call
Third person:	he *does* call	they *do* call

EMPHATIC FORMS—*PAST TENSE*

First person:	I *did* call	we *did* call
Second person:	you *did* call	you *did* call
Third person:	he *did* call	they *did* call

When *do, does,* and *did* are used in questions, the form is not used for emphasis. The use of *do, does,* and *did* in questions is an idiomatic way of asking questions in English. In the following questions *do, does,* and *did* are not the emphatic form of the verb:

<u>Did</u> he <u>buy</u> that hat last week?

<u>Do</u> you <u>know</u> her?

<u>Does</u> he <u>want</u> to pay the bill now?

Also, when *do, does,* and *did* are used to mean *accomplish, carry out,* etc., the form is not used for emphasis in these cases. This sentence is an example:

We *did* our homework quickly.

THE USE OF SHALL AND WILL

Many of the precise distinctions concerning the use of *shall* and *will* are rapidly passing out of informal speaking and writing. Careful writers, however, still observe some of these distinctions. The following are some of the distinctions that are most generally observed:

Simple Futurity

Use *shall* in the first person and *will* in the second and third persons to express **simple futurity.** Simple futurity means anticipation or expectation of what is likely to happen, or what one is likely to do. It follows the regular forms for the future tense:

First person: I *shall* go	we *shall* go
Second person: you *will* go	you *will* go
Third person: he *will* go	they *will* go

Determination, Threat, Promise

If you want to express determination, compulsion, threat, or promise (willingness to do something), reverse the order of *shall* and *will*. Use *will* in the first person, and *shall* in the second and third persons.

First person: I *will* go	we *will* go
Second person: you *shall* go	you *shall* go
Third person: he *shall* go	they *shall* go

Special Cases

When *shall* and *will* are followed by such expressions as *be glad, be sorry, be happy, be delighted, be pleased,* etc., use *shall* in the first person, and *will* in the second and third persons. If *will* is used in the first person, it would mean that you are determined *to be glad, sorry, delighted,* etc. If *shall* is used in the second and third persons, it would mean that you are compelling someone *to be glad, sorry,* etc. The following are the accepted ways of using such expressions:

I shall be glad to see you. (not *will*)
<u>first person</u>

We shall be delighted to help you. (not *will*)
<u>first person</u>

You will be sorry to learn of his misfortune. (not *shall*)
<u>second person</u>

He will be pleased to see you at four. (not *shall*)
<u>third person</u>

In giving courteous commands, you should use *will* in the second and third persons instead of *shall*. This is the form that is generally followed in giving military orders and instructions:

Corporal Smith *will report* to Captain Allen. (not *shall report*)

You *will hand* in your report on Wednesday. (not *shall*)

The meeting *will come* to order. (not *shall*)

Mr. Ames, you *will meet* with the committee today. (not *shall*)

SHOULD AND WOULD

Should is the past tense of *shall* and in general, follows the same rules that apply to the use of *shall*. *Would* is the past tense of *will* and follows the same rules that apply to the use of *will*.

Both *should* and *would* have special uses. *Would* is used in all three persons to express *habitual* or *customary* action. *Should* is often used in all three persons to express *obligation*. *Ought* and *should* both express obligation and are used interchangeably.

Every evening we *would play* cards for hours. (*habitual action*)

You *should read* something worth while every day. (*obligation*)

You *ought to read* something worth while every day. (*obligation*)

159

Study the following sentences carefully. Note especially the explanations given in parentheses. This will help you understand the distinctions which have been made in the preceding discussion:

I shall go to the theater this evening. (*simple futurity—expectation*)
first person

I will not see him today. (*determination* on the part of the speaker)
first person

You will enjoy meeting him. (*simple futurity* or *expectation*)
second person

He will enter Harvard in September. (*simple futurity*)
third person

I will accompany you to the clinic. (*promise—willingness*)
first person

He shall report to the judge every month. (*I am determined* that
third person
he shall.)

You shall have any assistance that you may need. (*I am determined*
second person
that you shall.)

We shall be pleased to grant you an interview. (*simple futurity*)
first person

You would drown if you ventured out in deep water. (*simple
second person
futurity*)

He would drown if he ventured out in deep water. (*simple
third person
futurity*)

We should be very happy if you would call for us. (*simple futurity*)
first person   second person

I should be the first one to volunteer. (*obligation*)
first person

You should read good books. (*obligation*)
second person

They should offer their services to the committee. (*obligation*)
third person

MIXED TENSES

Unless there is a good reason for making a change, the tenses of the verbs in a sentence or in a paragraph should agree. If you start out with a verb in the *past tense,* you should not change to another verb in the *present tense.* If you start with a verb in the *present tense,* you should not change to the *past tense.*

Tense means *time,* and when you change the tense, you also change the time. Tenses must be consistent; that is, there must be a logical sequence of time. It is illogical to shift from one tense to another tense. Study the following illustrations carefully:

Dr. Smith *examined* the patient and *calls* the nurse. (*incorrect*)

In this sentence, the verb *examined* is in the past tense. It is followed by the verb *calls* which is in the present tense. There is a shift from the past tense to the present tense. Both verbs should be in the past tense or both verbs should be in the present tense.

Dr. Smith <u>examines</u> the patient and <u>calls</u> the nurse. (*correct*)
<small>present</small>   <small>present</small>

    or

Dr. Smith <u>examined</u> the patient and <u>called</u> the nurse. (*correct*)
<small>past</small>   <small>past</small>

I <u>went</u> into the hall and there I <u>see</u> a strange man. (*incorrect*)
<small>past</small>   <small>present</small>

I <u>went</u> into the hall and there I <u>saw</u> a strange man. (*correct*)
<small>past</small>   <small>past</small>

The officer <u>stopped</u> the car and <u>speaks</u> to the driver. (*incorrect*)
<small>past</small>   <small>present</small>

The officer <u>stopped</u> the car and <u>spoke</u> to the driver. (*correct*)
<small>past</small>   <small>past</small>

THE "OF" ERROR

Careless speakers and writers often use the preposition *of* in place of the auxiliary verb *have*. The word *of* is a preposition and should never be used as part of a verb phrase.

The *"of"* error is generally caused by the use of contractions or by careless enunciation on the part of a speaker. The mistake is commonly made after the words *could, might, ought to, should,* and *would*. When *have* is used following any of these words, and the two words are contracted, the resulting combination sounds as if *of* were being used rather than *have: could've* sounds like *could of, should've* sounds like *should of,* etc.

Since in speech the contracted form of *have* cannot readily be distinguished from *of,* many persons have the mistaken belief that *of* is the word being said and that it is the correct word to use. As a result they carry over the mistake from their speech into their writing, and never know they are in error. To avoid making the *"of"* error when you are speaking, never contract *have* to *'ve*.

Study the following examples. The preposition *of* should never be used in place of *have* as part of a verb phrase.

We should *of* been more careful. (*incorrect*)

We should *have* been more careful. (*correct*)

He must *of* taken it. (*incorrect*)

He must *have* taken it. (*correct*)

They might *of* notified us. (*incorrect*)

They might *have* notified us. (*correct*)

I should *of* prepared the report. (*incorrect*)

I should *have* prepared the report. (*correct*)

In grammar, *tense* means *time*. The tense of a verb indicates the time of the action or the time of the state of condition (linking verb).

There are six tenses in English: *present* tense, *past* tense, *future* tense, *present perfect* tense, *past perfect* tense, and *future perfect* tense.

The *present tense* indicates present time: I *know* him.

The *past tense* indicates past time: John *was* ill yesterday.

The *future tense* indicates future time: I *shall see* you tomorrow.

The *present perfect tense* indicates an action that is completed at the time of speaking or writing:

I *have called* him twice today.

The *past perfect tense* indicates an action that was completed before some definite time in the past:

At the meeting, I recognized a delegate whom I *had met* in Boston.

The *future perfect tense* indicates an action that will be completed at some definite time in the future. The future perfect tense expresses the relation between two future times:

You will understand the subject of tense when you *will have finished* this unit.

The *progressive form* of the verb is the form that is used to indicate that the action is continuing at the time indicated by the tense:

We *have been planning* to go to Europe

The *emphatic form* of the verb is used to give added emphasis to a statement:

I *did write* that letter.

14

VERBS: VOICE AND MOOD

ACTIVE AND PASSIVE VOICE

A VERB not only undergoes certain changes to show *tense,* or the time of the action, but it changes in form to show *voice.* **Voice** is a grammatical term which is used to *tell whether the subject of the sentence is acting or is receiving the action expressed by the verb.*

When the subject is acting, we say that the subject is the *doer.* When the subject is receiving the action, we say that the subject is the *receiver.* If you keep these two terms, *doer* and *receiver,* in mind, you will have no difficulty in understanding what *voice* means in grammar.

Study the following sentences carefully. Note the changes that occur in the form of the verb. Note the change that occurs in the subject of the sentence:

Ned washed the car. (*Ned* is the *doer* of the action.)

The car was washed by Ned. (*Car* is the *receiver* of the action.)

In the first sentence, the subject is *Ned.* He is the *doer,* the one who is performing the action expressed by the verb *washed.* The *car* is receiving the action. In grammar we say that the verb in this sentence is in the **active voice** because the subject is the *doer,* or is doing the washing. The car is the *receiver* of the action.

The second sentence is written in the reverse order. The subject is now the receiver of the action instead of the doer. In order to express this idea, it was necessary to use another verb form, *was washed.* What happened to *Ned,* the doer? *Ned* is still in the sentence but is now in a phrase introduced by the preposition *by.*

The verb *was washed* is in the **passive voice** because it represents the subject of the sentence as the receiver of the action. In other words

164

the subject is not acting, but is *passive*. The doer, or the actor, appears in a phrase introduced by the preposition *by*.

A verb in the passive voice is *never* a simple verb. It is always a verb phrase. In the sentence, *Our car was stolen yesterday,* the verb *was stolen* is in the *passive voice*. The subject is the receiver of the action. Since the doer is unknown, the "*by* phrase" is omitted. But we know that it was stolen by someone. If we discover who stole the car, the doer might be added to the sentence:

Our car was stolen yesterday by two strangers.
 receiver   doer

If a verb is in the **active voice,** *the subject is the doer of the action.* If a verb is in the **passive voice,** *the subject is the receiver of the action.* When a verb is in the passive voice, the doer is often omitted. Sometimes the doer is unknown, and sometimes the doer is so evident that it is not necessary to include the "*by* phrase."

HOW THE PASSIVE VOICE IS FORMED

You cannot express an idea in the passive voice without using an auxiliary or helping verb. The verb *to be* is the auxiliary verb that is used to help form the six tenses of the passive voice. If you are familiar with the conjugation of the verb *to be*, you will have no difficulty in forming the passive voice of any verb that takes an object.

The passive voice is formed by combining the verb *to be* with the **past participle** of the principal verb. The principal verb is the verb that names the action.

The verb *was washed* in the sentence, *The car was washed by Ned,* is made up of the auxiliary verb *was,* which is a form of the verb *to be.* The *past participle* of the principal verb is added to the auxiliary *was.* The past participle of the verb *wash* is *washed.* The verb phrase is *was washed.* It is a verb phrase in the passive voice.

The verb phrases in the following sentences are in the passive voice. They are formed by combining some form of the verb *to be* with the past participle of the principal verb, or the verb that names the action.

The plans <u>will be made</u> by the general.
passive voice

Trees <u>have been planted</u> in the park by the commissioners.
passive voice

The verb in the first sentence is *will be made.* It is made up of the auxiliary *will be,* which is a form of the verb *to be,* and the past participle of the verb *make,* which is *made* (*will be made*).

The verb in the second sentence is *have been planted.* It is made up of the auxiliary verb *have been,* which is a form of the verb *to be* and the past participle of the verb *plant* (*planted*).

The six tenses of the verb *call* given in the previous chapter are the forms for the *active voice.* The forms for the *passive voice* follow. If you examine these forms carefully, you will see that the tenses follow the regular conjugation of the verb *to be.* The past participle of the verb *call* (*called*) is added to the forms of the verb *to be.*

Reference Table

SIX TENSES OF THE VERB "CALL"

PASSIVE VOICE

Present Tense

	Singular	**Plural**
First person:	I *am* called	we *are* called
Second person:	you *are* called	you *are* called
Third person:	he *is* called	they *are* called

Past Tense

	Singular	Plural
First person:	I *was* called	we *were* called
Second person:	you *were* called	you *were* called
Third person:	he *was* called	they *were* called

Future Tense

	Singular	Plural
First person:	I *shall be* called	we *shall be* called
Second person:	you *will be* called	you *will be* called
Third person:	he *will be* called	they *will be* called

Present Perfect Tense

	Singular	Plural
First person:	I *have been* called	we *have been* called
Second person:	you *have been* called	you *have been* called
Third person:	he *has been* called	they *have been* called

Past Perfect Tense

	Singular	Plural
First person:	I *had been* called	we *had been* called
Second person:	you *had been* called	you *had been* called
Third person:	he *had been* called	they *had been* called

Future Perfect Tense

	Singular	Plural
First person:	I *shall have been* called	we *shall have been* called
Second person:	you *will have been* called	you *will have been* called
Third person:	he *will have been* called	they *will have been* called

SIX TENSES OF THE IRREGULAR VERB "KNOW"

PASSIVE VOICE

Present Tense

	Singular	Plural
First person:	I *am* known	we *are* known
Second person:	you *are* known	you *are* known
Third person:	he *is* known	they *are* known

Past Tense

First person:	I *was* known	we *were* known
Second person:	you *were* known	you *were* known
Third person:	he *was* known	they *were* known

Future Tense

First person:	I *shall be* known	we *shall be* known
Second person:	you *will be* known	you *will be* known
Third person:	he *will be* known	they *will be* known

Present Perfect Tense

First person:	I *have been* known	we *have been* known
Second person:	you *have been* known	you *have been* known
Third person:	he *has been* known	they *have been* known

Past Perfect Tense

First person:	I *had been* known	we *had been* known
Second person:	you *had been* known	you *had been* known
Third person:	he *had been* known	they *had been* known

Future Perfect Tense

First person:	I *shall have been* known	we *shall have been* known
Second person:	you *will have been* known	you *will have been* known
Third person:	he *will have been* known	they *will have been* known

WHEN TO USE THE PASSIVE VOICE

Since you may show that the subject is either the doer or the receiver of the action, the question naturally arises, "Which form is better?" In many sentences, the use of the passive voice often results in a roundabout, awkward method of expression.

In the large majority of cases the *active voice is the better form to use.* Never use the passive voice, either in speaking or writing, when the active voice would be more natural or more direct. The following illustrations show clearly that the active voice would be more natural and more direct than the passive voice.

The concert was enjoyed by us. (*passive voice*)

We enjoyed the concert. (*active voice*)

Your order was sent by us by express today. (*passive voice*)

We sent your order by express today. (*active voice*)

The stranger was barked at by a dog. (*passive voice*)

A dog barked at the stranger. (*active voice*)

As a rule, the active voice is preferred for business writing, and for any other form of writing that requires the direct approach. The use of the *active voice increases vividness.* The passive voice expresses reversed action, since the receiver comes before the doer. Active verbs are often used in newspaper headlines because they are more vivid and take less space. The following headlines are all in the active voice:

"Bushman Gets Out of Cage"

"White Sox Capture First Title"

"Urges France to Begin Defense Plan"

"Governor Advises Aid for Workers"

The passive voice is generally used when the subject of the sentence is *indefinite, general,* or *unimportant.* In the sentence, *They mine coal in Pennsylvania,* the subject is so indefinite that it is not clear what is meant by *they.* It might mean the miners, the people, or the companies. This sentence, and sentences like it, are improved by putting the verb in the passive voice.

They *mine* coal in Pennsylvania. (*poor*)

Coal *is mined* in Pennsylvania. (*better*)

They *grow* wheat in many of our states. (*poor*)

Wheat *is grown* in many of our states. (*better*)

They *use* tractors on some farms. (*poor*)

Tractors *are used* on some farms. (*better*)

The passive voice is also used when *what was done* is more important than the doer of the action. Study the following sentences:

The play, "Man and Superman," *was written* by Shaw. (*passive*)

Shaw *wrote* the play "Man and Superman." (*active*)

America *was discovered* by Columbus. (*passive*)

Columbus *discovered* America. (*active*)

In the first sentence, if you wish to emphasize the play more than the author, put the verb in the passive voice. In the third sentence, if you wish to emphasize the discovery more than the discoverer, put the verb in the passive voice.

The use of the passive voice is generally used when you want to emphasize the *receiver* rather than the *doer.* However, in the great majority of cases the active voice is more effective than the passive voice.

MOOD OF VERBS

In addition to tense and voice, verbs have another property which is called **mood** (or *mode*). The word *mood* comes from a Latin word which means *manner*. When we apply the term mood to verbs, we mean *the manner in which the verb expresses the action or state of being*.

There are three moods in English, the *indicative mood,* the *imperative mood,* and the *subjunctive mood*. The *indicative mood* is used *to make statements* and *to ask questions*. Most of the verbs that you commonly use are in the indicative mood.

> The stenographer <u>wrote</u> the letter. (*statement of fact*)
> indicative mood

> <u>Did</u> you <u>hear</u> the President's address? (*question*)
> indicative mood

The imperative mood is used to *express a command* or *a request*. The imperative mood is found only in the present tense, second person. The subject is always the pronoun *you,* which is seldom expressed.

> <u>Come</u> here at once! (*command*)
> imperative mood

> <u>Close</u> the door, Jane. (*request*)
> imperative mood

The subjunctive mood is used to *express a wish* or *a condition which is contrary to fact.* By contrary to fact we mean something which is not true. A contrary to fact condition is usually introduced by the word *if* or *as if*.

> If he <u>were</u> here, I would give him the keys. (*He is not here.*)
> subjunctive mood

> I wish I <u>were</u> in Florida. (*expresses a wish*)
> subjunctive mood

The indicative and the imperative moods do not present any problems in English. The verb has the same form to express a statement or to ask a question. You can identify the imperative mood easily because the subject is *you*, which is usually understood. The imperative mood always expresses a command or a request.

Although most of the forms for the subjunctive have disappeared from our language, there are a few forms left that you should be able to recognize and to use. The verb *to be* still retains more of the subjunctive forms than any other verb. Compare the following indicative and subjunctive forms of the verb *to be*:

Reference Table

SUBJUNCTIVE FORMS OF VERB "TO BE"

Indicative Mood		Subjunctive Mood	

Present Tense—Singular and Plural

First person:	I am	we are	(If) I *be*	(If) we *be*
Second person:	you are	you are	(If) you *be*	(If) you *be*
Third person:	he is	they are	(If) he *be*	(If) they *be*

Past Tense—Singular

First person:	I was	(If) I *were*
Second person:	you were	(If) you were
Third person:	he was	(If) he *were*

Present Perfect Tense—Singular

First person:	I have been	(If) I have been
Second person:	you have been	(If) you have been
Third person:	he has been	(If) he *have* been

The subjunctive with *be* (present tense) is almost never used in informal speaking and writing. The subjunctive form *have been* instead of *has been* is also passing out of use.

In the preceding table, the forms for the subjunctive that are different from the indicative are printed in *italics;* that is, *be* in the present tense; *were* in the past tense, first person, singular, and third person, singular; *have* in the present perfect tense, third person, singular.

There is only one change that occurs in the subjunctive in the case of other verbs. In the present tense, third person, singular, the *s* is dropped in the subjunctive.

The verb *have* has only one form in the subjunctive that is different from the indicative. In the present tense, third person, singular, *have* is used in place of *has*:

If he *have* the time, he will meet with you. (subjunctive)

He *has* the time, and he will meet with you. (indicative)

If he fail— (not *fails*)

If he keep— (not *keeps*)

If he find— (not *finds*)

If he have— (not *has*)

If he call— (not *calls*)

The word *if* is not a part of the subjunctive. The forms for the subjunctive are usually given with the word *if* because the group of words in which the subjunctive is used is very frequently introduced by the word *if*.

Although the subjunctive mood is rapidly passing out of use in informal speaking and writing, there are certain uses that are still observed by discriminating writers and speakers. The subjunctive expressing a *wish* and the subjunctive in a *contrary to fact condition* are two of these uses.

USES OF THE SUBJUNCTIVE MOOD

As explained, careful writers and speakers use the subjunctive to express a wish, a condition that is contrary to fact (not true), and a condition of uncertainty (it may be true or not true). Sometimes careful writers and speakers also use the subjunctive *in making a suggestion, in making a demand,* or *in expressing a need.*

I wish I *were* a millionaire. (wish)

If I *were* you, I should give up the contest. (contrary to fact)

If this plan *fail,* we shall give up the project. (condition of uncertainty)

I suggest that he *work* full time in the future. (suggestion)

The supervisor insists that the bookkeeper *prove* his report. (a demand)

It is imperative that the play *begin* at once. (a necessity)

The subjunctive is used in certain parliamentary expressions, such as the following:

I move that the nominations *be closed.*

He moved that the report of the committee *be accepted.*

She moved that the minutes *be adopted* as read.

I move that the meeting *be adjourned.*

The *two most important* uses of the subjunctive are the subjunctive expressing a wish and the subjunctive in a contrary to fact condition after *if, as if,* and *as though.*

SUMMARY

Voice is that property of a verb which indicates whether the subject is performing the action or is receiving the action. There are two voices: active voice and passive voice.

A verb is in the **active voice** when it represents the subject as *performing* the action.

A verb is in the **passive voice** when it represents the subject as *receiving* the action.

Only a verb that takes an object (transitive verb) can be changed into the passive voice.

The passive voice is formed by combining some form of the verb *to be* with the past participle of the verb that names the action: Examples: *am called, will be elected, have been promoted, was interviewed.*

Mood indicates the manner in which the action or the state of being is expressed. There are three moods in English: indicative mood, imperative mood, and the subjunctive mood.

The **indicative mood** is used to state a fact or ask a question.

The **imperative mood** is used to express a command or make a request.

The **subjunctive mood** is used to express a wish, doubt, uncertainty, or a condition that is contrary to fact.

Although the subjunctive is rapidly passing out of use in informal speaking and writing, certain uses of the subjunctive are still observed by careful speakers and writers.

The subjunctive expresses certain distinctions in meaning which cannot be expressed by the indicative. This is true of the subjunctive of *wish,* and the subjunctive in a *contrary to fact condition. If I was you* does not express the same idea as *If I were you.* You can never be the other person. The subjunctive indicates that fact.

175

15

AGREEMENT OF SUBJECT AND VERB

ONE of the common errors made both in speaking and writing is the lack of agreement between the subject noun or pronoun and the predicate verb. In order to have harmonious relations between the parts of the sentence, you must have this agreement.

AGREEMENT IN PERSON AND NUMBER

The grammatical principle upon which agreement of subject and verb depends is very simple: *The verb must agree with its subject in person and number.* If the subject of the sentence is singular, the verb must also be in the singular. If the subject is plural, the verb must also be plural. If the subject is in the first person, the verb must also be in the first person. If the subject is in the second or third persons, the verb must agree.

> *He doesn't* know the answer. (correct—subject and verb are in third person)
>
> *He don't* know the answer. (incorrect—lack of agreement)
>
> *You were invited* to the meeting. (correct—subject and verb are in second person)
>
> *You was invited* to the meeting. (incorrect—lack of agreement)

In the first sentence the subject and verb agree. The subject *He* is in the third person, singular. The verb *doesn't* is also in the third person, singular. In the second sentence, *He don't* is incorrect. The correct form for third person, singular is *doesn't* not *don't*.

Although the rule is very simple, there are a number of problems involved in agreement of subject and verb. These problems are responsible for the errors that are commonly made. Sometimes the speaker or writer does not know whether the subject should be regarded as singular or plural. Sometimes he is not sure about the form of the verb for the singular and for the plural. Sometimes he does not know which word is the real subject of the sentence.

In this unit you will consider some of the problems that are responsible for the errors that occur in making the subject and the verb agree. Your first problem will be the one that occurs when you have a sentence with a compound subject.

AGREEMENT OF VERB WITH COMPOUND SUBJECT

The parts of a compound subject are usually connected by *and*, *or*, *nor*, *either-or*, and *neither-nor*. Usually, when two or more subjects are connected by *and*, the subject is plural and requires a plural verb. The following examples have compound subjects:

Mary and Jane are taking Spanish.
<u>compound subject</u>

The president and the vice-president speak at every meeting.
<u>compound subject</u>

In the first sentence, the two parts of the compound subject are connected by *and*. The subject is plural and takes a plural verb, *are*. In the second sentence, the two parts of the compound subject are also connected by *and*. The subject takes the plural form of the verb which is *speak*.

There is one exception to the "and" rule. Sometimes the two subjects connected by *and* form a unit. In this case, *the subject is regarded as singular and takes a singular verb.*

Bacon and eggs is a popular combination. *(Verb is singular.)*
<u>singular</u>

The Stars and Stripes flies overhead. *(Verb is singular.)*
<u>singular</u>

When two subjects connected by *and* refer to the same person or thing, the subject is *singular*.

His <u>companion and friend</u> <u>is</u> very devoted to him.
same person

The <u>secretary and treasurer</u> <u>was</u> present at the meeting.
same person

If the subjects in the preceding sentences referred to *two individuals,* the verbs would be plural. The sentences would read as follows:

His <u>companion</u> and his <u>friend</u> <u>are</u> very devoted to him.

The <u>secretary</u> and the <u>treasurer</u> <u>were</u> present at the meeting.

By placing the word *his* before friend and the word *the* before treasurer, you clearly indicate that there are two individuals.

Subjects Connected by "Or" or "Nor"

When two singular subjects are connected by the word *or*, the subject is singular. The sentence means *either the one or the other.* It does not mean *both.* The same rule applies when *nor* is used to join two singular subjects. *Either-or* and *neither-nor* follow the same rule.

Mary or Jane <u>is going</u> to the fashion show. (*the one or the other*)
singular

Neither the man nor the boy <u>was</u> responsible. (*neither the one nor the other*)
singular

When one of the subjects connected by *or, nor, either-or, neither-nor* is singular and the other is plural, the verb agrees with the subject that is nearer to it. If both subjects are plural, the verb is also plural.

Neither the <u>boy</u> nor the <u>men</u> <u>were</u> responsible. (*Verb is plural.*)
singular   plural

Neither the <u>men</u> nor the <u>boy</u> <u>was</u> responsible. (*Verb is singular.*)
plural   singular

Neither the <u>men</u> nor the <u>boys</u> <u>were</u> responsible. (*Verb is plural.*)
     plural   plural

In the first sentence, the plural subject is nearer to the verb. In the second sentence, the singular subject is nearer to the verb. In the third sentence, both subjects are plural. When one of the subjects is singular and the other is plural, you should put the plural subject nearer to the verb. It makes the verb plural and sounds better.

If the subjects connected by these words differ in *person,* the verb should agree with the subject nearer to it. Such sentences are often very awkward and should be avoided, if possible.

Either <u>I</u> or <u>they</u> are responsible for the small attendance.
    first   third

This sentence would sound better if it were written as follows:

Either <u>I</u> am responsible for the small attendance, or <u>they</u> are.

AGREEMENT OF VERB WITH COLLECTIVE NOUNS

A **collective noun** is a noun that represents a group or a collection of objects usually considered as a unit. Words like *crowd, troop, herd, people, flock,* and *jury* are collective nouns.

A collective noun that is singular in meaning requires a singular verb. A collective noun that is plural in meaning requires a plural verb.

If the collective noun in a particular sentence represents the individuals acting as a unit, the noun is singular. If the sentence indicates clearly that the individuals are acting separately, the noun is plural. The following examples will help you see this distinction:

The *committee is opposed* to the plan. (*acting as a unit*)

The *board of directors is* in session. (*as a unit*)

The *jury returned its* verdict. (*as a unit*)

The *jury have returned* to their homes. (*as individuals*)

The *family have given* their contributions. (*as individuals*)

In most cases where the individuals composing a group are acting separately, it is better to use such expressions as *the members of the jury, the members of the family,* etc. These expressions sound better and clearly indicate that the individuals are acting separately.

The members of the jury have returned to their homes.

The people in the audience were waving their hands.

The members of the band were wearing their uniforms.

INTERVENING PHRASES

Sometimes the subject is followed by prepositional phrases or such expressions as *accompanied by, in accordance with, together with, as well as, including,* etc. The subject of the sentence is not affected in any way by the introduction of such phrases. You will never find the subject of the sentence in a prepositional phrase or in any one of the expressions listed in the following sentences:

A *package* (of books) *was delivered* today.

Materials (for the building) *have been shipped.*

Important *papers,* as well as his will, *were found* in his desk.

The *checks,* including a statement, *were mailed* today.

In the first sentence, the subject is the word *package.* Since package is singular, the verb must be singular. In the second sentence, the subject is the word *Materials.* Since the subject is plural, the verb must be plural. The prepositional phrases, *of books,* and *for the building,* do not affect the number of the subject.

The subject of the third sentence is *papers,* which is plural. The verb must also be plural to agree with the subject. The group of words, *as well as his will,* does not affect the number of the subject. In the fourth sentence, the expression, *including a statement,* does not affect the number of the subject. The subject is *checks,* which is plural. The verb must also be plural, to agree with the subject.

AGREEMENT OF SUBJECT WITH CONTRACTIONS

Contractions are verbs that have been shortened by the omission of one or more letters. The omission of the letters is indicated by the use of an apostrophe. Many persons make mistakes in agreement of subject and verb when they use contractions. The use of the contractions *don't* and *ain't* are responsible for a great many of these errors.

Although the word *ain't* is frequently heard in informal conversation, most educated persons consider its use incorrect and unacceptable.

Do not use *ain't* for *am not, are not,* or *isn't.* The contraction *aren't* should be used for *are not.* There is no contraction for the words *am not.*

I *am not* interested in the position. (not *ain't*)

We *are not* going to the theater. (not *ain't*)

We *aren't* going to the meeting. (not *ain't*)

Isn't this a beautiful day! (not *ain't*)

Another error commonly made is the use of **don't** for **doesn't.** **Don't** is a contraction for *do not.* It should not be used in the third person, singular. The expressions, *it don't, he don't* and *she don't* are incorrect. Do not misuse them for *it doesn't, he doesn't,* and *she doesn't.*

It *don't* make any difference. (incorrect)

It *doesn't* make any difference. (correct)

He *don't* belong to our union. (incorrect)

He *doesn't* belong to our union. (correct)

She *don't* want the position. (incorrect)

She *doesn't* want the position. (correct)

AGREEMENT OF VERB WITH INDEFINITE PRONOUNS

The indefinite pronouns *one, no one, anyone, everyone, someone, anybody, nobody, everybody, somebody, each, either,* and *neither* are always singular. Since these pronouns are singular, they take a singular verb.

Only *one* of the candidates is eligible. (*singular verb*)

Each of these bags has been examined. (*singular verb*)

Neither has lost his ticket. (*singular verb*)

Somebody is responsible for the accident. (*singular verb*)

Anyone has the right to offer criticism. (*singular verb*)

Nobody has access to the vault. (*singular verb*)

When *many a, each,* and *every* are used to introduce a sentence and function as adjectives, the *subject* is singular.

Many a *man* wishes that he had gone to college.

Each *window* and *door* was locked securely.

Every *man, woman,* and *child* is expected to report.

The indefinite pronouns *several, few, both* and *many* are always plural.

Several were called to the platform. (*plural verb*)

A *few* were opposed to the bill. (*plural verb*)

Both were anxious to receive the award. (*plural verb*)

Many in the audience objected to his speech. (*plural verb*)

The indefinite pronouns *some, none, any,* and *all* are singular or plural according to the meaning of the sentence. When these words refer to a *quantity* or a *mass* taken as a whole, they are generally considered as singular. When they refer to a *number,* they are regarded as plural in meaning.

Some are going by plane. (*more than one*—plural)

Some of the ice cream *is* left. (*mass or quantity*—singular)

Are any of the men going by plane? (*more than one*—plural)

Is there *any* gasoline in the tank? (*mass or quantity*—singular)

None of these apples *are* ripe. (*more than one*—plural)

We needed a ball but *none was* available. (*not one*—singular)

All of the gasoline *has been sold.* (*mass or quantity*—singular)

All of the women *have brought* gifts. (*more than one*—plural)

Some nouns are plural in form, but singular in meaning. Examples of nouns that take a singular verb are *mumps, measles, news, summons, physics, mathematics.*

Physics is a very interesting subject. (*Verb is singular.*)

The news this week is startling. (*Verb is singular.*)

Measles is a contagious disease. (*Verb is singular.*)

The summons was served by the bailiff. (*Verb is singular.*)

Mathematics was his favorite study. (*Verb is singular.*)

SPECIAL CASES OF AGREEMENT

1. Words like *pants, trousers, pliers, scissors, shears,* and *tongs* are plural and take a plural verb. When the word *pair* is used as the subject, the subject is regarded as singular and takes a singular verb.

The *scissors* are very sharp. (*plural*)

A *pair* of scissors was left on the desk. (*singular*)

2. A plural noun which shows *weight, extent,* or *quantity* is singular, and takes a singular verb.

Ten miles is a long distance to walk. (*singular*)

Five dollars is the price of the hat. (*singular*)

Twelve inches is the proper length. (*singular*)

3. The words *half* and *part* are singular or plural according to the meaning of the sentence. When these words refer to a *mass* or a *section,* they are singular. When they refer to a *number* of individuals or things, they are plural.

Half of the boys are in camp. (*number*—plural)

Half of the pie is left. (*mass or section*—singular)

Part of the roof was destroyed. (*mass or section*—singular)

Part of the guests have arrived. (*number*—plural)

4. When the word *number* is preceded by the article *a,* it takes a plural verb. When it is immediately preceded by the article *the,* it takes a singular verb.

A number of men *were working* on the project. (*plural*)

The number of men present *was* small. (*singular*)

5. The name of a firm is often regarded as singular even when there

is a plural form in the title. If the entire name carries a plural idea, the name is regarded as plural.

Mandel Brothers are having a sale on furs. (*plural*)

The Macmillan Company publishes books. (*singular*)

General Motors Company has declared a dividend. (*singular*)

6. Sometimes a sentence begins with the word *there* or *here*. Neither of these words could be the subject of the sentence. The word *there* is used either as an expletive or as an adverb. The word *here* is an adverb. When a sentence begins with *here* or *there*, you should transpose it so that the true subject will appear at the beginning of the sentence. Then it will be possible for you to determine whether the subject is singular or plural.

There are six men on the committee.

Six <u>men</u> <u>are</u> on the committee. (*plural subject—plural verb*)

Here comes the general with his staff.

The <u>general</u> <u>comes</u> here with his staff. (*singular subject and verb*)

Sometimes a sentence beginning with the introductory *there* or *here* has a *compound subject*, which requires a plural verb. Mistakes in the number of the verb are frequently made because the speaker or the writer does not realize that the subject is *compound*. When the sentence is transposed, it is easy to determine whether the subject is simple or compound. The following sentences have compound subjects:

There goes the boy and his mother. (incorrect)

There go the boy and his mother. (correct)

The <u>boy and his mother</u> <u>go</u> there. (*compound subject—plural verb*)

Here comes John and Mary. (incorrect)

Here come John and Mary. (correct)

<u>John and Mary</u> <u>come</u> here. (*compound subject—plural verb*)

A verb must agree with its subject in **person** and **number.** If the subject is singular, the verb must be singular. If the subject is plural, the verb must be plural.

If the subject is in the first person, the verb must be in the first person. If the subject is in the second person, the verb must be in the second person. If the subject is in the third person, the verb must be in the third person.

A **compound subject** connected by *and* is usually plural and takes a plural verb. If the parts of the compound subject refer to a *unit* or to *one person,* the subject is singular and takes a singular verb.

Singular subjects connected by *or, nor, either-or, neither-nor,* take a singular verb. If both of the subjects are plural, the verb is plural. If one of the subjects is singular and the other is plural, the verb agrees with the subject that is *nearer* to it.

A **collective noun** that is *singular in meaning* takes a singular verb. A collective noun that is *plural in meaning* takes a plural verb. If the collective noun represents the individuals acting as a unit, the verb is singular. If the collective noun represents the individuals acting separately, the verb is plural. The meaning of the sentence will determine whether a collective noun should be regarded as singular or plural.

The subject of a sentence *is not affected* in any way by the introduction of phrases or other expressions that come between the subject and the verb. The subject of a sentence *is never found* in a prepositional phrase.

Some of the **indefinite pronouns** are always singular. Some are always plural. The indefinite pronouns *some, none, any,* and *all* are singular or plural according to the meaning of the sentence.

16

PREPOSITIONAL PHRASES

A PREPOSITION is a word that shows the relation between its object and some other word in the sentence.

A prepositional phrase consists of the preposition and its object. Sometimes the noun which serves as the object of the preposition has modifiers, but the important words in the phrase are the two words—the *preposition* and the *object*.

I walked down the winding street.
       <u>preposition</u>   <u>object</u>

The girl with red hair is an artist.
       <u>preposition</u> <u>object</u>

In the first sentence, the preposition is the word *down.* The object is *street.* The entire phrase is *down the winding street.* The two important words in the phrase are the preposition *down* and the object *street.*

In the second sentence, the preposition is *with* and the object is *hair.* The prepositional phrase is the group of words, *with red hair.*

In grammar, a **phrase** is a group of words, *without a subject and predicate,* that functions as *a single part of speech.* A prepositional phrase is a phrase that functions as an *adjective* or an *adverb.* Since adjectives and adverbs are modifiers, the prepositional phrase is also a modifier.

188

ADJECTIVE PHRASES

An *adjective phrase* is a prepositional phrase that modifies a *noun* or a *pronoun*. An adjective phrase is often the equivalent of an adjective, as you will readily see from the following illustrations:

The man <u>at the gate</u> sold us the tickets.
       adjective phrase

We followed the path <u>near the river.</u>
                     adjective phrase

In the first sentence, the prepositional phrase is *at the gate.* It is an adjective phrase because it modifies the noun *man.* The phrase, *at the gate,* is the equivalent of an adjective because it means the *gate* man.

In the second sentence, the prepositional phrase is *near the river.* This is also an adjective phrase because it modifies the noun *path.* The sentence means that we followed the *river* path. The phrase *near the river* is the equivalent of an adjective.

Like the adjective, the adjective phrase *describes* or *limits* the noun or pronoun which it modifies.

She wore a hat *with blue trimming.* (describes the hat)

He lives in the house *to your right.* (limited to a particular house)

An adjective phrase may follow the noun which it modifies, or it may be used in the predicate after a linking verb.

The accident *on the bridge* was not serious. (follows the noun)

The injured man seemed *in a daze.* (follows a linking verb)

You will not acquire skill in recognizing prepositional phrases unless you become familiar with the words that are commonly used, as prepositions. Refer to the following list until you are able to identify the prepositions that are in common use.

Commonly Used Prepositions

above	at	by	into	toward
about	before	down	like	through
across	behind	during	near	under
after	below	except	of	until
against	beneath	for	off	up
along	beside	from	on	upon
among	between	in	since	with
around	but (except)	inside	to	within

The fact that a word appears in this list does not mean that it is always used as a preposition. Many of the words that are commonly used as prepositions are also used as adverbs.

Planes were flying <u>above the city</u>. (*Above* is a preposition.)
prepositional phrase

Planes were flying <u>above</u>. (*Above* is an adverb.)
adverb

ADVERBIAL PHRASES

An *adverbial phrase* is a prepositional phrase that modifies a *verb*, an *adjective*, or an *adverb*. Like the adverb, the adverbial phrase answers the questions: *when? where? how?* and *to what extent?* Adverbial phrases express *time, place, manner,* and *degree.*

I shall return <u>at noon.</u> (Phrase expresses *time.*)

            adverbial phrase

The sailor was working <u>on the deck.</u> (Phrase expresses *place.*)

                        adverbial phrase

Tell the story <u>in your own words.</u> (Phrase expresses *manner.*)

              adverbial phrase

In the first sentence, the adverbial phrase is *at noon.* The phrase tells *when* or at what time I shall return. It modifies the verb *shall return.* The adverbial phrase in the second sentence is *on the deck.* This phrase tells *where* or *at what place* the sailor was working. It modifies the verb *was working.* The adverbial phrase in the third sentence is *in your own words.* It tells *how* or *in what manner* you should tell the story. The phrase modifies the verb *tell.*

Adverbial phrases that modify verbs are very easy to identify. Those that modify adjectives and adverbs are not always easy to identify. The adverbial phrase that modifies an adjective usually follows that adjective. Study the following illustration carefully:

The child seemed afraid <u>of the noise.</u> (modifies *afraid*)

                      adverbial phrase

In this sentence, the adverbial phrase *of the noise* modifies the predicate adjective *afraid.* Adverbial phrases that modify adjectives usually follow this pattern.

COMPOUND OR PHRASAL PREPOSITIONS

A preposition is not always a single word. There are a number of prepositions in common use that are made up of a group of two or more words. Such prepositions are called **compound prepositions** or **phrasal prepositions**.

Although the *compound preposition* consists of two or more words, it is regarded as a unit, or as a single preposition. The following list includes the compound prepositions that are in common use:

according to	for the sake of	in respect to
along side of	in addition to	in spite of
along with	in accordance with	instead of
because of	in case of	on account of
by means of	in consideration of	out of
by reason of	in apposition with	with reference to
by way of	in front of	with regard to
contrary to	in regard to	with respect to

Compound Prepositions in Sentences

In compliance with his request, we closed the account.
compound preposition

prepositional phrase

According to our schedule, the job will be completed tomorrow.
compound preposition

prepositional phrase

The president resigned on account of illness.
compound preposition

prepositional phrase

PRONOUNS USED AS OBJECTS OF PREPOSITIONS

You have already learned that the object of a preposition is always in the **objective case.** When nouns are used as objects of prepositions, they do not present a problem because nouns do not have different forms for the objective case.

Pronouns do present a problem in case because some of the *personal pronouns* and the pronoun *who* have one form for the nominative case and another form for the objective case. When a pronoun is used as the object of a preposition, the form for the objective case must be used.

It is incorrect to use the forms *I, he, she, we, they,* or *who* as objects of prepositions. They are **nominative case** forms. The correct forms to use are *me, him, her, us, them,* and *whom.* In the following sentences, all the pronouns that are used as objects of prepositions are in the **objective case:**

The speaker spoke to **me** after the meeting. (*me*—objective case)

I went to the Art Institute with **her.** (*her*—objective case)

We looked at **him** while he was dancing. (*him*—objective case)

The women prepared a dinner for **them.** (*them*—objective case)

The librarian found the books for **us.** (*us*—objective case)

For **whom** are you working now? (*whom*—objective case)

Watch the two words, *but* and *like,* carefully when they are followed by pronouns. The word *but* is a preposition when it means *except.* When the word *but* is used as a preposition, it must be followed by the objective case. Similarly, when the word *like* is used as a preposition, it must be followed by the objective case of the pronoun. As a preposition, *like* means *similar to,* or *in a manner similar to.*

No one knew the answer **but** me. (*but*—preposition)

His son looks **like** him. (*like*—preposition)

Other uses of *like* are given on page 226.

THE CORRECT USE OF PREPOSITIONS

Many of the common prepositions are often used incorrectly. Since a preposition expresses a relationship between the object and some other word in the sentence, the preposition that you use must be selected with care. Very often the speaker or writer is not aware of the distinctions in meaning that careful writers and speakers observe in using prepositions.

The following are some of the prepositions that you should use with discrimination. As a student of language, you should be aware of the distinctions in meaning that are indicated here. Success in writing and speaking depends to a great extent upon the choice of words. For that reason, care should be exercised in choosing words that convey the exact meaning intended.

Differences in Meaning

1. **Around, about.** *Around* means encircling. *About* often means approximately. Do not use *around* when you mean approximately.

The fish weighed *around* three pounds. (incorrect)

The fish weighed *about* two pounds. (correct)

She tied a ribbon *about* her head. (incorrect)

She tied a ribbon *around* her head. (correct)

2. **Agree to, agree with.** One *agrees to* a proposal, but *agrees with* a person.

The members *agreed with* the president. (correct—*person*)

I *agree to* your plan for saving money. (correct—*proposal*)

3. **Beside, besides.** *Beside* means by the side of. *Besides* means in addition to.

Margaret sat *beside* her father. (*by the side of*)

There were three *besides* Jerry in the boat. (*in addition to*)

4. **Between, among.** *Between* is used when referring to two. *Among* is used when referring to more than two.

Frank and Harry divided the money *between* them. (*two persons*)

The money was divided *among* the five heirs. (*more than two*)

5. **Differ with, differ from.** One differs *with a person* in the matter of opinion. A person or thing *differs from* another in certain respects; that is, the person or thing is *unlike* another in certain respects.

I *differ with* you about his qualifications. (*matter of opinion*)

Maine *differs from* Florida in many ways. (*in certain respects*)

6. **Different from, different than.** *Different from* is correct. Do not use *different than*, which is incorrect.

The motion picture is *different from* the book. (correct)

The motion picture is *different than* the book. (incorrect)

7. **In, into.** The preposition *in* indicates location or motion within a place. *Into* indicates motion *toward the inside* of a place from the outside.

The tea was held *in* the garden. (*within a place*)

The swimmer jumped *into* the pool. (*from the outside*)

He swam *in* the pool. (*motion within a place*)

8. **In back of, behind.** *In back of* should never be used for *behind*.

The car is *in back of* the house. (incorrect)

The car is *behind* the house. (correct)

9. **Over, more than.** *Over* expresses the idea of *place*. *More than* expresses the idea of *quantity*.

The actress has *over* a hundred dresses. (incorrect)

The actress has *more than* a hundred dresses. (correct)

She wore a cape *over* her shoulders. (correct—*place*)

10. **Outside of, except.** Do not use *outside of* when you mean *except*.

No one went *outside of* James. (incorrect)

No one went *except* James. (correct)

11. **To, too.** The preposition *to* should not be confused with the adverb *too*.

I am going *to* the Dunes. (preposition *to*)

Will you go, *too*? (adverb, meaning *also*)

12. **Within, inside of.** Do not use *inside of* to express time. Use *within*.

He will leave *inside of* a week. (incorrect)

He will leave *within* a week. (correct)

13. **In regard to, with regard to.** Do not say *in regards to* or *with regards to*. The correct expressions are *in regard to* and *with regard to*.

In regards to your order (incorrect)

In regard to your order (correct)

14. *Unnecessary prepositions.* Do not use *off of* for *off*. The *of* should not be added. Always omit the unnecessary prepositions in sentences like the following:

He jumped *off of* the pier. (*of* is superfluous)

He jumped *off* the pier. (correct)

Where is he *at*? (incorrect)

Where is he? (correct)

Where is he going *to*? (incorrect)

Where is he going? (correct)

Is the rain over *with*? (incorrect)

Is the rain over? (correct)

POSITION OF THE PREPOSITION

Many students believe that it is incorrect to end a sentence with a preposition. Very often it is more natural and more emphatic to place the preposition at the end of the sentence. In many questions, the preposition comes naturally at the end. But a preposition should not be used at the end of a sentence if it sounds awkward or changes the meaning of the sentence. The following sentences end with a preposition. The prepositions fall naturally and correctly at the end.

Whom are you looking *for?*

What kind of plane is he traveling *in?*

They sold the car you were looking *at.*

Ordinarily, the preposition should not be placed at the end of the sentence. However, many of our best writers and speakers occasionally end sentences in this way.

SUMMARY

A **preposition** is a word that shows the relation between its object and some other word in the sentence.

A *phrase* is a group of words, *without a subject and a predicate,* that functions as a single part of speech. A **prepositional phrase** is a phrase that functions as an *adjective* or an *adverb.*

Like the adjective and the adverb, an **adjective phrase** or an **adverbial phrase** is a modifier. An adjective phrase modifies a noun or a pronoun. An adverbial phrase modifies a verb, an adjective, or another adverb.

A **compound preposition** is a preposition that consists of two or more words. A compound preposition functions as a unit or as one word.

The *object* of a preposition is always in the **objective case**. The correct form of the pronoun for the objective case should always be used as the object of a preposition. The forms *me, him, her, us, them,* and *whom* are the correct forms to use as objects of prepositions.

The word *like* is always a preposition. The word *but* is a preposition when it means *except.* When *like* and *but* are used in prepositional phrases, they should be followed by the objective case.

Ordinarily, a preposition should not be placed at the end of a sentence. Many writers and speakers occasionally place the preposition in this position. This is done for emphasis. In many questions, the preposition comes naturally at the end of the sentence.

17

THE COMPOUND SENTENCE

ON PAGE 35 is an explanation of the four types of sentences: *declarative, interrogative, imperative,* and *exclamatory.* A particular sentence falls into one of these groups according to the purpose which it serves.

When you make a statement, you use a declarative sentence, but when you ask a question, you use an interrogative sentence. If your purpose is to issue a command or make a request, you use the imperative sentence. When you want to express strong feeling or sudden emotion, you use an exclamatory sentence.

KINDS OF CLAUSES

There is still another way of classifying sentences. This classification is determined by the internal structure of the sentence or the way in which it is built up. Specifically, this classification is based upon the number and kinds of clauses which a sentence contains. According to this classification, sentences are divided into four groups; *simple, compound, complex,* and *compound-complex.*

In order to understand the difference between a simple sentence and a compound or complex sentence, you must have a very clear idea of what is meant by a clause in grammar.

A **clause** is a group of words that has a *subject* and a *predicate.* There are two kinds of clauses: *independent* or *main clauses* and *dependent* or *subordinate* clauses.

INDEPENDENT CLAUSES

An **independent clause** is a group of words that has a subject and a predicate. An independent clause does not depend upon anything else for its meaning. It expresses a complete thought. An independent clause is a simple sentence when it stands alone.

The officer blew his whistle and the cars stopped.

independent clause   independent clause

In this sentence, there are two independent clauses. The first independent clause is *The officer blew his whistle.* The second independent clause is *the cars stopped.* These clauses could be written as two simple sentences by omitting the conjunction *and.* The conjunction *and* does not belong to either of the independent clauses. It simply brings the two independent clauses together in one sentence.

The officer blew his whistle.   The cars stopped.

simple sentence   simple sentence

SUBORDINATE CLAUSES

A **subordinate clause** is a group of words that has a subject and a predicate, *but the clause cannot stand alone.* A subordinate clause does not express a complete thought. It depends upon the main clause for its meaning. The connective, or the word that introduces the subordinate clause, plays an important part in making it a dependent clause. An illustration will make this clear:

The cars stopped when the officer blew his whistle.

main clause   subordinate clause

In this sentence, the group of words, *when the officer blew his whistle,* is a subordinate clause. It cannot stand alone although it has both a subject and a predicate. The word *when,* which introduces the clause, makes the words which follow it dependent upon the main clause for the meaning. That is the reason why the clause, *when the officer blew his whistle,* is called a dependent or a subordinate clause.

The group of words, *the cars stopped,* is an independent clause. It could stand alone. It is the main clause in the sentence because it states the main idea in the sentence.

THE SIMPLE SENTENCE

A **simple sentence** is a sentence having *one* subject and *one* predicate, either or both of which may be *compound*. A simple sentence consists of one and only one independent clause. All of the following sentences are simple sentences, but some have compound subjects or predicates. The last sentence has both a compound subject and a compound predicate.

John joined the Navy.

John and Fred joined the Marines.
compound subject

Mary sang and played at the concert.
compound predicate

Mary and Jane sang and played at the concert.
compound subject   compound predicate

Note that a compound subject does not mean two subjects. It means that *one* subject is made up of two or more nouns or pronouns. A *compound predicate* does not mean two predicates. It means that *one* predicate is made up of two or more verbs or verb phrases.

THE COMPOUND SENTENCE

A **compound sentence** is a sentence that *contains two or more independent clauses.* The independent clauses of a compound sentence must be joined in some way to indicate that the independent clauses form one sentence.

When you put two independent clauses or two simple sentences together to form one longer sentence, you have a compound sentence:

John joined the Navy. (simple sentence)

Harry joined the Marines. (simple sentence)

If you join these two simple sentences in order to make a compound sentence, you have the problem of punctuation and the problem of using a conjunction. The following sentences show the ways in which two simple sentences might be joined to form one compound sentence:

John joined the Navy, **but** Harry joined the Marines. *(comma and conjunction)*

John joined the Navy; Harry joined the Marines. *(semicolon)*

John joined the Navy **but** Harry joined the Marines. *(conjunction only)*

From these illustrations you can see that the independent clauses of of a compound sentence may be connected in one of three ways:

1. By using a comma before a conjunction

2. By using a semicolon without a conjunction

3. By using a conjunction without a comma

All three methods of writing a compound sentence are correct. However, you will use the first method, a comma before a conjunction, much more frequently than the other two methods.

IDENTIFYING THE COMPOUND SENTENCE

Some students have difficulty in distinguishing between a simple sentence with a compound subject or predicate, and a compound sentence. The point to keep in mind is that the compound sentence must be the equivalent of at least *two complete simple sentences*. Examine the following illustration carefully:

The Indian squaw cooks, sews, and builds the wigwam.

This is not a compound sentence. It is a simple sentence with a compound predicate. You could not possibly make two independent clauses out of the sentence as it is written. In order to turn it into a compound sentence, you would have to supply another subject and write the sentence as two independent clauses:

The Indian squaw cooks and sews, **and** she builds the wigwam.

independent clause   independent clause

COORDINATE CONJUNCTIONS

The independent clauses of a compound sentence are often connected by a coordinate conjunction. **Coordinate** means of the *same rank* or of *equal rank*. **Coordinate conjunctions** are used *to connect words, phrases, and clauses of equal rank*. The independent clauses of a compound sentence are of the same rank; therefore, we use a coordinate conjunction to connect them. The coordinate conjunctions that are commonly used for this purpose are *for, and, but, or, nor,* and *while* when it means the same as *but.*

Use of the Comma and Coordinate Conjunction

When a coordinate conjunction is used in a compound sentence, it is usually preceded by a comma. The comma should not be omitted unless the independent clauses are very short and the thought is closely connected. Observe the use of the comma and the coordinate conjunction in each of the following compound sentences:

Arthur washed our new car, **and** Ned polished it.
independent clause   independent clause

I may consider your plan, **or** I may disregard it.
independent clause   independent clause

I did not seek the position, **nor** do I want it.
independent clause   independent clause

Michael likes tennis, **but** he prefers to play golf.
independent clause   independent clause

Their team was untrained, **while** ours was highly trained.
independent clause   independent clause

Jack went to bed early, **for** he was very tired.
independent clause   independent clause

In modern writing, the comma is often omitted before the conjunctions *and* and *or.* Careful writers, however, usually place a comma before the conjunctions *but* and *for.* If a comma is not placed before the word *for* when it is used as a coordinate conjunction, *for* might be mistaken for a preposition.

USE OF THE SEMICOLON IN THE COMPOUND SENTENCE

As explained, a comma and a coordinate conjunction are often used to separate the clauses of a compound sentence. Sometimes the ideas combined in a compound sentence are so closely related that it is not necessary to use a conjunction. In that case, a semicolon is used to separate the two clauses. The following are two important uses of the semicolon in the compound sentence:

1. A semicolon should be used between the independent clauses of a compound sentence *when they are not joined by a coordinate conjunction.* In the following sentence, there is no conjunction between the two independent clauses; therefore, a semicolon is used.

> The doctor came in late; he did not stop to read the telegram.

2. When the independent clauses of a compound sentence are very long, or have *internal punctuation,* a semicolon is generally used before the coordinate conjunction. **Internal punctuation** means that there are commas within one or both of the independent clauses.

> Shakespeare, a great dramatist, wrote a great many plays; and he also wrote a number of sonnets.

> Temperamental and lazy, John managed to get along without working; but he was never contented or happy.

Both of these sentences have one or more commas in the first independent clause; that is, the first clause has *internal punctuation.* A semicolon is used between the two independent clauses even though a coordinate conjunction is used.

THE "COMMA FAULT"

You have just learned that two independent clauses may be joined by a semicolon when no conjunction is used. You have also learned that two independent clauses are often joined by a coordinate conjunction and a comma. The point to keep in mind is that two independent clauses should not be joined by a comma unless a coordinate conjunction is used. When a writer uses a comma between the independent clauses of a compound sentence, he makes an error known as the "comma fault." The following sentence illustrates the "comma fault."

The author wrote many stories for children, she also wrote a number of historical novels. *(comma fault)*

In this sentence, two independent clauses are joined by means of a comma. This is known as the *"comma fault"* because the comma is the sole connection between two independent clauses. This error may be eliminated by punctuating the sentence in any one of the three ways that have been given in this unit:

1. Use a coordinate conjunction after the comma:

   The author wrote many stories for children, and she also wrote a number of historical novels. *(correct)*

2. Use a semicolon between the two independent clauses:

   The author wrote many stories for children; she also wrote a number of historical novels. *(correct)*

3. Punctuate the two independent clauses as two simple sentences:

   The author wrote many stories for children. She also wrote a number of historical novels. *(correct)*

A skillful writer sometimes puts commas between the independent clauses of a compound sentence. This is done deliberately for the purpose of producing a certain effect. The clauses are usually very short and similar in length and structure. The following sentence is a famous example:

"I came, I saw, I conquered."

THE RUN-ON SENTENCE

The **run-on sentence error** is very similar to the *"comma fault."* The only difference is that the run-on sentence consists of two or more independent statements that are run together without any mark of punctuation, or without any connecting word. The following sentence is an illustration of the run-on sentence:

> Money provided by stockholders has helped the company purchase equipment and supplies it has also enabled the company to expand its production.

In this sentence, two independent statements have been run together without any punctuation or without any connecting word or words. The sentence might be correctly written by following any of the suggestions given for removing the *"comma fault."*

Since the run-on sentence error is commonly made, you should check your writing carefully. Be sure that you do not run sentences together without punctuation or proper connectives.

TRANSITIONAL WORDS

There is another type of connecting word that you may use between the independent clauses of a compound sentence. The words that belong in this group are not coordinate conjunctions. They are sometimes called **transitional words** because they are not pure conjunctions.

Some of these words have a slight connecting force. Others have some adverbial force. But they all belong to the independent clause which they introduce or in which they are found. Connectives that belong to this group *are always preceded by a semicolon.*

Since many of these words are regarded as independent elements, they are usually set off by commas. Words like *moreover, however, therefore,* and *nevertheless* are usually set off. Words like *then, still, yet,* and *so* are seldom set off by commas when they retain their adverbial force.

Sometimes the connection is made by a group of words. Expressions like the following are transitional words and are regarded as a single connecting word: *in fact, on the other hand, that is,* etc. Study the following illustrations carefully:

The road was unpaved; **nevertheless,** we drove on in the rain.

I missed the first boat; **however,** I arrived on time.

The president introduced the speaker; **then** he sat down.

Ethel was sick; **in fact,** she had one of her usual colds.

We arrived early; **as a result,** we had time to visit with our friends.

We cannot get materials; **consequently,** we cannot finish the job.

I became tired of doing his work; **moreover,** I had my own work to do.

I did not dislike the play; **on the contrary,** I enjoyed it immensely.

Commonly Used Transitional Words

accordingly	indeed	as a result
afterwards	likewise	at last
again	meanwhile	at the same time
anyhow	moreover	for example
besides	namely	for instance
consequently	nevertheless	for this reason
doubtless	next	in any case
eventually	otherwise	in fact
evidently	perhaps	in like manner
finally	possibly	in short
furthermore	still	on the contrary
hence	then	on the other hand
however	therefore	that is
yet	thus	in addition

SUMMARY

According to the way in which they are constructed, sentences are classified into four groups: *simple, compound, complex,* and *compound-complex.* The structure of a particular sentence is determined by the number and kinds of clauses which it contains.

1. A **clause** is a group of words that has a *subject* and a *predicate.* There are two kinds of clauses—*independent* clauses and *dependent* or *subordinate* clauses.

2. An **independent clause** is a group of words that has a subject and a predicate. It expresses a complete thought. An independent clause is the equivalent of a simple sentence.

3. A dependent or **subordinate clause** is a group of words that has a subject and a predicate, but does not express a complete thought. It depends upon the main clause for its meaning.

4. A **simple sentence** is a sentence that has one subject and one predicate, either or both of which may be compound.

5. A **compound sentence** is a sentence that contains two or more independent clauses. The independent clauses of a compound sentence must be connected in some way. They are often connected by a comma used with a coordinate conjunction.

6. A **coordinate conjunction** is a conjunction that connects words, phrases, and clauses of *equal rank.*

7. The two independent clauses of a compound sentence are often connected by transitional words. **Transitional words** are words that are used to show the relation between two independent clauses. Many of these transitional words have some adverbial force; that is, they modify the verb in the independent clause of which they are a part. Transitional words are always preceded by a semicolon. They are usually followed by a comma.

8. A **run-on sentence** is a sentence in which two independent clauses are written as a single sentence without a coordinate conjunction or any mark of punctuation between them.

9. The **"comma fault"** is the use of a comma as the sole connection between two independent statements. If the comma is used for this purpose, a coordinate conjunction should also be used.

THE COMPLEX SENTENCE-ADJECTIVE CLAUSES

THE COMPOUND sentence explained in the previous chapter is an important type of sentence because it enables us to combine two or more related ideas. However, it is just as ineffective to use a number of compound sentences strung along with *ands* and *buts* as it is to use a number of short, choppy, simple sentences. Less important ideas should be put in subordinate positions within a sentence. A sentence containing subordinate ideas is called a *complex sentence.*

A **complex sentence** is a sentence that consists of *one independent clause* and *one or more subordinate clauses. Subordinate* means lower in rank, power, or importance. A subordinate clause is less important than an independent clause because it depends upon the independent clause for its meaning. The independent clause is also called the *main* or the *principal* clause. As previously explained, an independent clause is a group of words that has a subject and a predicate, and does not depend upon anything else for its meaning. It expresses a complete thought, and can stand alone.

A **subordinate clause** is a group of words that has a subject and a predicate, but *cannot stand alone.* A subordinate clause does not express a complete thought. It should never be punctuated as if it were a complete sentence.

A subordinate clause is usually introduced by some type of *subordinate conjunction* or by a *relative pronoun.* These connecting words make it clear that the clause expresses an idea that is subordinate to the main clause. They also join the subordinate clause to some word in the independent clause.

Complex Sentences

I shall be at the station when you arrive.
  independent clause   *subordinate clause*

I shall not go to the park if it rains.
  independent clause   *subordinate clause*

She wore a beautiful dress which her grandmother had worn.
  independent clause   *subordinate clause*

In the first sentence, the subordinate clause is *when you arrive.* The clause is introduced by the **subordinate conjunction** *when.* The group of words, *when you arrive,* has a subject and a predicate, but it cannot stand alone. That is the reason why the clause is called a *subordinate clause.* It depends upon the main clause for its meaning.

The subordinate clause in the second sentence is *if it rains.* This group of words cannot stand alone. The clause is introduced by the subordinate conjunction *if.* This conjunction helps the subordinate clause express the idea that there is a condition upon which *my going* depends.

The subordinate clause in the third sentence is *which her grandmother had worn.* This clause is introduced by the relative pronoun *which.* The word *which* refers to the word *dress* in the independent clause. It also introduces the subordinate clause. A **relative pronoun** always joins a clause to the *antecedent* of the pronoun. In this sentence, the antecedent of the relative pronoun is *dress. Dress* is the word to which the pronoun refers.

The relative pronoun also has an important function in the subordinate clause. It might be the subject of the clause, the object of the verb in the clause, the object of a preposition, or a predicate pronoun after a linking verb.

KINDS OF SUBORDINATE CLAUSES

There are three kinds of subordinate clauses: *adverbial clauses, adjective clauses,* and *noun clauses.* Each of these different types is used as a part of speech. That is why subordinate clauses are called adverbial clauses, adjective clauses, and noun clauses.

The **adverbial clause** functions as an adverb. The **adjective clause** functions as an adjective, and the **noun clause** functions as a noun.

Adverbs modify verbs, adjectives, and other adverbs. Adverbial clauses also modify verbs, adjectives, and adverbs. Adjectives modify nouns and pronouns. Adjective clauses also modify nouns and pronouns. Nouns are used as subjects of sentences, as objects of verbs, and as objects of prepositions. Noun clauses are used in the same ways.

Subordinate Clauses

The man <u>who received the medal</u> was my uncle.
<small>adjective clause</small>

We always stop working <u>when the bell rings.</u>
<small>adverbial clause</small>

I believe <u>that the bookkeeper is honest.</u>
<small>noun clause</small>

In the first sentence, the subordinate clause is the group of words, *who received the medal*. The subordinate clause is an **adjective clause** and modifies the word *man*. In the second sentence, the subordinate clause is *when the bell rings*. It is an **adverbial clause** and modifies the verb *stop*. This clause expresses *time* just as an adverb expresses *time*. The subordinate clause in the third sentence is the group of words, *that the bookkeeper is honest*. This subordinate clause is a **noun clause** and is used as the object of the verb *believe*.

ADJECTIVE CLAUSES

An **adjective clause** *is a subordinate clause that functions as an adjective.* Adjectives are used to describe or limit nouns or pronouns. An adjective clause is also used to describe or limit a noun or a pronoun.

An adjective clause is usually introduced by a relative pronoun. A **relative pronoun** *is a pronoun that joins an adjective clause to some word in the independent or main clause.* The word to which it joins the clause is the *antecedent* of the relative pronoun. The relative pronouns used in this way are *who* (*whom*), *which*, and *that*.

Adjective Clauses Introduced by Relative Pronouns

John brought the books <u>that you ordered.</u> (*that* — relative
<small>adjective clause</small>
pronoun)

I favored the plan <u>which the senator proposed.</u> (*which*—relative
<small>adjective clause</small>
pronoun)

Men <u>who are thinkers</u> look for facts. (*who*—relative pronoun)
<small>adjective clause</small>

I saw the salesman <u>whom I met at the office.</u> (*whom*—relative
<small>adjective clause</small>
pronoun)

The subordinate clause in the first sentence is *that you ordered.* It is an adjective clause and modifies the noun *books.* This clause is introduced by the relative pronoun *that.* The antecedent of the relative pronoun *that* is the word *books.* The pronoun *that* joins its clause to the word *books* in the main clause.

The subordinate clause in the second sentence is *which the senator proposed.* It is an adjective clause and modifies the noun *plan.* The antecedent of the relative pronoun *which* is the word *plan.* The adjective clause limits the meaning to the *plan which the senator proposed.*

The subordinate clause in the third sentence is *who are thinkers.* The main clause is *Men look for facts.* In this sentence the subordinate clause comes between the subject and the predicate of the main clause. The subordinate clause is introduced by the relative pronoun *who.* The antecedent of *who* is *men.*

The adjective clause in the fourth sentence is *whom I met at the office.* This clause is introduced by the relative pronoun *whom.* The antecedent of the pronoun is the word *salesman. Whom* is in the objective case because it is the object of the verb *met* in the subordinate clause.

Relative Adjectives

Sometimes an adjective clause is introduced by the word *whose,* which is the possessive form of the pronoun *who.* In such cases the word *whose* modifies a noun which follows it. When the word *whose* is used in an adjective clause, it is called a **relative adjective.** The word *relative* is used to show that the word *whose* refers to its antecedent in the main clause.

That is the *man* **whose** car was stolen. (*man—*antecedent)

In this sentence the word *whose* is a relative adjective, modifying the word *car.* The antecedent of *whose* is the word *man* in the main clause. The word *whose* connects the clause *whose car was stolen* to the word *man.*

ADJECTIVE CLAUSES INTRODUCED BY RELATIVE ADVERBS

Adjective clauses are often introduced by the relative adverbs *where, when,* and *why.* When these adverbs introduce adjective clauses they relate to some word in the main clause in much the same way as a relative pronoun does. A relative adverb always has an antecedent and joins its clause to that antecedent. In addition, a relative adverb performs the function of an adverb in its own clause. It is called a *relative adverb* because it relates to an antecedent.

I found the house where the poet lived. (*where*—relative adverb)
                             adjective clause

The doctor selected a time when I was not working. (*when*—
relative adverb)   *adjective clause*

I discovered the reason why he is leaving. (*why*—relative adverb)
                             adjective clause

In the first sentence, the relative adverb is *where*. It introduces the clause, *where the poet lived*. It also refers to its antecedent, *house*. As an adverb, it modifies the verb *lived* in the subordinate clause.

The relative adverb in the second sentence is *when*. Its antecedent is *time*. The relative adverb *when* joins the clause, *when I was not working,* to its antecedent *time*. It also functions as an adverb, modifying the verb *was working.*

The relative adverb in the third sentence is *why*. Its antecedent is *reason*. It modifies the verb *is leaving* in its own clause.

The only difference between a relative adverb and a simple adverb is the fact that the relative adverb is found in an adjective clause and refers to its antecedent in the main clause. Both relative adverbs and simple adverbs modify verbs.

"WHO" AND "WHOM" IN SUBORDINATE CLAUSES

It is often difficult to determine whether to use "who" or "whom" when one of these words is used to introduce a subordinate clause. Always keep in mind that *who* is the correct form for the nominative case, and *whom* is the correct form for the objective case.

When a relative pronoun introduces a clause, it has a double function. It joins the clause to its antecedent which is in the main clause, and in addition it performs one of the following three functions in the subordinate clause:

1. The pronoun may be the *subject* of the subordinate clause.

2. The pronoun may be used as a *predicate pronoun* after a linking verb.

3. The pronoun may be used as the *object* of the verb or a preposition.

In order to determine how the pronoun is used, it is often necessary to put the subordinate clause in grammatical order, or to transpose it.

Allen was the one *who published the report.* (*who*—subject)

In this sentence, it is clear that *who* is the subject of the subordinate clause. The form *who* is correct because the subject is in the nominative case.

The president is a man *whom everyone admires.* (*whom*—direct object)

In this sentence, the word *whom* is the direct object of the verb *admires.* By transposing the clause, you will be able to see this clearly: *everyone admires whom.* The subject of the clause is *everyone,* not *whom.*

Jack is the boy *to whom they gave the camera.* (*whom*—object of preposition)

In this sentence, the pronoun *whom* is the object of the preposition *to.* When the subordinate clause is transposed, the use of *whom* becomes clear: *they gave the camera to whom.* *They* is the subject of the clause, not *whom.*

RESTRICTIVE AND NONRESTRICTIVE CLAUSES

Adjective clauses present a problem in meaning and in punctuation. Sometimes the adjective clause is set off by commas. Sometimes the adjective clause is not set off by commas. The following sentences are illustrations of adjective clauses that are *not* set off by commas:

I spoke to the woman *who was giving the demonstration.*

This is the man *who discovered the leak in the pipe.*

I dislike driving in a town *where there are no stop signals.*

In the first sentence, the adjective clause is *who was giving the demonstration.* If you leave the clause out, the meaning of the sentence is changed. The sentence now gives no indication of *who* the woman was. Since the clause identifies that woman, it is essential to the meaning of the sentence.

In the second sentence, the clause is *who discovered the leak in the pipe.* This clause identifies the man and is essential to the meaning of the sentence. The clause restricts the meaning of the sentence to the man *who discovered the leak in the pipe.* Therefore, it is essential to the meaning of the sentence.

The third sentence does not mean that *I dislike driving in a town.* The meaning is restricted to driving in a certain type of town; that is, in a town *where there are no stop signals.*

Clauses that are necessary to the meaning of the sentence are called *restrictive clauses.* A restrictive clause is not set off by commas. A **restrictive clause** identifies the word it modifies.

Some adjective clauses are not essential to the meaning of the sentence. They give added information, but the essential meaning of the sentence would not be changed if such clauses were omitted. Study the following sentences carefully:

Mr. Miller, *who lived next door,* moved to Canada.

Will James, *who was once a cowboy,* wrote many stories.

Father, *who was working in the garden,* missed the broadcast.

The speaker, *who was accompanied by his wife,* left early.

In the first sentence, the clause, *who lived next door,* gives additional information about Mr. Miller, but the meaning of the sentence is not changed if you leave the clause out. The clause does not place any restrictions on the meaning. Therefore it is called a *nonrestrictive clause.* Nonrestrictive clauses are set off by commas.

A **nonrestrictive clause** is a clause that is not essential to the meaning of the sentence. All the clauses in the preceding illustrations are nonrestrictive clauses. They are set off by commas. They are not needed in the sentence to identify the person who is mentioned in the main clause.

A nonrestrictive clause is a subordinate clause which is not essential to the meaning of the sentence. A nonrestrictive clause functions more like an appositive or a parenthetical expression. You might call it a thrown-in remark. That is the reason why the nonrestrictive clause is set off by commas.

SUMMARY

A **complex sentence** is a sentence that consists of one independent clause and one or more subordinate clauses.

A **subordinate clause** is a group of words that has a subject and a predicate, but cannot stand alone. A subordinate clause depends upon the main clause for its meaning.

There are three kinds of subordinate clauses: *adjective clauses, adverbial clauses,* and *noun clauses.*

An **adjective clause** is a subordinate clause that functions as an adjective. An adjective clause may be introduced by a *relative pronoun,* a *relative adverb,* or a *relative adjective.*

A **relative adverb** is an adverb that refers to an antecedent in the main clause and functions as an adverb in the subordinate clause. *When, where,* and *why* are commonly used as relative adverbs.

A **relative pronoun** is a pronoun that joins the subordinate clause to its own antecedent in the main clause. A relative pronoun also has an important function in the subordinate clause. *Who, whom, which,* and *that* are relative pronouns.

A **relative adjective** is a relative pronoun that is used as an adjective. It refers to its antecedent in the main clause and modifies a noun in the subordinate clause. *Whose* is commonly used in this way.

A **restrictive adjective clause** is a clause that is essential to the meaning of the sentence. A restrictive clause explains or identifies the word in the main clause to which it refers. A restrictive clause is *not* set off by commas. A **nonrestrictive adjective clause** is *not* essential to the meaning of the sentence. A nonrestrictive clause *is* set off by commas.

19

ADVERBIAL CLAUSES

A N ADVERBIAL CLAUSE functions in the same way as an adverb functions. Adverbs tell *how, when, where,* and *to what extent* the action is performed. Adverbial clauses answer the same questions and, in addition, express several other ideas which the simple adverb does not express.

Adverbs modify verbs, adjectives, and other adverbs. Adverbial clauses also modify verbs, adjectives, and adverbs. The adverbial clause modifies a verb more often than it modifies an adjective or an adverb.

SUBORDINATE CONJUNCTIONS

An adverbial clause is usually introduced by a *subordinate conjunction.* This connecting word is called a subordinate conjunction because it makes the idea expressed by its clause *subordinate to the main idea in the sentence.* The subordinate conjunction also shows the relation between the subordinate clause and the word in the main clause which the subordinate clause modifies.

The **subordinate conjunction** is used to show that the clause which it introduces is a subordinate clause, and not a main clause. The subordinate conjunction also indicates the exact type of relationship that the subordinate clause has to the main clause.

The following illustrations will make clear the function of the *subordinate conjunction* in a subordinate clause:

We listened to the radio because we wanted to hear the news.
    verb   adverbial clause—modifies listened

She will find the telegram on her desk when she returns.
  verb phrase   adverbial clause—modifies will find

In the first sentence, the subordinate clause is *because we wanted to hear the news*. It is an adverbial clause and modifies the verb *listened* in the main clause. The subordinate conjunction is the word *because*.

If you leave out the word *because,* the words that follow no longer express a subordinate idea. They express a complete thought. It is the word *because* that makes the group of words, *we wanted to hear the news*, subordinate to the main clause. The **subordinate conjunction** is the key to the adverbial clause.

You should become familiar with the subordinate conjunctions that are commonly used to introduce *adverbial clauses*. The subordinate conjunction will help you identify the adverbial clause. It will also help you determine the **kind** of adverbial clause which it introduces.

WORDS USED AS SUBORDINATE CONJUNCTIONS

after	because	provided that	unless
although	before	since	until
as	even if	so—as	when
as—as	even though	so that	whenever
as if	except	than	where
as long as	if	that	wherever
as soon as	in order that	till	whether
as though	provided	though	while

KINDS OF ADVERBIAL CLAUSES

Adverbial clauses are used to express a number of different ideas. The following are the ten important ideas which are expressed by adverbial clauses: *time, place, manner, degree, comparison, purpose, result, condition, concession, cause (reason).*

Since the subordinate conjunction helps the adverbial clause express the idea intended, you should become familiar with the conjunctions that are used to express certain ideas, such as *time, place,* etc. The following is a list of the subordinate conjunctions commonly used in adverbial clauses of the various types:

Time: after, before, when, whenever, since, until, as soon as, while

Place: where, wherever

Manner: as, as if, as though

Degree: that, as—as, not so—as, than

Comparison: as, than, so—as, as—as

Purpose: that, so that, in order that

Result: that, so that

Condition: if, provided, provided that, unless

Concession: although, though, even if

Cause: as, because, since

Ideas Expressed by Adverbial Clauses

Time: I watched the crowd while I was waiting for you.

Place: Put the notice where it can be seen.

Manner: The soldier walks as if he were lame.

Degree: Marvin is not so industrious <u>as his brother</u> (is industrious).

Comparison: The train was later <u>than it usually is.</u>

Purpose: Ted practiced every day <u>so that he might win the contest.</u>

Result: The salesman was so persuasive <u>that I finally bought the car.</u>

Condition: I shall attend the meeting <u>if I have the time.</u>

Concession: Frances will sing at the concert <u>although she has a cold.</u>

Cause or Reason: Gerald read the book <u>because I recommended it.</u>

CLAUSES OF DEGREE

An *adverbial clause of degree* that is introduced by the subordinate conjunction *that* usually expresses a **result** idea as well as the idea of **degree.** The degree idea is expressed by words like *such, such a,* and *so* which precede the subordinate clause.

Jane practiced <u>so</u> long <u>that she became very tired.</u>

Harold made <u>such</u> a poor sales record <u>that he lost his position.</u>

In both these sentences, the adverbial clauses introduced by *that* express a *degree idea* and a *result idea.*

An adverbial clause of degree usually modifies an adjective or an adverb in the main clause.

He talked <u>so</u> loud <u>that he annoyed the speaker.</u>

In this sentence, the adverbial clause *that he annoyed the speaker* is introduced by the subordinate conjunction *that.* The adverbial clause modifies the adverb *so* in the main clause.

THE POSITION OF THE ADVERBIAL CLAUSE

In all of the preceding illustrations, the adverbial clause follows the main clause. An adverbial clause is often placed at the beginning of the sentence for emphasis, or for variety in sentence patterns. When the subordinate clause precedes the main clause, it is usually set off by a comma.

He went to the office <u>when it was convenient</u>. (follows main clause)
adverbial clause

<u>When it was convenient</u>, he went to the office. (precedes main clause) adverbial clause

The men work overtime <u>whenever it is necessary</u>. (follows main clause) adverbial clause

<u>Whenever it is necessary</u>, the men work overtime. (precedes main clause) adverbial clause

In the first sentence, the adverbial clause *follows* the main clause. In the second sentence, the same adverbial clause *precedes* the main clause. The adverbial clause is placed at the beginning of the sentence for emphasis. Since the adverbial clause is in inverted or transposed order, it is set off by a comma.

The adverbial clause in the third sentence *follows* the main clause. In the fourth sentence, this same clause is placed at the beginning of the sentence for emphasis. The adverbial clause is set off by a comma because it is in transposed order.

Sometimes it is necessary to change the position of a noun and a pronoun when the adverbial clause is placed at the beginning of a sentence:

I shall visit **Margaret** in Texas if she sends me her address.

If Margaret sends me her address, I shall visit **her** in Texas.

CLAUSES OF COMPARISON

In both speaking and writing, words are often omitted that are necessary to the grammatical completeness of the sentence. Certain words are sometimes omitted because the meaning of the sentence is perfectly clear without them. Sometimes they are omitted in order to avoid using a sentence that is awkward or monotonous.

Certain words are usually omitted in an *adverbial clause of comparison* for the reasons just given. The verb is often omitted because it can be readily supplied. It is important to realize that the verb has been omitted in order to decide upon the correct form of the pronoun that should be used as the subject of the verb. We often hear sentences like the following, which are incorrect:

I am younger than **him.** (incorrect)

John can run as fast as **us.** (incorrect)

In both sentences the *incorrect form* of the pronoun is used in the adverbial clause of comparison. If the speaker had finished the clause, he would have used the correct form of the pronoun. When the clause is finished, it becomes evident that the pronoun is the *subject* of the clause. A pronoun used as the subject should be in the *nominative case.*

I am younger than **he** (is young). (*he*—subject)

John can run as fast as **we** (can run). (*we*—subject)

In the unfinished clause of comparison the word *than* is a conjunction, and not a preposition. The word *than* introduces a clause which must be finished grammatically. When we supply the words that are necessary to complete the clause, we realize that the form of the pronoun should be *he* and not *him. He* is the correct form to use for the subject. The subject requires the *nominative case.*

Study the following illustrations carefully. Pay special attention to the form of the pronoun used in the *adverbial clause of comparison.*

The filling in of the words that have been omitted shows what the proper form of the pronoun should be:

You have lived longer than *I* (have lived). (not *me*)

Martha sews as well as *she* (sews). (not *her*)

Some of the men worked harder than *we* (worked). (not *us*)

I speak as correctly as *he* (does). (not *him*)

"As—As" and "Not So—As" in Comparisons

The connectives *as—as* and *not so—as* are often used in sentences that contain adverbial clauses of comparison. Careful writers and speakers make a distinction in the use of these combinations. They use *as—as* when the comparison is **positive,** and *not so—as* when the comparison is **negative.**

The comparison is said to be positive when the two things compared are approximately the same or equal. The comparison is said to be negative when there is an inequality between the two things compared. An illustration will help make this clear.

John is **as** tall **as** his brother. (positive comparison)

John is **not so** tall **as** his father. (negative comparison)

In the first sentence, the comparison is *positive.* The two persons compared are approximately *equal* in height. The combination *as—as* is used to indicate this type of comparison. In the second sentence, the combination *not so—as* is used to show an *inequality* in height, or a *negative* comparison.

In speaking and in informal writing *as—as* is commonly used to show both types of comparison—positive and negative. However, in formal writing it is advisable to observe the distinctions that discriminating writers make.

Use of "Like" in Clauses

The word *like* is commonly used as a preposition. When the word *like* is used as a preposition, it should be followed by an object. If the object is a pronoun, the pronoun should be in the *objective case.* This usage was explained on page 193.

Many careful speakers and writers feel that *like* should not be used as a conjunction to introduce a subordinate clause of manner or comparison. The words *as, as if,* and *as though* should be used to introduce this type of clause.

> I shall write the letter *like* you advised me. (colloquial)
>
> I shall write the letter *as* you advised me. (preferred)

> You look *like* you were tired. (colloquial)
>
> You look *as if* you were tired. (preferred)

> It looks *like* it might snow. (colloquial)
>
> It looks *as if* it might snow. (preferred)

In the last few years, the colloquial use of *like* as a conjunction has increased. This use sometimes appears in print. We often hear the word *like* used as a conjunction in popular television programs. However, in general, it has not been accepted as standard English for written use.

When *like* is used as a preposition, it means *similar to,* or *in a similar manner to.*

> Mary's hat is *like* the one I bought in Paris. (*like*—preposition)

> John is *like* his father in temperament. (*like*—preposition)

An *adverbial clause* is a **subordinate clause** that functions as an adverb. An adverbial clause may modify a verb, an adjective, or an adverb.

An *adverbial clause* is usually introduced by a **subordinate conjunction**. A *subordinate conjunction* is a conjunction that is used to connect a subordinate clause to the main clause.

An adverbial clause may express any one of the following ideas: *time, place, manner, degree, comparison, purpose, result, condition, concession, cause (reason).*

An adverbial clause may follow the main clause or precede it. If the adverbial clause precedes the main clause, it is usually set off by a comma.

An **adverbial clause of degree** introduced by the word *that* usually expresses the idea of *result* as well as the idea of *degree.* A clause of degree modifies an adjective or an adverb in the main clause.

Adverbial clauses of comparison are often grammatically incomplete. It is necessary to supply the missing words in order to determine the case of the pronoun that is used as the subject of the clause of comparison.

The combination *as—as* is used to express a **positive comparison**. The combination *not so—as* is used to express a **negative comparison**.

The word *like* is frequently used as a preposition. Its use should be avoided as a conjunction to introduce an adverbial clause of manner. Use *as, as if,* or *as though* to introduce that type of clause.

20

NOUN CLAUSES

ADJECTIVE CLAUSES and adverbial clauses are used as modifiers in the same way that adjectives and adverbs are used as modifiers. Noun clauses are not used as modifiers. They perform the same functions that a noun performs.

FUNCTION OF THE NOUN CLAUSE

Noun Clause — Subject of a Sentence

A noun is commonly used as the *subject* of a sentence. A *noun clause* may also be used as the **subject** of a sentence. The following illustrations show how the noun clause is used as the subject of a sentence:

What the chairman proposed was not practical.
<u>noun clause—subject</u>

How you manage on your income is a puzzle to me.
<u>noun clause—subject</u>

That their house is for sale is a well-known fact.
<u>noun clause—subject</u>

Where we could find an apartment was our problem.
<u>noun clause—subject</u>

The subject of a sentence usually tells what we are talking about. The noun clause in the first sentence tells *what* was not practical; namely, *What the chairman proposed.* In the second sentence, the subject, or the noun clause, tells *what* it is that is a puzzle to me; namely, *How you manage on your income.* In the third sentence, the noun clause tells *what* is a well-known fact; namely, *That their house is for sale.* The noun clause in the last sentence tells *what our problem was.*

If you examine the preceding illustrations, you will see that the following words introduce the noun clauses: *what, how, that,* and

228

where. These same words are often used to introduce adjective or adverbial clauses. The only way to be sure that you are dealing with a *noun clause* is to determine how the clause is used in the sentence. If it functions in the way that a noun functions, it is a noun clause.

Noun Clause — Direct Object of a Verb

A *noun clause* is frequently used as the **direct object** of a verb. A noun used as an object completes the meaning of the verb and answers the question *What?* A noun clause used as the direct object of a verb completes the verb and in almost all cases answers the question *What?* Study the following illustrations. They show how noun clauses are used as objects of verbs:

I hope (*what?*) that you will be promoted. (object of *hope*)

We knew (*what?*) where we could park the car. (object of *knew*)

Tell the manager (*what?*) why you are leaving. (object of *tell*)

I believe (*what?*) that it is going to rain. (object of *believe*)

He understood (*what?*) what we were trying to do. (object of *understood*)

The noun clause in the first sentence tells *what I hope.* It is used as the object of the verb *hope.* The noun clause in the second sentence tells *what we knew.* It is the object of the verb *knew.* The noun clause in the third sentence tells *what you should tell the manager.* It is the object of the verb *tell.* The noun clause in the fourth sentence tells *what I believe.* The noun clause in the last sentence tells *what he understood.*

Noun Clause—Predicate Noun

A *noun clause* may be used as a **predicate noun** after one of the linking verbs. Like the predicate noun, a noun clause used after a linking verb means the same as the subject. It is also used to complete the verb. The noun clauses in the following sentences are used as *predicate nouns* after linking verbs:

The rumor was <u>that he had left the city</u>. (means the same as *rumor*)

That is <u>what we agreed to do</u>. (means the same as *that*)

My first impression was <u>that I had seen him before</u>. (means the same as *impression*)

The report was <u>that he was drowned</u>. (means the same as *report*)

The noun clause in the first sentence is *that he had left the city*. It completes the verb *was* and means the same as the subject *rumor*. The noun clause in the second sentence is *what we agreed to do*. It completes the linking verb *is* and means the same as the subject *that*. The noun clause in the third sentence is *that I had seen him before*. It completes the linking verb *was* and means the same as the subject *impression*. The noun clause in the last sentence means the same as *report* and completes the linking verb *was*.

Noun Clause—Object of a Preposition

Like the noun, a *noun clause* is sometimes used as the **object of a preposition.** You may often find it difficult to determine whether the noun clause is the object of the preposition or whether some word in the clause is the object of the preposition. If you study the following illustrations carefully, you will see why an entire *clause* is the object of the preposition.

Give the message to <u>whoever is in the office</u>. (noun clause—object of the preposition *to*)

We did not agree about <u>what the doctor ordered</u>. (noun clause —object of the preposition *about*)

Do the job in <u>whatever way you wish</u>. (noun clause—object of *in*)

In the first sentence, the noun clause *whoever is in the office* is the object of the preposition *to*. *Whoever* could not be the object of the preposition because it is the subject of the clause. In addition, the sentence does not mean that you should give the message to *whoever*. It means that you should give the message to *whoever is in the office*. The entire clause is the object of the preposition *to*.

In the second sentence, the noun clause *what the doctor ordered* is the object of the preposition *about*. The sentence does not mean that we did not agree about *what*. It means that we did not agree about *what the doctor ordered*. The word *what* could not be the object of the preposition because it has another function to perform in the clause. It is the object of the verb *ordered*.

The noun clause in the third sentence must be the object of the preposition. The word *way* could not be the object of the preposition because that is not the meaning intended. The sentence does not mean that you should do the job in *whatever way,* but it means that you should do the job in *whatever way you wish*. The entire clause is the object of the preposition *in*.

OMISSION OF THE CONNECTING WORD

Sometimes the word that introduces a subordinate clause is omitted. The reason for this omission is to bring the main idea and the subordinate idea closer together. Although the best writers and speakers often omit the connecting word, you should supply it whenever there is any doubt about the construction of the clause.

I believe <u>that</u> you will be promoted. (*that*—subordinate conjunction)

I believe you will be promoted. (subordinate conjunction omitted)

NOUN CLAUSE USED AS AN APPOSITIVE

A noun is often used *in apposition* with another noun. The word **apposition** comes from two Latin words which mean *"placed by"* or *"put near to."* A word in *apposition* is placed near another word to explain it or to identify it in some way. We often speak of a person and then add something to explain who the person is, or to identify him in some way.

Mike, our *janitor,* is very accommodating.

We called on Dr. Allen, a famous *scientist.*

Paris, a *city* in France, is famous as a fashion center.

In the first sentence, the noun *janitor* is in apposition with the noun *Mike.* It explains who Mike was. In the second sentence, *scientist* is in apposition with *Dr. Allen.* It identifies him as a scientist. In the third sentence, *city* is in apposition with *Paris.*

In all three sentences the nouns that are in apposition with other nouns are set off by commas. Sometimes the appositive is so closely connected with the noun that no commas are required. It is not good practice to set off the appositive by commas in sentences like the following:

My brother Andrew is in London.

The poet Whittier wrote "Snowbound."

Like the noun, a *noun clause* is often used in **apposition** with a word or a group of words. When the noun clause is used in apposition, it usually explains such words as *idea, fact, belief, report, rumor,* etc. Noun clauses used in apposition are not set off by commas.

The rumor <u>that John would be elected</u> spread rapidly.
apposition with rumor

The fact <u>that the contract was signed</u> was important.
apposition with fact

The announcement that the strike was over was received with

cheers.
> apposition with announcement

We entertained the hope that the crew had survived.
> apposition with hope

NOUN CLAUSE AND THE INTRODUCTORY "IT"

Sometimes a sentence begins with the introductory word *it*. In sentences of this type the word *it* is not the real subject of the sentence. The grammatical or real subject appears later. The real subject is often a *noun clause*. Sentences are arranged in this way either for emphasis or for smoothness.

It is obvious that you do not have the money.
> noun clause—subject

(It) That you do not have the money is obvious. (*transposed order*)

This sentence begins with the introductory word *it*. The real or grammatical subject appears later in the sentence. The subject is the noun clause, *that you do not have the money*. When the sentence was transposed, the word *it*, which has no grammatical connection with any part of the sentence, was dropped, and the real subject was put in its proper place.

The word *it* has only one purpose in sentences of this type. It fills in the place normally occupied by the subject. Its function is similar to that of the introductory word *there*, which was explained in Grammar Unit Four. When the word *it* is used in this way, it is called an **expletive**.

Sentences that begin with *it* as an expletive, or "filling in" word, are easily recognized because they always follow the same pattern:

It is important that you see him at once.
> expletive   noun clause—subject

(It) That you see him at once is important. (*transposed order*)
> expletive   noun clause—subject

WORDS THAT INTRODUCE NOUN CLAUSES

A *noun clause* may be introduced by a **subordinate conjunction**. The subordinate conjunctions commonly used in this way are *that*, *whether*, and *whether - or*. The sole duty of the subordinate conjunction is to connect the noun clause to the main clause.

I wonder <u>whether</u> they will recognize me.
<small>subordinate conjunction</small>

John knows <u>that</u> he will be nominated for an office.
<small>subordinate conjunction</small>

Whether (not *if*) should be used to introduce noun clauses used as the direct object of the verbs *say, learn, understand, know, doubt, ask, tell, discover, wonder,* etc.

Ask John **if** he has washed the car. (incorrect)

Ask John **whether** he has washed the car. (correct)

I did not know **if** he would leave or stay. (incorrect)

I did not know **whether** he would leave or stay. (correct)

A noun clause is often introduced by a **relative pronoun:** *who, what, whatever, whoever, whomever, whichever. Whoever* and *whomever* are seldom used in informal writing and speaking.

The agent does not know <u>what</u> he should do about repairs.
<small>relative pronoun</small>

Give to the fund whatever you can afford.
<small>relative pronoun</small>

A copy of the speech was given to <u>whoever</u> wanted it.
<small>relative pronoun</small>

The relative pronoun that introduces a noun clause is sometimes called an **indefinite relative pronoun** because it does not have an antecedent expressed in the sentence.

Sometimes the relative pronoun is used as an *adjective* in the noun clause. A pronoun used in this way is called a **relative adjective,** or an **indefinite relative adjective** because it has no antecedent.

I shall accept <u>whatever</u> <u>salary</u> is offered me. (*whatever*— adjective)
modifies salary

The manager always knows <u>what course</u> he should follow. (*what*— adjective)
modifies course

Noun clauses are also introduced by the adverbs *how, when, why,* and *where*. The introductory adverb also modifies the verb in the noun clause.

<u>How we should invest the money</u> is the question. (*how*—adverb)
noun clause

He asked <u>where the president lived</u>. (*where*—adverb)
noun clause

I do not know <u>when the speaker will arrive</u>. (*when*—adverb)
noun clause

He did not tell <u>why he left the firm</u>. (*why*—adverb)
noun clause

A **noun clause** is a subordinate clause that is used as a *noun*. A noun clause may function as the **subject** of the sentence, as the **direct object** of a *verb*, as the **object** of a *preposition*, as a **predicate noun** after a linking verb, as an **appositive,** or as the **delayed subject** after the introductory word *"it."*

A *noun clause* may be introduced by a **subordinate conjunction,** by a **relative pronoun,** a **relative adjective,** or an **adverb.** The relative pronoun that introduces a noun clause is sometimes called an *indefinite relative pronoun* because it has no antecedent expressed in the sentence. The relative adjective is called an *indefinite relative adjective* for the same reason.

The only function of a *subordinate conjunction* in a noun clause is to connect the noun clause to the main clause. The *relative pronoun* has a special function in the noun clause, such as *subject, object,* etc. The *relative adjective* and the *adverb* not only introduce the noun clause, but also modify some word in it.

The word that introduces a subordinate clause is often omitted. The reason for this omission is to bring the main clause and the subordinate clause closer together.

The subordinate conjunction *whether* (not *if*) should be used to introduce a noun clause that is used as the direct object of the verbs *say, learn, know, doubt, wonder, understand,* etc.

A *noun clause* is often the real subject of a sentence that begins with the expletive *it.* Such sentences should be transposed and put in normal or grammatical order. The *noun clause* is the logical subject of the sentence.

21

PARTICIPLES

THE NATURE OF VERBALS

THERE are three verb forms in English that are known as verbals: *participles, gerunds,* and *infinitives.* Participles are discussed here, and gerunds and infinitives are explained in the following chapters. These verb forms are called verbals because they are derived from verbs and retain many of the characteristics of the verb.

A **verbal** may take any kind of modifier or any kind of complement that a verb might take. In addition to this verb-like function, a verbal has a special function of its own. A verbal usually performs the work of two parts of speech at the same time.

There is one function that a *verbal* cannot perform. It cannot function as the predicate verb in a sentence because it is an incomplete form of the verb. A verbal cannot make a statement or ask a question.

A **participle** is a verbal (verb form) which is *used as an adjective.* Since a participle is a verb form and partakes of the nature of a verb, it may take modifiers and complements.

Participles do not always take modifiers or complements. Very often they are used as **pure adjectives** and are placed directly before the nouns which they modify. Sometimes they are used as **predicate adjectives** after linking verbs. The following illustrations show the participle used as a simple adjective:

He conducts a <u>flourishing</u> business. (*flourishing* — modifies
participle
or
adjective
business)

The reports were <u>discouraging</u>. (*discouraging*—modifies *reports*)
participle
or
predicate adjective

We are reading an <u>interesting</u> book. (*interesting*—modifies *book*)
participle
or
adjective

The participle that is most commonly used as an adjective is the participle that ends in *ing*. This is called the **present participle.** In the following illustrations the *present participles* are placed directly before the nouns which they modify. When used in this way, they are generally regarded as pure adjectives.

running water	*singing* brook
shaking knees	*rustling* leaves
murmuring pines	*dangling* modifiers
coming events	*whistling* boy
soaring prices	*sleeping* child

The participles found in the preceding illustrations are *running, shaking, murmuring, coming, soaring, singing, rustling, dangling, whistling,* and *sleeping.* All these forms are derived from verbs.

Many participles are used as pure adjectives. When the participle is used as a pure adjective, it is usually placed directly before the noun which it modifies. When the participle is used as a **predicate adjective,** it is found in the predicate and modifies the subject.

The game was <u>exciting</u>. (*exciting*—used as a predicate adjective)
               participle

The book is <u>interesting</u>. (*interesting*—predicate adjective)
           participle

The rumors were <u>startling</u>. (*startling*—used as a predicate adjective)
                  participle

In the first sentence, the participle *exciting* is used as a predicate adjective, modifying the noun *game.* The participle *interesting,* in the second sentence modifies the noun *book.* In the third sentence, the participle *startling* is used as a predicate adjective, modifying the subject noun *rumors.* The participles *exciting, interesting,* and *startling* are forms of verbs.

**A participle is a verb form
which is frequently used as an adjective.**

238

FORMS OF THE PARTICIPLE

There are three participles that are commonly used as adjectives: the *present participle* (active voice); the *past participle* (passive voice); and the *perfect participle* (active voice). There is no active past participle in English.

These participles are easily recognized. The **present participle** always ends in *ing;* the **past participle** usually ends in *ed, d, t, n,* or *en.* The past participles of some of the irregular verbs do not have distinctive endings: *swum, drunk, gone, sung,* etc. The **perfect participle** is always formed by prefixing the word *having* to the past participle: *having sung, having called, having driven, having seen,* etc.

Regular Verbs

Present Participle	Past Participle	Perfect Participle
(*active*)	(*passive*)	(*active*)
calling	called	having called
watching	watched	having watched

Irregular Verbs

singing	sung	having sung
driving	driven	having driven
going	gone	having gone

PAST PARTICIPLES AND PERFECT PARTICIPLES

The past participle ending in *ed* is commonly used as an adjective. The following illustrations show how *past participles* function as *adjectives*:

A doctor, **called** to the scene, examined the injured man.

The **neglected** and **forgotten** child was picked up by an officer.

The army, **surprised** by the attack, fled into the woods.

The street was littered with paper, **thrown** from the windows.

In the first sentence, the past participle, *called,* is used as an adjective to modify *doctor.* The participle is modified by the adverbial phrase, *to the scene.* There are two past participles in the second sentence, *neglected* and *forgotten.* One ends in *ed* and the other ends in *en.* These participles modify the noun *child.* In this sentence, the participles are placed directly before the noun *child,* which they modify.

The past participle *surprised* in the third sentence modifies *army.* The participle is modified by the adverbial phrase *by the attack.* The past participle *thrown* in the last sentence is modified by the adverbial phrase *from the windows.* The participle *thrown* modifies the noun paper.

The following sentences show the adjective use of the *perfect participle*:

Having finished the dress, Mary packed it carefully in a box.

Having completed the job, the men left early.

Having accomplished his mission, the ambassador returned home.

Having recovered completely, Ted left the hospital.

The perfect participles in the preceding illustrations are *having finished, having completed, having accomplished,* and *having recovered.* The first three take direct objects—*dress, job,* and *mission.* The last one, *having recovered,* is modified by the adverb *completely.* They are all in the active voice.

The perfect participle, *having finished,* modifies the noun *Mary. Having completed* modifies the noun *men; having accomplished* modifies *ambassador,* and *having recovered* modifies *Ted.* These participles are used as adjectives.

THE PARTICIPIAL PHRASE

Since the participle is derived from a verb, it retains many of the characteristics of a verb. Like the verb, a participle may take **modifiers** and **complements**. The participle with its *modifiers* or *complements*, or with both complements and modifiers is called a **participial phrase**.

MODIFIERS OF PARTICIPLES

A participle is often modified by an adverb or an adverbial phrase:

Looking up suddenly, Robert saw a rainbow in the sky.
     adv. adv.

Coming close to the rock, we saw a strange sight.
     adv. adv. ph.

In the first sentence, the participle *looking* modifies the noun *Robert*. The participle *looking* is modified by the adverb *up* and the adverb *suddenly*. *Looking up suddenly* is a **participial phrase**.

In the second sentence, the participle *coming* modifies the pronoun *we*. The participle *coming* is modified by the adverb *close* and the adverbial phrase *to the rock*. *Coming close to the rock* is a **participial phrase**.

The participles in the following sentences also take *adverbial modifiers*:

Trembling with excitement, Sara waited for her friends.
       participial phrase
(Participial phrase modifies the noun *Sara*.)

The house, remodeled recently, is very attractive.
        participial phrase
(Participial phrase modifies the noun *house*.)

We saw an old man lying on the road.
           participial phrase
(Participial phrase modifies the noun *man*.)

In the first sentence, the participial phrase consists of the participle *trembling* and its modifier, the adverbial phrase *with excitement*. The

241

phrase, taken as a whole, modifies the noun *Sara.* The participial phrase *trembling with excitement* is used as an adjective, modifying *Sara.*

In the second sentence, the participial phrase consists of the participle *remodeled* and the adverbial modifier, the adverb *recently.* The entire phrase, *remodeled recently,* is used as an adjective, modifying the noun *house.*

In the third sentence, the participial phrase is *lying on the road.* It consists of the participle *lying* and the adverbial phrase *on the road.* The entire phrase, *lying on the road,* modifies the noun *man.*

COMPLEMENTS OF PARTICIPLES

1. Like the verb, a participle may take a direct object if the verb expresses action.

Carrying a suitcase, the porter entered the train.
— participle — dir. obj.
participial phrase

Realizing the danger, the captain ordered a retreat.
— participle — dir. obj.
participial phrase

In the first sentence, the noun *suitcase* is the direct object of the participle *Carrying.* The entire expression, *Carrying a suitcase,* is a participial phrase. The participial phrase modifies the noun *porter.*

In the second sentence, the noun *danger* is the direct object of the participle *realizing.* The entire expression, *Realizing the danger,* is a participial phrase. The participial phrase modifies the noun *captain.*

2. Like the verb, a participle may be followed by a predicate noun or a predicate adjective.

Participles that take predicate nouns or predicate adjectives as complements are forms of *linking verbs.*

Being an invalid, he could not climb the steep hill.
participle — pred. noun
participial phrase

Becoming weary, the traveler sat down to rest.
participle — pred. adj.
participial phrase

242

In the first sentence, the participle *being* is followed by the predicate noun *invalid*. The noun *invalid* refers to the same person as the subject *he*. The entire expression, *being an invalid,* is a participial phrase. The participial phrase modifies the subject pronoun *he*. *Being* is a form of the linking verb *to be*.

In the second sentence, the participle *becoming* is followed by the predicate adjective *weary*. The entire expression, *becoming weary,* is a participial phrase, modifying the noun *traveler*. *Becoming* is a form of the linking verb *to become*.

PARTICIPLES USED IN INDEPENDENT CONSTRUCTIONS

Sometimes a participle is used with a noun in an independent construction; that is, the participle and the noun which it modifies are not related grammatically to any other part of the sentence. Such a construction is called the **nominative absolute construction.**

The term *absolute* is used because the entire expression is an *independent construction*. It forms part of a sentence, but is not connected with the rest of the sentence grammatically. The term *nominative* is used because the noun which the participle modifies is in the *nominative case*. The following illustrations will make this use of the participle clear:

The sun having set, we decided to return home.
<u>Independent construction</u>

The train being late, the soldiers missed the boat.
<u>Independent construction</u>

In the first sentence, the expression, *The sun having set,* consists of the perfect participle *having set* and the noun *sun* with its modifier *The*. The entire expression, *The sun having set,* is used *absolutely* or independently. It has no grammatical connection with the rest of the sentence. The noun *sun* is in the nominative case.

The expression, *The train being late,* in the second sentence is also a *nominative absolute construction;* that is, it has no grammatical relation to the rest of the sentence. The noun *train* is in the nominative case. It is modified by the expression *being late,* which consists of the participle *being* and the predicate adjective *late*.

DANGLING PARTICIPLES

Participles are often used incorrectly in speaking and writing. One of the most common mistakes in English is to use what is commonly referred to as the **dangling participle.** Anything that dangles is said *to hang loosely,* without secure attachment. A participle "dangles" when there is no word in the sentence which it could properly modify, or when it seems to be related to a word which does not convey the meaning intended.

It is easy to detect these loose participial modifiers. Sometimes the use of a *dangling modifier* gives a ridiculous or a humorous slant to the meaning of the sentence. You can avoid this error if you think through your sentences carefully and relate the participle to the proper word.

When the participial phrase is placed at the beginning of a sentence, it should refer to the subject. When it could not possibly modify the subject from the standpoint of meaning, the sentence must be rewritten and a suitable subject supplied which it could logically modify.

Walking through the tunnel, a wallet was picked up.

dangling modifier

Entering the harbor, the Statue of Liberty came into view.

dangling modifier

Taking the test, the teacher gave me a passing grade.

dangling modifier

In the first sentence, the participial phrase *walking through the tunnel* modifies the subject of the sentence, which is *wallet.* A participle used at the beginning of a sentence modifies the subject. It is evident that the wallet was not walking through the tunnel; however, that is the meaning conveyed by the sentence as it is written. Very often the best way to get rid of a dangling participle is to substitute a clause for it.

While we were walking through the tunnel, we picked up a wallet.

In the second sentence, the participial phrase modifies *Statue of Liberty.* But it was not the *Statue of Liberty* that was entering the harbor. The phrase seems to be related to a word which it could not modify. The word which the participial phrase really modifies is not in the sentence. The sentence might be revised as follows:

As we entered the harbor, the Statue of Liberty came into view.

In the last sentence, the participial phrase modifies the word *teacher.* If you read the sentence carefully, you will readily see that it was not the teacher who took the test. The sentence would be correctly written if a clause were substituted for the dangling phrase.

After I took the test, the teacher gave me a passing grade.

MISPLACED MODIFIERS

Sometimes there is a word in the sentence which the participial phrase properly modifies, but the participle is not placed correctly. As a result, the meaning is confused. This error is commonly referred to as a **misplaced modifier.**

Jumping into the water, the children were rescued by the life guard. misplaced modifier

Several soldiers passed by in their uniforms recently drafted.
misplaced modifier

If you read the first sentence carefully, you will see that the word which the participle modifies is in the sentence. It is the word *lifeguard.* It was the *lifeguard* who jumped into the water. It was not the *children.* The trouble with the sentence is that the participial phrase should modify the subject. As the sentence is written, the subject is *children.* The subject should be the word *lifeguard.* The sentence might be rewritten as follows:

Jumping into the water, the lifeguard rescued the children.
participial phrase

In the second sentence, a participial modifier is also misplaced. As the sentence is written, the participial phrase modifies the word *uniforms.* But it was not the *uniforms* that were recently drafted; it was the *soldiers.* The sentence might be rewritten as follows:

Several recently drafted soldiers passed by in their uniforms.
participial phrase

PARTICIPLES USED IN VERB PHRASES

Participles are not always used as adjectives. One of their most important uses is to help form a *verb phrase.* When the participle forms part of a verb phrase, it is not considered as a separate word, but as part of the verb phrase.

A participle is never used alone as the predicate verb in a sentence because it is an incomplete form of the verb. It is used as part of a verb phrase. The following illustrations show how the participle is used as part of a verb phrase:

The janitor is washing the windows. (*washing*—part of verb phrase)

The gardener has planted the shrubs. (*planted*—part of verb phrase)

In the first sentence, the verb phrase *is washing* is made up of the auxiliary verb *is* and the present participle of the verb *wash,* or the *ing* participle, *washing.* In the second sentence, the verb phrase *has planted* is made up of the auxiliary *has* and the past participle of the verb *plant,* which is *planted.*

Sometimes it is difficult to determine whether the participle is part of the verb phrase, or whether it is used as an adjective modifying the subject. This is often true when a participle follows a linking verb. The meaning of the sentence will help you determine which use is intended by the speaker or writer. Study the following sentences carefully:

The talk was **inspiring.** (participle, used as an *adjective*)

We **were inspired** by his talk. (participle, part of *verb phrase*)

In the first sentence, the verb is *was,* not *was inspiring.* The verb *was* is a linking verb and requires a complement. In this sentence the complement is *inspiring,* which is used as a predicate adjective modifying the noun *talk.* The sentence means *inspiring talk. Inspiring* is a participle used as an adjective.

In the second sentence, the verb is *were inspired.* In this sentence, the past participle *inspired* is part of the verb phrase, *were inspired.* Study the following sentences carefully. Try to determine whether the participle is used as an adjective or is part of the verb phrase:

Robert was elected secretary at our last meeting. (*elected*—part
of the verb phrase)

The old man looked neglected. (*neglected*—participle used as
adjective)

The milk seems frozen. (*frozen*—participle used as adjective)

The house was furnished by an interior decorator. (*furnished*—
part of verb phrase)

I have been sitting here for an hour. (*sitting*—part of verb
phrase)

We were exhausted after the swim. (*exhausted*—participle used
as adjective)

When the participle follows a linking verb, it is used as an adjective
if it describes the state or the condition of the subject. In the second
sentence, the participle *neglected* describes the condition of the old
man. In the third sentence, the participle *frozen* describes the condition
of the milk. Both participles are used as adjectives. In the last sentence,
the participle *exhausted* also describes the condition of the subject, *we*.

SUMMARY

A **verbal** is a form of a verb which is used as another part of speech. There are three verbals in English—*participles, gerunds,* and *infinitives.*

A *verbal* retains many of the characteristics of a verb, but it cannot function as the predicate verb in a sentence because it is an incomplete verb form. A verbal cannot make a statement, ask a question, or express a command.

A *verbal* may take any **complement** or any adverbial **modifier** that a verb may take. When verbals take complements or modifiers, they function as two parts of speech at the same time.

A **participle** is a verbal (verb form) which is used as an *adjective.*

A **participial phrase** consists of a participle and any modifiers or complements that the participle may have in the sentence. A participial phrase functions as an *adjective.*

A **dangling participle** is a participle which does not modify any word in the sentence. *Dangling participles* usually appear at the beginning of a sentence. When a participle is placed at the beginning of a sentence, it logically modifies the subject. If the subject is not the word which the participle properly modifies, the participle "dangles."

A **misplaced modifier** is a modifier that is incorrectly placed in the sentence. The modifier must be attached to the word which it modifies and not to some other word. When a modifier is misplaced, it often leads to a wrong interpretation of the sentence.

A participle or a participial phrase is often used with a noun or a pronoun in an independent construction. Such an expression is often called a **nominative absolute.** An absolute expression is one that is *grammatically independent* of the rest of the sentence. A noun or a pronoun used in a *nominative absolute* construction is in the *nominative case.*

248

22
GERUNDS

Nature of the Gerund

IF you understand the dual nature of the participle, you will have little difficulty in understanding the dual nature of the gerund. Remember that the participle is both *verb* and *adjective.* The gerund is both *verb* and *noun.*

Gerunds are like participles in many respects. Gerunds and participles are *verbals;* that is, they are *forms derived from verbs.* Both participles and gerunds have the same *"ing"* forms. Both take the same kinds of complements and modifiers that verbs take.

Gerunds differ from participles in one fundamental respect. **Gerunds** *are verb forms used as nouns.* Participles are verb forms used as adjectives. Because a gerund functions as a noun, it can take certain modifiers that a participle cannot take. Like the noun, a gerund is often modified by an *adjective* or by an *adjective phrase.* Participles cannot take adjective modifiers.

Since the gerund functions as a noun, it may be used as the *subject* of a sentence, the *direct object* of a verb, the *object of a preposition,* or as a *predicate noun* after one of the linking verbs. Gerunds are often called *verbal nouns* because they are derived from verbs.

Painting is Martha's hobby. (gerund used as *subject*)
<u>subject</u>

Martha enjoys painting. (gerund used as *direct object*)
<u>direct object</u>

Martha earns a living by painting. (gerund used as *object of a preposition)*
<u>object of preposition</u>

Martha's hobby is painting. (gerund used as a *predicate noun*)
<u>predicate noun</u>

In the first sentence, the word *painting* is a gerund. It is a verb form that is used as a noun. *Painting* is the subject of the sentence. In the second sentence the same verb form *painting* is used as the direct object of the verb *enjoys.* In the third sentence *painting* is used as the object of the preposition *by,* and in the fourth sentence it is used as a predicate noun after the linking verb *is.*

THE GERUND PHRASE

Like the participle, the gerund retains many of the characteristics of a verb. Because the gerund is a verb form, it may take any of the complements or any of the modifiers that a verb might take. The gerund with its complements and modifiers is called a **gerund phrase.**

COMPLEMENTS OF GERUNDS

Like the verb, a *gerund* may take a **direct object.** Study the following sentence carefully. You will readily see that although the gerund is used as a noun, it retains the characteristics of a verb because it takes a *direct object.*

Sweeping the floor was one of Jack's duties.
gerund   dir. object
     gerund phrase

In this sentence the word *sweeping* is a gerund. It is used as the *subject* of the sentence. This is its noun function. Since the gerund is a verb form, it retains some of the characteristics of a verb. The verb *sweep* is an action verb and may take a *direct object.* The gerund *sweeping* may also take a direct object. In this sentence the direct object of the gerund *sweeping* is the noun *floor.*

Some verbs take both a direct and an indirect object. Gerunds formed from such verbs may also take a **direct** and an **indirect object.**

Giving the girls a holiday will please them.
gerund   indir. obj.   dir. obj.
     gerund phrase

In this sentence, *giving* is a gerund used as the subject of the sentence. This is its use as a **noun.** As a **verb form,** it takes the direct object *holiday* and the indirect object *girls.* The entire expression, *giving the girls a holiday* is a **gerund phrase.**

If the gerund is a form of a linking verb, it may take a **predicate noun** or a **predicate adjective** as a *complement.* Study the following sentences carefully. In both sentences the gerund requires a complement to complete its meaning. The gerunds are forms of linking verbs.

His <u>becoming</u> a <u>captain</u> involved certain responsibilities.
    gerund   pred. noun
        gerund phrase

I had not heard of Jane's <u>being</u> <u>ill.</u>
                   gerund pred. adj.
                   gerund phrase

In the first sentence, the gerund *becoming* takes the predicate noun *captain* as a complement. In the second sentence, the gerund *being* takes the predicate adjective *ill* as a complement.

ADVERBIAL MODIFIERS OF GERUNDS

The gerund, like the participle, may be modified by an **adverb** or an **adverbial phrase.** You should have no trouble in identifying the adverbial modifiers of the gerunds in the following sentences:

<u>Sitting</u> <u>on a park bench</u> was his favorite pastime.
gerund   adv. ph.
      gerund phrase

<u>Driving</u> a truck <u>in the city</u> is difficult.
gerund   adv. ph.
      gerund phrase

I do not advise your <u>seeing</u> him <u>now.</u>
                      gerund   adv.
                      gerund phrase

The gerund *sitting* in the first sentence is modified by the adverbial phrase *on a park bench*. The gerund *driving* in the second sentence is modified by the adverbial phrase *in the city*. The gerund *seeing* in the third sentence is modified by the adverb *now*.

ADJECTIVE MODIFIERS OF GERUNDS

Because the gerund functions as a noun, it may be modified by an *adjective,* or by a *noun* or a *pronoun* used as an *adjective.*

The <u>slow</u> <u>driving</u> in the mountains irritated Max.
gerund

(*slow*—adjective, modifying the gerund *driving*)

The <u>dog's</u> <u>barking</u> saved the child's life.
gerund

(*dog's*—noun used as an adjective, modifying *barking*)

The critics praised <u>her</u> <u>wonderful</u> <u>dancing.</u>
gerund

(*her*—pronoun used as an adjective, modifying *dancing*)

(*wonderful*—adjective, modifying *dancing*)

In the first sentence, the gerund *driving* is modified by the adjective *slow.* In the second sentence, the gerund *barking* is modified by the word *dog's,* which is a noun in the possessive case used as an adjective. In the third sentence, the gerund *dancing* is modified by the possessive adjective *her* (pronoun used as an adjective) and the adjective *wonderful.*

Like the noun, a gerund is often modified by an *adjective phrase.* In the following sentences, the gerunds take adjective phrases as modifiers:

We heard the <u>rustling</u> <u>of the leaves.</u>
gerund   adj. ph.

The villagers listened to the <u>tolling</u> <u>of the bell.</u>
gerund   adj. ph.

In the first sentence, the gerund *rustling* is modified by the adjective phrase *of the leaves.* You can readily see that the adjective phrase modifies *rustling* because the sentence means that we heard the *leaves' rustling.* The second sentence means that the villagers listened to the *bell's tolling.*

THE POSSESSIVE CASE BEFORE THE GERUND

The gerund is frequently modified by a noun or a pronoun in the *possessive case.* A mistake commonly made is to forget to put the noun or pronoun in the possessive case to show that it is a modifier. The important word in such sentences is the *gerund,* and not the modifier. The following illustration will help to make this clear:

The men objected to <u>me</u> <u>playing</u> on the team. (*incorrect*)
pro.   gerund

The men objected to <u>my</u> <u>playing</u> on the team. (*correct*)
pro.   gerund

The first sentence is incorrect because it conveys the wrong meaning. The sentence does not mean that the men objected to *me.* The word *me* is not the object of the preposition *to.* The object of the preposition *to* is the gerund *playing.* The sentence means that the men objected to the *playing.* The use of the form *me* before the gerund is incorrect. The possessive form *my* should be used.

The following sentences are incorrect because the wrong form of the noun or pronoun is used before the gerund:

I am interested in <u>William</u> <u>advancing</u> in his profession (*incorrect*)
noun   gerund

Mother did not like <u>me</u> <u>taking</u> part in the contest. (*incorrect*)
pro.   gerund

The first sentence does not mean that I am interested in *William* primarily. but that I am interested in *William's advancing.* The object of the preposition *in* is the gerund *advancing,* and not the proper noun *William.* Since the noun is a modifier of the gerund, it must be put in the possessive case (*William's* advancing).

The second sentence does not mean that Mother did not like *me.* It means that she *did* not like the *taking part in the contest.* The correct form of the pronoun before the gerund is *my* (*my* taking part).

THE DANGLING GERUND

Gerunds are often found in prepositional phrases which are placed at the beginning of the sentence. The gerund or the gerund phrase is the *object of the preposition*. The entire prepositional phrase should modify some word in the main part of the sentence. If there is no such word, the phrase *"dangles"* in the sentence; that is, the phrase is an unattached modifier.

The gerund almost always expresses action. There must be some word in the sentence to indicate the *doer* of this action. That word would logically be the subject of the sentence. Examine the following sentence carefully:

Upon <u>receiving</u> the telegram, the <u>trip</u> was canceled.
     gerund
           dangling gerund

This sentence begins with a prepositional phrase. The object of the preposition *upon* is the gerund phrase, *receiving the telegram*. The gerund *receiving* implies that someone received the telegram. The way the sentence is written, the *trip* received the telegram. The trouble with the sentence is that the subject has no logical relation to the gerund. The subject of the sentence should indicate *who* is doing the *receiving*. The following sentences are written correctly:

Upon <u>receiving</u> the telegram, **we** canceled the trip.
     gerund

    or

<u>After we had received the telegram</u>, we' canceled the trip.
   clause substituted for gerund phrase

This error might be corrected in one of two ways as shown in the preceding illustrations:

1. By supplying the word which the prepositional phrase logically refers to.

2. By substituting a subordinate clause for the gerund phrase.

When the gerund phrase at the beginning of a sentence does not have a logical relation to the subject of the sentence, the result is often humorous. The careful study of a sentence like the following will help you understand the error and the reason for the correction:

By pressing a button, the table comes out of the wall. (*incorrect*)
gerund phrase

(*pressing*—dangling gerund)

This sentence clearly indicates that *someone must press a button* before *the table* will come out of the wall. According to the way in which the sentence is written, *the table* performs that function. Such an interpretation would be absurd.

The trouble with the sentence is that the *subject* has no logical relation to the *gerund*. The subject of the sentence should be a word that would indicate the *doer* of the action expressed by the gerund. That word does not appear in the sentence as it is written. The sentence would be correctly written in either one of the following ways:

By pressing a button, *you* will release the table from the wall.
gerund phrase

If you press a button, the table will come out of the wall.
subordinate clause

SUMMARY

A **gerund** is a verb form (verbal) that functions as a *noun*. A gerund may function as the *subject* of a sentence, the *direct object* of a verb, the *object of a preposition,* or as a *predicate noun* after a linking verb. It may also be modified by an adjective, an adjective phrase, or by a noun or a pronoun in the possessive case.

Because the gerund retains the characteristics of a verb, it may take a *direct object,* an *indirect object,* a *predicate noun,* or a *predicate adjective* as a complement. It may also be modified by an *adverb* or an *adverbial phrase.*

If the gerund is a form of an action verb, it expresses *action.* If it is a form of a linking verb, it expresses *state of condition.*

The gerund ends in *ing.* The present participle also ends in *ing.* The only way to tell whether a word ending in *ing* is a participle or a gerund, is to study its use in the sentence. If it functions as an **adjective,** it is a **participle.** If it functions as a **noun,** it is a **gerund.**

A gerund is frequently modified by a noun or a pronoun in the *possessive case.* A common error in English is to fail to put the noun or pronoun before the gerund in the possessive case. Failure to do this often leads to statements which are misleading and illogical.

A prepositional phrase containing a gerund should modify some word in the sentence. If there is no word in the sentence which the gerund phrase could logically modify, the phrase is called a *dangling modifier.* The gerund is called a *dangling gerund.*

23

INFINITIVES

Nature of the Infinitive

PARTICIPLES, gerunds, and infinitives are called *verbals* because they are derived from verbs and function like verbs in many respects. They are unlike verbs because they cannot function as the predicate verb in a sentence. They are incomplete forms that cannot be used to make statements, ask questions, or give commands or requests. This is an important fact regarding verbals that you should always keep in mind.

The infinitive is easy to identify because it carries a definite sign which indicates that it is an infinitive. An infinitive is usually preceded by the word **to**, which is commonly called the *sign of the infinitive.*

When the word *to* is used with a verb form to complete the infinitive, it is *not a preposition.* It is merely the *sign* of the infinitive. The way to be sure that the expression is an infinitive, and not a prepositional phrase, is to look at the word which follows *to.* If this word is a verb form, the expression is an infinitive, and not a prepositional phrase.

Like the gerund, the infinitive is *used as a noun.* It may also function as an *adjective* or as an *adverb.* An infinitive may take any complement or any modifier that a verb might take.

The sign of the infinitive (*to*) is usually omitted after certain verbs in order to avoid awkward or stilted expressions. The *to* is usually omitted after the following verbs: *hear, feel, watch, let, dare, help, see, make, please, bid, need,* etc.

USES OF THE INFINITIVE

Previous chapters explained the two-sided character of the participle and the gerund. The participle functions as an adjective and retains some of the characteristics of a verb. The gerund functions as a noun and also retains some of the characteristics of a verb. The **infinitive** retains its verb nature, and in addition may function as a *noun,* an *adjective,* or an *adverb.*

The noun function of an infinitive is very similar to the noun function of a gerund. An infinitive may be the *subject* of a sentence, the *direct object* of a verb, the *object of a preposition,* or a *predicate noun* after a linking verb.

To write was his ambition.
subject

His ambition was to write.
predicate noun

He did nothing except (to) write.
object of preposition

He likes to write.
direct object

In the first sentence, the infinitive *To write* is the subject of the sentence. In the second sentence, the infinitive *to write* is used as a predicate noun after the linking verb *was.* In the third sentence, the infinitive *to write* is used as the object of the preposition *except.* In this sentence, the sign of the infinitive is omitted. In the fourth sentence, the infinitive *to write* is used as the direct object of the verb *likes.*

INFINITIVES USED AS ADJECTIVES

The infinitive is often used as an *adjective* or an *adverb*. When the infinitive is used as an adjective, it usually modifies a noun which precedes it. It is easy to identify the adjective use of the infinitive because an adjective could be readily substituted for the infinitive. Study the following illustrations carefully:

The desire **to win** was apparent. (the *winning* desire)

They asked permission **to leave.** (*leaving* permission)

He obtained a permit **to build.** (*building* permit)

We had fresh water **to drink.** (*drinking* water)

In the first sentence, the infinitive *to win* is used as an adjective. It modifies the noun *desire*. In the second sentence, the infinitive *to leave* modifies the noun *permission*. In the third sentence, the infinitive *to build* modifies the noun *permit*. In the last sentence, the infinitive *to drink* modifies *water*.

INFINITIVES USED AS ADVERBS

The infinitive is often used as an *adverb* to modify a verb, an adjective, or an adverb. When the infinitive is used as an adverb, it usually expresses *purpose* or *degree*.

It is easy to identify an infinitive used as an adverb when it modifies a verb. In almost every case, the infinitive expresses *purpose*. It tells why, or for what purpose the action is performed. When an infinitive is used in this way, it is often called the *infinitive of purpose*. The infinitives in the following illustrations express purpose and modify the verb:

The traveler stopped **to rest.** (*to rest*—expresses purpose)

The composer came **to listen.** (*to listen*—expresses purpose)

The officer returned **to help.** (*to help*—expresses purpose)

In the first sentence, the infinitive *to rest* modifies the verb *stopped*. The infinitive expresses purpose; that is, it tells why the traveler stopped. The infinitive *to listen* modifies the verb *came*. This infinitive also expresses purpose. It tells why the composer came. The infinitive in the third sentence tells why the officer returned. It modifies the verb and expresses purpose.

An infinitive used as an adverb frequently modifies an *adjective*. This use of the infinitive is also easy to identify. In most cases, the infinitive modifies an adjective which follows a linking verb. Examine the following illustrations carefully:

The cake was ready **to bake.** (*to bake*—modifies the adjective *ready*)

The men were anxious **to work.** (*to work*—modifies the adjective *anxious*)

We are sorry **to leave.** (*to leave*—modifies the adjective *sorry*)

I shall be glad **to help.** (*to help*—modifies the adjective *glad*)

In the first sentence, the linking verb *was* is followed by the predicate adjective *ready*. The adjective *ready* is modified by the infinitive *to bake* which is used as an adverb. As you have learned, only adverbs can modify adjectives. The sentence means that the cake was ready *for baking*. The infinitive *to bake* could readily be turned into an adverbial phrase. This should make its adverbial function clear.

In the second sentence, the linking verb *were* is followed by the predicate adjective *anxious*. The adjective *anxious* is modified by the infinitive *to work*. In the third sentence, the predicate adjective *sorry* is modified by the infinitive *to leave*. In the last sentence, the predicate adjective *glad* is modified by the infinitive *to help*.

In all of the preceding illustrations a linking verb is followed by a predicate adjective. The predicate adjective is modified by an infinitive which is used as an adverb.

COMPLEMENTS OF INFINITIVES

Like the gerund and the participle, the infinitive may take any kind of complement a verb might take. Sometimes the infinitive takes a *direct object*. Sometimes it takes both a *direct* and an *indirect object*. If the infinitive is a form of a linking verb, it may take a *predicate noun* or a *predicate adjective* as a complement.

Arlene wanted to buy a fur coat. (*coat*—object of *to buy*)

The tailor promised to make me a suit. (*me*—indirect object)

(*suit*—direct object)

John would like to be an aviator. (*aviator*—predicate noun)

His ambition is to become rich. (*rich*—predicate adjective)

In the first sentence, the infinitive *to buy* takes the direct object *coat*. In the second sentence, the infinitive *to make* takes both an indirect object and a direct object. *Me* is the indirect object and *suit* is the direct object. In the third sentence, the infinitive *to be* takes the predicate noun *aviator* as a complement. In the last sentence, the infinitive *to become* takes the predicate adjective *rich* as a complement.

MODIFIERS OF INFINITIVES

1. Like the verb, an infinitive may be modified by an *adverb* or by an *adverbial phrase*.

The boys like to swim fast. (*fast*—adverb, modifies *to swim*)
<u>adverb</u>

The boys like to swim in Lake Michigan. (adverbial phrase—
<u>adverbial phrase</u>
modifies *to swim*)

To write well is an accomplishment. (*well*—adverb—modifies
<u>adverb</u>
To write)

To fish in that stream is a pleasure. (adverbial phrase—modifies
<u>adverbial phrase</u>
To fish)

261

2. Sometimes the infinitive has both a complement and a modifier.

To do the job properly would require a month's time.
        dir. obj. *adv.*

In this sentence the infinitive *To do* takes the direct object *job*. The infinitive is also modified by the adverb *properly*.

THE INFINITIVE PHRASE

In the preceding illustration, the entire phrase, *To do the job properly,* regarded as a whole, is the **complete subject** of the sentence. This group of words is called an **infinitive phrase.** An *infinitive phrase* consists of an infinitive with its complements or its modifiers, or both, if it takes both.

Ted's aim was to please others. (infinitive with a *direct object*)
              infinitive phrase

We did not want to travel by plane. (infinitive with an *adverbial*
               infinitive phrase
phrase as a modifier)

The men would like to begin the project now. (infinitive with a
               infinitive phrase
direct object and an *adverb* as modifier)

The infinitive phrase in the first sentence is *to please others.* The phrase consists of the infinitive *to please* and its object *others.* The infinitive phrase in the second sentence is *to travel by plane.* It consists of the infinitive *to travel* and the adverbial phrase *by plane,* which modifies the infinitive. The infinitive phrase in the last sentence is *to begin the project now.* The infinitive takes the direct object *project* and the adverbial modifier *now.*

THE OMISSION OF THE SIGN "TO"

The sign of the infinitive (*to*) is omitted when the infinitive is used after certain verbs. The sign is not used because the sentence would sound awkward or stilted with the sign placed before the verb form. You should become familiar with the verbs that are followed by the infinitive without the sign *to*.

The sign of the infinitive is usually omitted when the infinitive is used after the following verbs: *hear, feel, let, watch, dare, help, see, make, please, bid, need, do,* etc. The following sentences illustrate the use of the infinitive without the sign. The *to* is enclosed in parentheses to show you that you should supply it mentally in order to recognize the infinitive construction.

INFINITIVES WITHOUT THE SIGN

1. I felt the floor (to) shake under me.

2. We heard him (to) sing some old ballads.

3. I saw her (to) enter the theater.

4. They bid us (to) leave immediately.

5. They dare not (to) create a disturbance.

6. Help me (to) carry the luggage.

7. Let his friend (to) help him.

8. They made him (to) wait for an hour.

9. They watched him (to) play.

10. There was nothing to do but (to) read.

11. We need not (to) climb the cliff.

12. They helped us (to) build the garage.

13. Please (to) pass the sugar.

14. Let the old man (to) have his way.

15. The janitor does everything except (to) clean the windows.

An *infinitive* is a verb form (verbal) which is used as a *noun,* an *adjective,* or an *adverb.* An infinitive is usually preceded by the word *to* which is commonly called the sign of the infinitive. When *to* is used in this way, it is *not a preposition.*

An infinitive is often used as a **noun.** Like the noun, an infinitive may be used as the *subject* of a sentence, the *direct object* of a verb, the *object of a preposition,* or as a *predicate noun* after a linking verb.

The infinitive is also used as an **adjective** or an **adverb.** When the infinitive is used as an adjective, it usually modifies a preceding *noun.* When the infinitive is used as an adverb, it modifies a *verb,* an *adjective,* or an *adverb.* When the infinitive modifies a verb, it usually expresses *purpose.*

Like the gerund and the participle, an infinitive may take any kind of **complement** or **modifier** that a verb might take. Sometimes the infinitive takes a *direct object.* Sometimes it takes both an *indirect* and a *direct object.* If the infinitive is a form of a linking verb, it is usually followed by a *predicate noun* or a *predicate adjective.* An infinitive may be modified by an *adverb* or an *adverbial phrase.*

An infinitive with its complement or complements and its modifier or modifiers constitutes an **infinitive phrase.** The infinitive phrase may be used as a *noun,* an *adjective,* or an *adverb.*

Like the participle and the gerund, the infinitive *cannot* function as the **predicate verb** of a sentence.

24

PROBLEMS IN THE USE OF INFINITIVES

THE INFINITIVE CLAUSE

A NOUN clause is often used as the direct object of a verb. The infinitive is often used in a construction which is similar to this use of a noun clause.

Sometimes the infinitive has its own *subject*. With this subject, the infinitive is used in a construction which is commonly called the **"infinitive clause."** *The infinitive clause is not a true clause* because the infinitive cannot function as a predicate verb. An infinitive cannot function as the predicate verb in a clause because it is an incomplete verb form. The following illustrations will help make this clear:

The officers want <u>the men to sing at the Rotary Club.</u>
<small>infinitive clause</small>

We believed <u>him to be capable.</u>
<small>infinitive clause</small>

In the first sentence, the group of words, *the men to sing at the Rotary Club,* is called an **"infinitive clause."** This expression is called a clause because the infinitive has a subject, and the entire group of words functions in the same way as a **noun clause** would function. The *infinitive clause* is used as the direct object of the verb *want.*

In the second sentence, the group of words *him to be capable* is an infinitive clause. The subject of the infinitive is the pronoun *him.* The entire expression *him to be capable* is used as the direct object of the verb *believed,* but it is not a true clause. The infinitive *to be* is not a predicate verb.

Jean asked <u>me to go with her.</u> (*me*—subject of the infinitive *to go*)
<small>infinitive clause</small>

Father advised <u>him to buy the bonds.</u> (*him*—subject of the infinitive *to buy*)
<small>infinitive clause</small>

265

He believed <u>her to be honest</u>. (*her*—subject of the infinitive
to be)
infinitive clause

We want <u>them to build a house</u>. (*them*—subject of the infinitive
to build)
infinitive clause

The underlined expression in each of the preceding sentences is the
object of the preceding verb. In the first sentence, *me to go with her*
is the object of the verb *asked*. The sentence does not mean that she
asked *me*. It means that she asked *me to go with her*. The entire expression, *me to go with her*, is the object of the verb *asked*.

The group of words, *me to go with her*, is called an "infinitive clause."
It consists of the subject *me* and the infinitive *to go* with the modifier
of the infinitive, the adverbial phrase *with her*. You can readily see
that this is not a true clause because the infinitive *to go* is an incomplete verb form and cannot function as the predicate verb.

The important fact to keep in mind about this construction is that
the *subject* of the infinitive is always in the **objective case**. This is an
exception to the rule that subjects of sentences and subjects of clauses
are always in the nominative case.

Examine the preceding illustrations again. In the second sentence,
him is the subject of the infinitive clause, *him to buy the bonds. Him*
is in the objective case. In the third sentence, *her* is the subject of the
infinitive clause, *her to be honest. Her* is in the objective case. In the
last sentence, *them* is the subject of the infinitive clause *them to build
a house. Them* is in the objective case.

You will not have any difficulty with the **case** of the subject of the
infinitive. No one would think of saying, "Jean asked *I* to go with her,"
or "Father advised *he* to buy the bonds." It is natural to use the *objective
case* as the subject of the infinitive. However, it is important to keep
the following rule in mind. It will help you understand some of the
other problems connected with the use of infinitives.

The subject of an infinitive is always in the objective case.

Sometimes the sign of the infinitive is omitted in the "infinitive clause." You must learn how to recognize such "clauses" even if the sign is omitted.

The manager made <u>Mary copy the report again.</u>
infinitive clause

The manager made <u>Mary (to) copy the report again.</u>
infinitive clause

I saw <u>her dance at the carnival.</u>
infinitive clause

I saw <u>her (to) dance at the carnival.</u>
infinitive clause

In the first sentence, the infinitive clause, *Mary (to) copy the report again,* is the direct object of the verb *made.* The sign of the infinitive *(to)* is omitted in this sentence. In the second sentence, the infinitive clause *her (to) dance at the carnival* is the object of the verb *saw.* The sign of the infinitive is omitted before *dance.*

VERB "TO BE" IN AN INFINITIVE CLAUSE

When we use the infinitive *to be* in an "infinitive clause," we have a problem in agreement of subject and complement which is often confusing. You have just learned that the subject of an infinitive is always in the objective case. This rule applies in the case of *action verbs* and *linking verbs.*

The problem arises when the infinitive is a form of a linking verb. You learned in your previous study that the noun or pronoun used after a linking verb is in the *nominative case* to agree with the subject of the sentence. Up to this point, every word used as the subject of a sentence or of a clause has been in the nominative case. In the case of the "infinitive clause" we are dealing with a subject that is in the **objective case.**

The verb *to be*, as well as other linking verbs, always takes the same case after it as it takes before it. If the case before it is the *objective case,* the *objective case* must follow it. A noun or pronoun following a linking verb must be in the same case as the subject. Since the noun or pronoun that follows a linking verb means the same person or thing as the subject, it must agree with the subject in case. Therefore, the noun or pronoun that follows the verb *to be* in an infinitive clause is in the objective case to agree with the *subject,* which is in the objective case. This is the logical agreement of *subject* and *complement* after a linking verb functioning as an infinitive in an infinitive clause.

A few illustrations will make this clear. Notice the form of the pronoun after the linking verbs in the "infinitive clauses."

I should like the chairman to be him. (*chairman*—objective case
       <u>infinitive clause</u>   *him*—objective case)

Many of the guests thought us to be them. (*us*—objective case—
                 <u>infinitive clause</u>   *them*—objective case)

In the first sentence, the subject of the infinitive clause is *chairman,* which is in the objective case. The infinitive *to be* is followed by the predicate pronoun *him.* The pronoun used as the complement of a linking verb must agree in case with the subject. Since the subject is in the objective case, the pronoun must be in the objective case to agree with the subject.

In the second sentence, the pronoun *us* is the subject of the infinitive clause. *Us* is in the objective case. The pronoun that follows the infinitive *to be* must be in the same case as the subject. *Them* is in the objective case to agree with the case of the subject, *us.*

THE SPLIT INFINITIVE

The parts of an infinitive (*to* with a verb form) are regarded as a unit. They should not be separated unless there is a good reason for doing so. The usual method of separating the parts of the infinitive is to place an adverb between the *to* and the *verb form*. When the parts of the infinitive are separated in this way, we refer to the infinitive as a **"split infinitive."** The adverbial modifier "splits" the infinitive.

As a rule, the infinitive should *not* be split by a modifier. Sometimes it is both desirable and effective to split the infinitive, as many authorities in grammar are pointing out. Ordinarily, it is not the best practice, as you will readily see from the following illustrations:

I asked you **to** <u>immediately</u> **return** my camera.
       <small>modifier</small>

The judge was determined **to** <u>intently</u> and <u>carefully</u> **examine** the
                              <small>modifier</small>   <small>modifier</small>
evidence.

In the first sentence, the infinitive is *to return:* The adverbial modifier, *immediately,* is placed between the sign of the infinitive and the verb form. In this particular sentence there is no justifiable reason for splitting the infinitive. The sentence would sound much better if it were written as follows:

I asked you **to return** my camera immediately.

In the second sentence, two adverbial modifiers connected by *and* are placed between the parts of the infinitive. This sentence would sound better if the infinitive were not split in this manner:

The judge was determined **to examine** the evidence intently and carefully.

Many authorities in English call our attention to the fact that some of the best writers split infinitives. When writers do this, they have a good reason for the "split." They also know how to do it so that the sentence will not sound awkward or stilted. When a writer splits an infinitive, his purpose is to throw the emphasis in a certain direction. The following are examples of split infinitives found in good writing:

1. "I feel like inviting them to <u>first</u> consider ...."

2. "I desire to <u>so</u> arrange my affairs ...."

3. .... "his ability to <u>effectually</u> carry on ...."

4. .... "to enable him to <u>properly</u> perform his work ...."

5. .... "to <u>better</u> acquaint myself with the problems ...."

6. "Our object is to <u>further</u> cement trade relations."

7. "He worked silently and swiftly, hoping to <u>speedily</u> end his patient's discomfort."

8. "All they have to do is to sit down and <u>faithfully</u> copy it."

Although there is plenty of evidence that good writers sometimes split the infinitive, ordinarily it is better practice to keep the parts of the infinitive together. A writer or speaker should certainly avoid using such awkward sentences as the following:

Edwin was eager for me to <u>especially</u> see the art exhibit. (*to see*—
_{modifier}
infinitive)

Eugene promised to <u>never</u> <u>again</u> be late to work. (*to be*—
_{modifier} _{modifier}
infinitive)

The committee wanted to <u>beautifully</u> decorate the hall. (*to dec-*
_{modifier}
orate—infinitive

I want to <u>next year</u> go to Europe. (*to go*—infinitive)
_{modifier}

In the first sentence, the infinitive *to see* is "split" by placing the adverb *especially* between the sign of the infinitive *to* and the verb form *see*. In the second sentence, two adverbial modifiers "split" the infinitive. In the third sentence, the adverb *beautifully* "splits" the infinitive. In the fourth sentence, the adverbial modifier *year* is placed between the sign *to* and the verb form, *go*. *Year* is a noun used as an adverb.

SPECIAL USES OF THE INFINITIVE

The infinitive is often used in **apposition** with a noun to explain or identify that noun. This is a very useful construction, for it enables us to explain the noun in a very few words. The infinitive used as an *appositive* is usually set off by commas. Sometimes a dash is used:

His first proposal, to borrow money, was rejected.
infinitive phrase

We were given our orders—to finish the job before ten.
infinitive phrase

In the first sentence, the infinitive phrase, *to borrow money,* is in apposition with the word *proposal.* It explains the nature of the proposal or tells what the proposal was. In the second sentence, the infinitive phrase, *to finish the job before ten,* is in apposition with the word *orders.* It explains what our orders were.

The infinitive is also used as the **delayed subject** in a sentence that begins with the introductory word *it.* In this case *it* is an **expletive.**

It always pays to tell the truth.
infinitive phrase

(It)   To tell the truth always pays.
expletive   subject

It is your duty to protect your interests.
infinitive phrase

(It)   To protect your interests is your duty.
expletive   subject

Sentences that begin with the pronoun *it* used as an expletive should always be transposed in order to see the grammatical relations more clearly.

THE THREE-SIDED CHARACTER OF THE INFINITIVE

NOUN USES OF THE INFINITIVE

1. **Subject** of the sentence

2. **Direct object** of a verb

3. **Object** of a *preposition*

4. **Predicate noun** after a *linking verb*

5. **Appositive**

6. **Delayed subject** after an expletive

7. May take an *adjective modifier*

THE INFINITIVE AS A MODIFIER

1. May function as an **adjective**, modifying a noun

2. May function as an **adverb** expressing purpose or degree

VERB CHARACTERISTICS OF THE INFINITIVE

1. Expresses *action* or *state of being,* but *cannot* function as the predicate verb in a sentence

2. May take a complement: *direct object, indirect object, predicate noun,* or *predicate adjective*

3. May take modifiers: *adverbs* and *adverbial phrases*

4. May form part of an infinitive clause

An *infinitive* is often found in a construction which is commonly called the *"infinitive clause."* This construction is called a clause because the infinitive has a *subject,* and the entire expression is the equivalent of a noun clause. *The infinitive clause is not a true clause* because an infinitive cannot function as a predicate verb.

The **subject** of an infinitive in an infinitive clause is always in the **objective case.** This presents a problem in agreement when we are dealing with verbs like the verb *to be.* A linking verb always takes the same case after it as before it. If the subject is in the *objective case,* the noun or pronoun that follows the linking verb must also be in the *objective case.* This is the logical agreement of subject and predicate noun or pronoun. The pronoun that follows a linking verb in an infinitive clause must be in the objective case. Example: I knew it to be him. *Him* is in the objective case to agree with the pronoun *it.*

An *infinitive* is often **"split"** by placing an adverbial modifier between the sign (to) and the verb form. The parts of an infinitive are regarded as a unit and should not be split unless there is a good reason for doing so. But there are times when it is desirable to split an infinitive. Examples of *split infinitives* are found in good modern prose. Ordinarily, it is not the best practice to split an infinitive because it often results in an awkward or unnatural expression.

The infinitive is often used as the **delayed subject** in a sentence that begins with the introductory word "it." In such cases, the word *it* is used as an **expletive** and the infinitive is the logical subject of the sentence. Example: It is his duty to check the accounts. The true subject of the sentence is the infinitive *to check the accounts.*

25

PUNCTUATION REVIEW

A LL punctuation marks are "signals" from the writer to the reader. A period shows that a sentence has been ended or that an abbreviation has been used. A comma may show a slight break in thought, separate the two parts of a compound sentence, or be used in one of several other ways.

Keep in mind that *some sentences may be punctuated in more than one way* and that, in some instances, a punctuation mark may or may not be used at the writer's discretion.

Remember, also, that *some professions and businesses have their own style of punctuation.* A journalist, for example, may omit some punctuation marks which normally are included in a business letter. A lawyer, on the other hand, uses many more punctuation marks when preparing a legal form than are essential for most types of business writing.

OPEN AND CLOSED PUNCTUATION

The terms *open* and *closed* punctuation apply only to the business letter and only to the heading and inside address of the letter. They do not apply to the salutation and complimentary close. If your company uses *open* punctuation, as most firms do, *omit all commas and periods at the ends of lines in the heading and inside address* unless the line ends in an abbreviation. If your firm uses *closed* punctuation, *include commas and periods at the ends of the lines in the heading and in the inside address.* The following examples illustrate the two styles of punctuation. Remember that most firms prefer open punctuation.

Open Punctuation	Closed Punctuation
Acme Rug Cleaners, Inc.	Acme Rug Cleaners, Inc.,
1823 Timber Avenue	1823 Timber Avenue,
Cleveland, Ohio	Cleveland, Ohio.

The salutation and complimentary close of a business letter are usually punctuated by a colon after the salutation and a comma following the complimentary close, regardless of open or closed punctuation. Some writers, however, no longer punctuate either the salutation or the complimentary close.

USE OF THE PERIOD

1. The period (.) is used after a declarative or an imperative sentence.

> She went to the office.   (declarative)
> Close the car door.   (imperative)

Exception: If you wish to give a declarative or an imperative sentence the force of an exclamatory sentence, use an exclamation point rather than a period.

> I was so shocked that I was speechless!   (declarative)
> Bring the Pulmotor quickly!   (imperative)

2. After requests, use a period rather than a question mark.

> May I send you a copy of our latest bulletin.   (request)
> Will you send me any further information which you have available.
> (request)

3. The period is used after abbreviations and initials.

Dr.	Mrs.	A. M.	Jan.
Ill.	Sat.	C. I. Jones	Inc.
B.S.	Ph.D.	U.S.A.	Gen.

Note: When a sentence ends with an abbreviation, one period is sufficient for both the abbreviation and the sentence.

> Mail the package to Conley and Green, Inc.

4. **The period is used to indicate the omission of words in quoted passages.**

(a) Use three periods (. . .) to indicate the omission of words within a quoted passage.

> "I pledge allegiance to the flag of the United States . . . one nation, indivisible, with liberty and justice for all."—Francis Bellamy

(b) Use four periods (. . . .) to indicate the omission of words at the end of a quoted passage.

> "Fame is the spur . . . ."—John Milton

USE OF THE COMMA

1. The comma (,) is used after an adverbial dependent clause when the dependent clause precedes the main clause. When the dependent clause does not begin the sentence, the comma is usually unnecessary.

<u>After the director had read the minutes of the meeting</u>, he called for
adverbial clause
the financial report. (comma)

The director called for the financial report <u>after he had read the
minutes of the meeting.</u> (no comma)
adverbial clause

2. The comma is used after a participial phrase or an absolute phrase at the beginning of a sentence.

<u>Seeing the address across the street</u>, he wrote a note in his little book.
participial phrase

<u>The rain having stopped</u>, we went to lunch.
absolute construction

3. The comma is used after an introductory infinitive phrase.

<u>To be successful</u>, you must read widely.
infinitive phrase

Note: When the subject of the sentence is an infinitive, do not separate the subject from the rest of the sentence.

<u>To be successful</u> was his goal.
subject

4. The comma is used to set off parenthetical expressions, whether words, phrases, or clauses.

(a) Transitional words such as *however, therefore, moreover, besides, consequently* should be set off by commas.

> Consequently, I did not receive an answer to his letter.

Exception: The word *also* is not set off by commas unless the writer wishes *also* to be emphasized strongly. In such a case, *also* is generally placed in an unusual position in the sentence.

> We also noticed that the salaries declined after the first of the year.
>   (no emphasis)
> Also, we noticed that the salaries declined after the first of the year.
>   (emphasis intended)

(b) Phrases such as *so to speak, in short, as a result, of course* should be set off by commas.

> We found, in short, many errors in his work.
> Of course, there are many ways to tackle the problem.

(c) Clauses such as *I think, we suppose, he says* should be set off by commas.

> Someone, I suppose, should check the report.

(d) Explanatory expressions, such as *and I agree with him, so far as he is concerned,* etc., which break the logical sequence of words should be set off by commas.

> The president disliked the policy, and I agreed with him, of letting all
>   employees name their vacation time.

5. The comma is used after introductory expressions such as *yes, indeed, surely* (when it means *yes*), *well*.

> Well, the next thing we knew he had shot the deer.
> Yes, I will attend to the matter.

6. The comma is used to set off a nonrestrictive clause. A nonrestrictive clause is set off because *it is not essential to complete the meaning of a sentence.* A nonrestrictive clause is similar to a parenthetical expression in that it gives added information about the word it modifies.

Restrictive clauses are never set off by commas. *A restrictive clause is a clause that is necessary to complete the meaning of the sentence* because the clause identifies the word it modifies. A restrictive clause cannot be left out of a sentence, whereas a nonrestrictive clause can be.

The girl who lives next door came to work in our office. (The clause *who lives next door* is restrictive because it is needed to identify the word *girl*. The clause is not set off by commas.)

Mary Jones, who lives next door, came to work in our office. (The clause *who lives next door* is nonrestrictive because it is not needed to identify the name *Mary Jones*. The name *Mary Jones* clearly identifies the person being talked about, and the clause merely gives added information about the person *Mary Jones*.)

7. The comma is used to set off words in apposition. An appositive is a word or phrase that defines or identifies another word. An appositive means the same as the word it defines.

Jones, our office manager, is ill.
      appositive

Reverend Brown, our minister, is an intelligent man.
            appositive

Note 1: An appositive at the end of a sentence should be preceded by a comma.

I sent the memorandum to Jones, our office manager.

Note 2: Very closely related appositives do not require a comma.

| my cousin Mary | Louis the Fourth |
| his friend Bill | Mary Queen of Scots |

8. The comma is used to set off words used in direct address.

We regret, Mr. Thomas, that your order was unsatisfactorily filled.
Henry, bring me the December file.

9. The comma is used to separate a series of three or more words, phrases, or clauses.

Alice planned to have steak, potatoes, beans, lettuce, and ice cream for dinner.
He stalked off the stage, turned around, came back, and glared at the audience.
At the meeting it was decided to (1) give two weeks' vacation with pay, (2) give pensions at age sixty-five, (3) establish a profit-sharing plan.

Note 1: A comma should always be placed before the conjunction joining the last two members of a series.

She asked for paper, pencils, and a ruler.

Note 2: A comma should separate pairs of words in a series. A comma should not be placed before a conjunction joining words of a series that are considered as one unit.

> Typing and shorthand, spelling and vocabulary, grammar and punctuation are the most popular courses. (pairs of words in a series)

> For breakfast she ordered orange juice, toast, coffee, and ham and eggs. (*Ham and eggs* is considered to be one unit.)

10. The comma is used to separate coordinate adjectives which modify the same noun. Adjectives are coordinate if the word *and* can be used between them.

> The efficient, business-like secretary received an advance in pay. (Comma—the efficient *and* business-like secretary. Both adjectives modify *secretary*.)

> The five silver spoons were very expensive. (No comma—you would not say *five and silver spoons*.)

11. The comma is used in a compound sentence to separate independent clauses joined by one of the coordinate conjunctions *and, but, for, or, nor,* and *while* when it means the same as *but.*

> I dictated the letter as you ordered, but she did not transcribe it correctly.

> Minneapolis is a large industrial center, and it has many cultural attractions.

(a) If the clauses of a compound sentence are very short and closely connected, the comma may be omitted.

> He looked but he did not see her.

(b) Do not use a comma between two independent clauses unless a coordinate conjunction is used. The use of a comma without a coordinate conjunction between two independent clauses is called the *comma fault.* The following sentence illustrates the comma fault:

> The men in the shipping department will not follow instructions, they repeatedly make serious errors. (Incorrect—comma should not be used without a coordinate conjunction.)

Note 1: The comma fault may be eliminated by punctuating the sentence in one of the three following ways:

(a) Use a coordinate conjunction after the comma:

The men in the shipping department will not follow instructions, and they repeatedly make serious errors. (correct)

(b) Use a semicolon between the two independent clauses:

The men in the shipping department will not follow instructions; they repeatedly make serious errors. (Correct—see Rule 1 under semicolons.)

(c) Punctuate the two independent clauses as two simple sentences:

The men in the shipping department will not follow instructions. They repeatedly make serious errors. (correct)

Note 2: When the independent clauses of a compound sentence are very long or have *internal punctuation,* a semicolon is generally used before the coordinate conjunction. Internal punctuation means that there are commas within one or both of the independent clauses.

Copyboy, take this folder to Alan Toms, the fellow in brown over there; and be sure to come back.
Quietly efficient, Joan continued in her position; but she never got the raise.

Both of these sentences have one or more commas in the first independent clause. Since the first clause has internal punctuation, a semicolon is used between the two independent clauses even though a coordinate conjunction is used. (See Rule 3 under semicolons.)

12. The comma is used to set off words or phrases expressing contrast.

I asked you to file the contract, not destroy it.
You may be excused from the conference this time, but never again.

13. The comma is used to set off a definite place, month, or year.

Cleveland, Ohio   July 12, 1922
Cook County, Illinois   the third of December, 1931

Or, in sentence form, the comma is used in the following manner:

The president was born April 8, 1872, at 1224 Elm Street, Cleveland, Ohio.

14. The comma is used to set off a direct quotation.

The director asked, "How many of you are in favor of this change in policy?"

15.   The comma is used as a substitute for an exclamation point after a mild interjection.

Well, I'm glad that's over.
My, it's really raining.

16.   The comma is used after inverted names in lists.

Thackeray, William M.
Whittier, John Greenleaf

17.   The comma is used to indicate the omission of a word.

Fishing forms a quiet man; hunting, an eager man; racing, a greedy man.

18.   The comma is used to set off a proper name when followed by an academic degree or honorary title. The comma is used to separate two or more degrees or titles.

Philip F. Adams, A.B., M.A., Ph.D., lecturer in English.

19.   The comma is used to point off the thousands in figures of four digits or more.

| 1,117 | 20,718 | 1,817,000 |

Note: Do not use, the comma in telephone, house, page, and policy numbers, or in years.

the year 1933   Policy No. 903451
page 2348   Arlington 7-8903
                  1117 North Pensacola Avenue

20.   The comma is used to separate two sets of figures or two identical words.

John told you, you should apply immediately.
Send me 10, No. 1234 and 7, No. 138.
Since 1933, 12,000 new machines have been sold.

21.   The comma is used to separate a declarative clause and an interrogative clause which immediately follows.

The plane will arrive on time, will it not?
Jack is to get a promotion, isn't he?

22.   The comma is used to separate a phrase from the rest of the sentence when the phrase is inverted or out of its natural order.

Like you, I think the policy is a worthwhile one.
For me, it will mean extra work and less pay.
In spite of his promise, he was late to work again.

USE OF THE SEMICOLON

The semicolon (;) is used to show a stronger separation between the parts of a sentence than does a comma. In practical writing, however, avoid using the semicolon because it is generally too stiff and formal. If you use a great many semicolons, the chances are that you are either using them incorrectly, or you are writing sentences which are too long. Semicolons produce rather involved sentence patterns. Use them sparingly.

1.   The semicolon is used to separate independent coordinate clauses closely connected in meaning when no coordinate conjunction is used.

> The sales staff meets every other Tuesday; the production staff meets only once a month.

> He would not approve the art layout as presented; he suggested several drastic changes.

Note: An example of this rule, as used to avoid the comma fault, was given in Rule 11 under commas.

2.   The semicolon is used between coordinate clauses of a compound sentence when they are joined by transitional words and phrases. The following is a list of commonly used transitional words and phrases:

accordingly	indeed	as a result
afterwards	likewise	at last
again	meanwhile	at the same time
anyhow	moreover	for example
besides	namely	for instance
consequently	nevertheless	for this reason
doubtless	next	in any case
eventually	otherwise	in fact
evidently	perhaps	in like manner
finally	possibly	in short
furthermore	still	on the contrary
hence	then	on the other hand
however	therefore	that is
yet	thus	in addition

Note: Transitional words are usually set off by commas. When you use a semicolon in place of a comma before the transitional word, you usually put a comma after the transitional word. However, when the transitional word retains its adverbial force and is not regarded as an independent element, it is seldom set off with a comma. (See Rule 4 (a) under commas.)

> The members of the board of directors approved the change in distribution; consequently, you should appeal to them.

> The weather was cold and icy; therefore we didn't go.

3. The semicolon is used before a coordinate conjunction (*and, but, for, or, nor*) between two independent clauses when either one or both have internal punctuation. (See Rule 11 under commas.)

> The president, a well-read man, predicted a cost of living increase for the first of the year; but his prediction, which spread throughout the plant, proved to be wrong.

> The staff housekeeper ordered carpets, divans, lamps, tables, and chairs; but her order was incorrectly filled.

4. The semicolon is used before such words as *for example, for instance, that is,* and *namely* that introduce an example, enumeration, or a list in a sentence. A comma is placed after such words.

> These special artist's pencils are available in three colors; namely, red, green, and blue.

> Many of our policies will be changed this year; for example, salesmen will be paid a commission instead of a salary.

5. The semicolon is used in lists where a comma is insufficient to separate the members clearly.

> Guests at the convention were Mr. Leonard Key, the past president of the corporation; Mrs. F. K. Small, the wife of the founder; and Mr. Paul Wells, the speaker of the evening.

USE OF THE COLON

The colon (:) indicates the strongest possible break within a sentence.

1. The colon is used before a list of items or details.

> Please send out the following items: No. 378, No. 315, No. 519, and No. 570.
>
> His actions were as follows: He went to the drugstore, purchased a hypodermic needle, got into his car, and drove away.

Note 1: Capitalize the first letter of each item in a list when the list is in column form.

> You should know how to use the following office machines:
>
> 1. Typewriter
> 2. Duplicator
> 3. Dictaphone

Note 2: Do not capitalize the first letter of each item in a list when the items are included in a sentence.

> You should know how to use the following office machines: typewriter, duplicator, dictaphone, and calculator.

2. The colon is used before an appositive phrase or clause.

> Our company has always had this motto: The customer is always right.
> These are your duties: Sort the mail, open all that is not personal, throw away the envelopes, and bring the letters to me.

Note: Capitalize the first letter of the word which follows the colon when that word introduces a complete sentence, as in the above examples.

3. The colon is used after the salutation of a business letter.

> Dear Mr. Roe:　　　　　Gentlemen:　　　　　My dear Madam:

Note: Never use a semicolon after a salutation. A comma may be used after the salutation of a friendly or informal letter. Some modern writers do not use any punctuation after the salutation.

> Dear Jane,　　-　　　　Dear Father,　　　　　Dear Jones,

4. The colon is used to divide the parts of references, titles, formulas, and numerals.

> The time was 9:15 P.M.
> He assigned Chapter XII: Section 19.

USE OF PARENTHESES

1. Parentheses ( ) are used to set off words, phrases, clauses, or sentences which are used by way of explanation, translation, or comment, but which are independent constructions:

> Hilda (my sister's roommate at college) is coming to visit us.
> The motto read as follows: *"De gustibus non disputandum est."* (In matters of taste there is no dispute.)

2. Parentheses are used to enclose a number, letter, or symbol when used as an appositive.

> She ordered twelve (12) night stands for the hotel.
> The bookkeeper ornamented his letterhead with the percent symbol (%).

Note 1: When using parentheses with other punctuation marks, punctuate the main part of the sentence as if the parenthetical portion was not there. A punctuation mark comes after the second parenthesis if the punctuation mark applies to the whole sentence and not just to the parenthetical portion.

> He analyzed and presented standards of evaluation (business and technical), but his conditions proved nothing.

Note 2: Place the punctuation mark inside the second parenthesis if the punctuation mark applies only to material within the parenthetical portion.

> A simplified fire-fighting plan will help you. (See the back cover of this brochure.)

USE OF THE DASH

The dash (—) is used to indicate an abrupt change of ideas, but should be used sparingly. Excessive use of the dash usually indicates that the writer does not know what punctuation mark to use.

There are times you may want to use the dash for visual effect or emphasis. A glance at advertisements in a newspaper shows that copy writers make frequent use of the dash. However, in business writing, such as letters, reports, minutes, and in social correspondence, use the dash with caution.

1. The dash may be used to indicate a sudden change of thought in a sentence.

> I was certain that the manager—indeed, all of the office force— wanted John to receive the promotion.

2. The dash may be used to indicate a summarizing thought or an afterthought added to the end of the sentence.

> I shall make out an estimate, draw up a contract, send out a man to interpret it for you—give you every help I can.

3. The dash may be used to set off a word or phrase repeated for emphasis.

> We invited them for one meeting—one meeting only—not for the entire convention!

4. The dash may be used between numbers or dates to indicate *to* and *and*.

> His chapter covered from 1860—1868.
> My appointment was scheduled from 12:15—1:15.

Note on the punctuation of parenthetical matter: Close study of the rules on commas, parentheses, and dashes will show you that any one of the three punctuation marks may be used to set off parenthetical words, phrases, or clauses. When should you use the comma, dash, or parentheses? No strict rule can be stated. In general, follow this practice: In punctuating parenthetical matter, use dashes mainly for visual effect; use commas if the material is short; and use parentheses if the material is long.

USE OF BRACKETS

1. Brackets [ ] are used to enclose material added by someone other than the writer; for example, editorial additions or comments.

> The investigation [from June 1, 1950 to April 8, 1951] caused considerable speculation.

> The poet [Robert Browning] did not approve of the excessive adulation during the meeting.

2. Brackets are used to enclose parenthetical matter within parenthetical matter.

> Your order (including items No. 391, No. 394, and No. 286 [No. 288 was out of stock]) was filled last week.

Note: Brackets are rarely used in business and social writing. Generally they are found only in printed material of a scholarly or technical nature.

USE OF THE QUESTION MARK

1. The question mark (?) is used after all interrogative sentences that ask direct questions.

> Where are the current files?
> Are you going to the next meeting of the club?

Note: After requests, use a period instead of a question mark. (See Rule 2 under periods.)

2. The question mark may be used after each separate part of a sentence containing more than one question.

> Can we be sure of his willingness? his capability? his honesty?

Note: If the question is not complete until the end of the sentence, place a question mark at the end only.

> Will delivery be made today, tomorrow, or Friday?

3. The question mark is used in several ways when only part of the sentence is a question. In such sentences the question is generally introduced by a comma or colon; a semicolon or dash may also be used.

> May I ask, what is his purpose?
> This is our problem: What should be done to prevent further damage?
> Our questions are, what date will you arrive? where will you stay? and, do you desire us to furnish transportation?

USE OF THE EXCLAMATION MARK

1. The exclamation mark (!) is used after all exclamatory sentences—sentences that express surprise, emotion, or deep feeling.

> Look out for that train!
> Headlines read, "Peace Treaty Signed!"
> Your answer was hard to believe!

2. The exclamation mark is used after an interjection or a word used as an interjection. At times, the sentence following the interjection may be exclamatory.

> Hurry! The train will pull out in three minutes!
> Oh! I haven't heard that before.

3. The exclamation mark is used after statements which are commands or which imply need for immediate action.

> Return the card today! Don't delay!
> Hurry! Send your order now!

4. The exclamation point is used after an interrogative sentence that is exclamatory in form or intended to be exclamatory.

> Oh, how could he say that!
> But can he be trusted!

5. The exclamation point is sometimes used to add emphasis.

> Realize what this means!
> This offer absolutely expires April 6!

USE OF QUOTATION MARKS

1. Quotation marks (" ") are used to enclose a direct quotation. Each part of an interrupted quotation begins and ends with quotation marks.

> The inspector said, "Well, your case is not hopeless."
> "Where," he asked, "are you going to keep it?"
> "What will we do?" he asked. "Where can we raise the money?"

Note: Capitalize the first word of a direct quotation. Do not capitalize the first word in the second part of an interrupted quotation unless the second part begins a new sentence. Do not use quotation marks or capital letters in an indirect quotation.

> The inspector said that your case is not hopeless. (Many indirect quotations are introduced by the word *that.*)
> He asked where we would keep it.

2. Quotation marks are used to enclose the titles of magazine articles, chapters of books, names of songs, titles of poems, and other titles.

> *The New Yorker* includes a section entitled "The Talk of the Town."
> She asked Ellen to sing "Because" at her wedding.
> "Rabbi Ben Ezra" is one of my favorite poems.

Note: In typing or writing, underline the titles of books, magazines, operas, and any other works of art long enough to appear in book form. Underlining signifies italics for printing. The words, "The New Yorker" in the first sentence above are printed in italic type.

> The anthology, Toward Liberal Education, includes A. E. Housman's "Introductory Lecture" and S. I. Hayakawa's "Poetry and Advertising."
> The soprano sang "If Madam Should Call You" from Mozart's Marriage of Figaro.

3. Quotation marks are used to set off words, phrases, or sentences referred to within a sentence.

> The word "proceed" is frequently mispronounced.
> The phrase "on the other hand" is sometimes used as a transitional phrase.
> The sentence "Now is the time for all good men to come to the aid of their party" is an excellent typing exercise.

4. Quotation marks are used to set off slang words or expressions.

> She said that the office party was held at a "swank" hotel.

Note: Some offices prefer to use underlining instead of quotation marks in situations covered by Rules 3 and 4.

5. If several paragraphs are quoted, use quotation marks at the beginning of each paragraph, but at the end of the last paragraph only. Long quotations are usually introduced by a colon instead of a comma. Quotations of three or more lines are usually indented and set apart from the body of the text.

USE OF QUOTATION MARKS WITH OTHER PUNCTUATION

(a) The period and comma are always placed before ending quotation marks.

> He said, "They are not here."
> "They are not here," he said.

(b) The question mark and exclamation point are placed before quotation marks when they refer only to the quoted material.

> She asked, "When are you going to be promoted?"

(c) The question mark and exclamation point follow ending quotation marks when they refer to the entire sentence.

> Did she say, "You are to be promoted next month"?

(d) The semicolon and colon follow ending quotation marks unless they are part of the quoted matter.

> She said, "You are to be promoted next month"; consequently, I expected to be promoted.

USE OF SINGLE QUOTATION MARKS

1. Single quotation marks are used to set off a quotation within a quotation.

> "Jane," I asked, "did you tell me how to spell the word 'pathologically'?"
> The irate mother said, "You must get all of this 'junk' out of the living-room at once."

Note: Other punctuation marks are used with single quotation marks in the same way as with double quotation marks.

USE OF THE APOSTROPHE

1. The apostrophe (') is used in nouns to show possession.

Note: Keep in mind that the sign of the possessive case is always added to a word. It is not something that is inserted within a word.

(a) If the singular form of the noun does not end in *s* or an *s* sound, add the apostrophe and *s* (*'s*).

Singular	Singular Possessive
boy	boy's
girl	girl's
lady	lady's

(b) If the singular ends in *s* or an *s* sound, add the apostrophe (') or the apostrophe and *s* (*'s*) if the additional *s* sound is desired.

Singular	Singular Possessive
boss	boss' or boss's
dress	dress' or dress's
box	box' or box's

(c) If the plural form of the noun does not end in *s*, add the apostrophe and *s* (*'s*).

Plural	Plural Possessive
men	men's
children	children's
mice	mice's
teeth	teeth's
geese	geese's

(d) If the plural form of the noun ends in *s*, add the apostrophe (').

Plural	Plural Possessive
boys	boys'
girls	girls'
ladies	ladies'

(e) The possessives of proper nouns are formed in the same way as the possessives of common nouns. If the singular form of the name does not end in *s*, add the apostrophe and *s*. If the singular ends in *s* or an *s* sound, add the apostrophe (') or the apostrophe and *s* (*'s*). The plural possessive is always formed by adding the apostrophe to the plural form.

Proper Noun	Singular Possessive	Plural	Plural Possessive
John	John's	Johns	Johns'
Phyllis	Phyllis' or Phyllis's	Phyllises	Phyllises'
Jane	Jane's	Janes	Janes'

(f) Certain expressions relating to *time, distance,* and *value* are also written with an apostrophe.

the day's task	five cents' worth
a year's time	six miles' distance
a minute's notice	three weeks' vacation

(g) The singular possessive and the plural possessive of compound nouns are formed by adding the apostrophe to the end of the compound word.

Singular	Plural
brother-in-law's	brothers-in-law's
father-in-law's	fathers-in-law's

(h) Joint ownership is shown by making the last word in the series possessive. Individual ownership is shown by making both parts possessive.

Alice and Jack's apartment. (joint ownership)
Alice's and Jack's apartments. (individual ownership)

2. The apostrophe is used in indefinite pronouns to show possession. The possessive case of indefinite pronouns is formed in the same way as the possessive case of nouns.

everybody's duty	others' positions
one's coat	someone's hat

3. The apostrophe is used with **s** to form the plural of numbers, letters, signs, and symbols.

Your "r's" look like "n's."
He used twelve "%'s" to decorate his paper.

4. The apostrophe is used to indicate the omission of a word, letters, or numerals.

don't	let's	o'clock
hadn't	it's	she's
isn't	'tis	wouldn't

The accident happened in '18.

GLOSSARY OF TERMS

The following reference list contains definitions of the grammatical terms used in this Handbook. The terms are listed here so that you may quickly refer to them whenever necessary.

Active voice	A verb is in the active voice when it represents the subject as performing the action.
Adjective	An adjective is a word used to modify a noun or a pronoun.
Adjective clause	An adjective clause is a subordinate clause that functions as an adjective.
Adjective phrase	An adjective phrase is a prepositional phrase that functions as an adjective.
Adverb	An adverb is a word that modifies a verb, an adjective, or another adverb.
Adverbial clause	An adverbial clause is a subordinate clause that functions as an adverb.
Adverbial phrase	An adverbial phrase is a prepositional phrase that functions as an adverb.
Antecedent	The antecedent of a pronoun is the noun or pronoun to which it refers.
Appositive	An appositive is a word or a group of words that identifies or explains another word or group of words.
Article	The articles are *a, an,* and *the.* They are regarded as adjectives. *The* is the definite article. *A* and *an* are the indefinite articles.
Auxiliary verb	An auxiliary verb is one that helps the principal verb form a verb phrase.
Case	Case is that property of a noun or pronoun that shows the relation of the noun or pronoun to other words in the sentence.
Clause	A clause is a group of words having a subject and a predicate.

Collective noun	A collective noun is the name of a group or a collection of objects.
Comma fault	The comma fault is the use of a comma as the sole connection between two independent clauses. A comma should not be used for this purpose *unless* a coordinate conjunction is used with the comma.
Common noun	A common noun is the name of any one of a class of persons, places, or things.
Comparative degree	The comparative degree is used when a comparison is made between two persons or things. The comparative degree of *large* is *larger*. (My house is *larger* than yours.)
Comparison	Comparison is the change in the form of an adjective or an adverb to show a difference in degree. There are three degrees of comparison: *positive, comparative,* and *superlative.*
Complement	A complement completes the meaning of the verb.
Complete subject	The complete subject is the simple subject with all its modifiers.
Complete predicate	The complete predicate is the predicate verb or verb phrase with its complements and modifiers.
Complex sentence	A complex sentence is a sentence that consists of one independent clause and one or more subordinate clauses.
Compound complex sentence	A compound complex sentence is a sentence that consists of two independent clauses and one or more subordinate clauses.
Compound predicate	A compound predicate is made up of two or more connected verbs or verb phrases.
Compound relative pronoun	A compound relative pronoun is a pronoun formed by adding *ever* or *soever* to certain relative pronouns.

294

Compound sentence	A compound sentence is a sentence that consists of two or more independent clauses.
Compound subject	A compound subject is made up of two or more connected simple subjects.
Conjugation	The conjugation of a verb is the systematic arrangement of all its forms.
Conjunction	A conjunction is a word used to join words or groups of words.
Coordinate conjunction	A coordinate conjunction is a conjunction that connects words, phrases, and clauses of equal rank.
Dangling modifier	A dangling modifier is a modifier that does not refer to any word in the sentence. The word that it should modify has been left out of the sentence.
Declarative sentence	A declarative sentence makes a statement. A declarative sentence ends with a period.
Demonstrative pronoun	A demonstrative pronoun points out a specific person, place, or thing.
Dependent clause	A dependent clause (subordinate clause) is a group of words that has a subject and a predicate, but does *not* express a complete thought.
Direct address	A noun or pronoun that is used in addressing some person (or persons) is used in direct address.
Direct object	The direct object of a verb names the receiver of the action.
Emphatic form of a verb	The emphatic form of a verb is a form used to give greater emphasis to the idea expressed by the verb. The auxiliaries *do, does,* and *did* are used to give this emphasis.
Exclamatory sentence	An exclamatory sentence expresses strong feeling or sudden emotion. An exclamatory sentence ends with an exclamation mark.

Expletive	An expletive is an introductory word which fills in the place of the grammatical subject. The real subject appears after the verb. An expletive has no grammatical connection with any part of the sentence. The words *it* and *there* are commonly used as expletives.
Future perfect tense	The future perfect tense denotes action that will be completed at some definite time in the future.
Future tense	The future tense denotes future time.
Gerund	A gerund is a verb form (verbal) that is used as a noun.
Gerund phrase	A gerund phrase is a gerund with any complement or modifier that it may take.
Imperative mood	The imperative mood is the mood which expresses a command or a request.
Imperative sentence	An imperative sentence gives a command or makes a request. An imperative sentence ends with a period or an exclamation mark.
Indefinite pronoun	An indefinite pronoun does not point out a definite person, place, or thing.
Independent clause	An independent clause (main clause) is a group of words that has a subject and a predicate and expresses a complete thought. An independent clause is the equivalent of a simple sentence.
Independent element	An independent element is a word or group of words that has no grammatical connection with the rest of the sentence.
Indicative mood	The indicative mood is the mood that is used to make a statement or ask a question.
Indirect object	The indirect object of a verb tells to or for whom something is done.

296

Infinitive	An infinitive is a verb form (verbal) that is used as a noun, an adjective, or an adverb. An infinitive is usually preceded by the word *to*, which is commonly called the sign of the infinitive.
Infinitive phrase	An infinitive phase is an infinitive with any complement or modifier that it may take.
Interjection	An interjection is a word that expresses strong feeling or sudden emotion.
Interrogative adverb	An interrogative adverb introduces a question and modifies the verb.
Interrogative pronoun	An interrogative pronoun asks a question.
Interrogative sentence	An interrogative sentence asks a question. An interrogative sentence ends with a question mark.
Intransitive verb	An intransitive verb is a verb that does not have an object.
Inverted order	The sentence is in inverted order when the predicate, or part of the predicate precedes the subject.
Linking verb	A linking or copulative verb is one that is used to connect the subject with a word that explains or describes the subject. The explanatory word, which may be a noun, a pronoun, or an adjective, follows the verb.
Misplaced modifier	A misplaced modifier is a modifier that is incorrectly placed in the sentence. It seems to modify the wrong word because it is placed nearer to this word than to the correct word.
Modifier	A modifier is a word or group of words that limits or qualifies the meaning of another word.

297

Mood	Mood is the form that the verb takes to show the manner in which the action or state of being is to be regarded—as a *fact*, a *command*, as a *wish, doubt, uncertainty*, etc.
Nominative case	The nominative case is the case of the subject. A predicate noun is also in the nominative case. Nouns have no special form to indicate the nominative case.
Nonrestrictive clause	A nonrestrictive clause is a subordinate clause that is not essential to the meaning of the sentence. A nonrestrictive clause is usually set off by commas.
Normal order	The normal or grammatical order of a sentence is subject first, followed by the predicate.
Noun	A noun is a word used as the name of a person, place, thing, idea, or action.
Noun clause	A noun clause is a subordinate clause that is used as a noun.
Objective case	The objective case is the case of the direct object of a verb or a preposition. Nouns have no special form to show the objective case.
Participial phrase	A participial phrase is a participle with any complement or modifier that it may take.
Participle	A participle is a verb form (verbal) which is used as an adjective.
Parts of speech	Words are classified as parts of speech according to the work they do in sentences. The eight parts of speech are: *nouns, pronouns, verbs, adjectives, adverbs, prepositions, conjunctions,* and *interjections*.
Passive voice	A verb is in the passive voice when it represents the subject as receiving the action.

298

Past perfect tense	The past perfect tense denotes action that was completed at some definite time in the past.
Past tense	The past tense denotes past time.
Person	The *first person* is the person speaking. The *second person* is the person spoken to. The *third person* is the person or thing spoken of.
Personal pronoun	A personal pronoun shows by its form whether it refers to the person speaking, the person spoken to, or the person or thing spoken of.
Phrase	A phrase is a group of words, without a subject and a predicate, that is used as a part of speech.
Positive degree	The positive degree is used when there is no suggestion or comparison. It is the simple form of the adjective or the adverb. The positive degree of the adjective *large* is *large*.
Possessive case	The possessive case shows ownership. Nouns have special forms to show the possessive case.
Predicate	The predicate is the part of a sentence that makes a statement about the subject.
Predicate adjective	A predicate adjective is an adjective that completes the verb and modifies the subject. A predicate adjective is found in the predicate.
Preposition	A preposition is a word that shows the relation between its object and some other word in the sentence.
Prepositional phrase	A prepositional phrase is a group of words which consists of a preposition and its object. The object of the preposition may have modifiers.
Present perfect tense	The present perfect tense denotes action that is completed at the time of speaking or writing.

Present tense	The present tense denotes present time. The present tense is also used to express habitual action, and to express an idea which is generally accepted as true.
Progressive form of a verb	The progressive form of a verb is the form which shows that the action is continuing at the time indicated by the particular tense.
Pronoun	A pronoun is a word used in place of a noun.
Proper noun	A proper noun is the name of a particular member of a class.
Reflexive pronoun	A reflexive or intensive pronoun is a pronoun formed by adding *self* or *selves* to some form of a personal pronoun.
Relative adjective	A relative adjective is a relative pronoun that is used as an adjective. A relative adjective refers to an antecedent in the main clause.
Relative adverb	A relative adverb is an adverb that refers to an antecedent in the main clause and modifies some word in the subordinate clause.
Relative pronoun	A relative pronoun is a pronoun that joins a clause to its antecedent.
Restrictive clause	A restrictive clause is a clause that is essential to the meaning of the sentence. A restrictive clause is *not* set off by commas. A restrictive clause defines, limits, or identifies the word it modifies.
Run-on sentence	A run-on sentence is a sentence in which two independent clauses are written as a single sentence, without the use of a conjunction or any mark of punctuation to separate them.
Sentence	A sentence is a group of words that expresses a complete thought. A sentence must have both a subject and a predicate. Sentences are classified into the following four groups, according to the purpose they serve: *declarative, interrogative, imperative,* and *exclamatory.*

300

Simple predicate	The simple predicate is the verb or verb phrase.
Simple sentence	A simple sentence is a sentence having one subject and one predicate, either or both of which may be compound.
Simple subject	The simple subject names the person, place, or thing that is talked about.
Subject	The subject of a sentence is the part about which something is said.
Subjunctive mood	The subjunctive mood is the mood that is used to express doubt, wish, uncertainty, or a condition that is contrary to fact.
Subordinate conjunction	A subordinate conjunction is a conjunction that is used to connect a subordinate clause with the main clause.
Superlative degree	The superlative degree is used when more than two persons or things are compared. The superlative degree of *large* is *largest*. (My house is the *largest* house in the block.)
Tense	The tense of a verb is the change in the form of the verb to show the time of the action or state of condition.
Transitive verb	A transitive verb is a verb that has an object. The action expressed by the verb passes over to a receiver.
Verb	The verb is a word that expresses action or state of being. Verbs that express state of being are called linking verbs, or copulative verbs.
Verbal	A verbal is a verb form that is used as another part of speech. Participles, gerunds, and infinitives are verbals.
Verb phrase	A verb phrase is a verb that consists of more than one word. It is composed of a principal verb and one or more auxiliary verbs.
Voice	Voice is that property of a verb which shows whether the subject is performing the action or is receiving the action.

COMPREHENSIVE INDEX

COMPREHENSIVE INDEX

A

Antecedent (*con't*):
defined 74
indefinite or vague 81
of compound personal pronoun 64
pronoun agreement with 74-84
any, anybody, see Indefinite pronoun
Apostrophe, use of 101-107, 291
Appositive:
infinitive used as 271
noun clause used as 232
punctuation 232, 278, 284
are (form of *to be*) see *be*
around, about 194
Articles, definite and indefinite 19
as—as, not so—as 225
as if, as though 226
Auxiliary verb:
defined 15
list of, commonly used 16
to indicate tense 135-141, 149-151
Awkward expressions:
with passive voice 169
with split infinitive 269

B

bad, badly 130
band, see Collective noun
be, linking verb:
complements of, see Complement
forms of 13, 90
gerund forms 251
in infinitive clause 267
modifiers of, see Modifier
participial forms 242
subjunctive forms 171-174
tense of 151-152
use with passive voice 166
use with progressive forms 155
because, see Subordinating conjnction
become 90
behind, in back of 196
beside, besides 194
between, among 195
between you and me 61
Book titles, capitalization 50
underlining, punctuation 289
Brackets, rules for use 287
Business names, capitalization 46-52
but, as preposition 133, 193
as conjunction, see Conjunction

C

call, conjugation of 153-157, 167
came, come 137-141
can't in double negative 132
also see Contraction
can't help but 133
Capitalization, rules and examples 46-52
appositive statement after colon 285
book, song titles, etc. 50
building, monument, street names 47
business names 48, 51-52
clubs, political parties 48
compound words 52
days, months, holidays 49
department names 48, 52
geographic names 46
governmental bodies 48, 52
historical events and periods 47
items in lists 284
names of persons, etc. 48, 52
personified seasons 49
planet names, etc. 49
proper adjectives 46
proper nouns 46-52
regions, localities 47
religious books 51
school subjects 51
sections of country (North, etc.) 49
titles of rank, etc. 48, 52
words derived from proper nouns 50
words showing relationships 52
Case:
defined 95
following linking verb 96, 99
following action verb 96, 100
nominative and objective 95-100
of noun 95-105
of pronoun 98-108, 193, 215, 266-268
possessive 101-108, 253
with infinitive 266-268
Clause:
adjective 212-214
adverbial 219-227
coordinate and subordinate 199-200
independent in compound sentence 199-203
independent in complex sentence 210
infinitive 257-273
interrogative 281, 287

306

D

Dangling modifier:
   gerund 254
   participle 244
Dash, rules for use 286
Dates, punctuation 281, 286
Declarative sentence 35, 275
Definite article, *the* 25
Degree:
   adverbs of 124
   clauses of 222
Degrees of Comparison:
   adjective 116-119
   adverb 127
Delayed subject 41, 271
Demonstrative adjective 70
Demonstrative pronoun 62, 67, 83
Dependent clause, see Subordinate clause
Descriptive adjective 113
did, done 137-141
differ from, differ with 195
different from different than 195
Direct address, noun in 40, 278
Direct object: also see Object
   defined 85-88
Direct quotation 289-290
do, did, done 137-141, 157
don't, doesn't 176, 182
Double negative 132
dove, dived 137-141
drank, drunk 137-138

E

each, each one, see Indefinite pronoun
-ed, -d suffixes 143
Editorial comments with brackets 287
either, neither, see Indefinite pronoun
either . . . or 177-179
-er, -est suffixes of degree 116-118
Ellipsis (omitted words) 276
Emotion:
   expressed by exclamatory sentence 35
   expressed by interjection 25
Emphasis:
   by emphatic use of pronoun 64
   by punctuation 286, 288
   by use of active or passive voice 169
   by word order 37, 223, 233
   position of adverb for 21
Emphatic forms of verb 157
ever, soever 68

every 183
everybody, everyone, see Indefinite
   pronoun
Exclamation mark 18, 36
   rules for use of 275, 288
Exclamatory sentence, defined 35
   punctuation of 275, 288
   word order in 39
Exclamatory word, see Interjection
Expletive:
   it with infinitive 271
   it with noun clause 233
   there 41, 186
except, meaning expressed by *but* 133
except, outside of 196

F

farther, further 119
Faulty reference (antecedent) 81
Feminine words, see Gender
for, see Conjunction and Preposition
for example, see Transitional word
from, with *different* or *differ* 195
Fragmentary sentence 32
Function of words 9, 26
further, farther 119
Future perfect tense, see Tense
Future tense, see Tense

G

Gender:
   agreement of antecedent and pronoun
     74-84
   of indefinite pronoun 77-79
   of noun 75-76
   of pronoun, special forms 75-76
Geographical names, capitalization 46
Gerund:
   clause substituted for 254
   complements of 250
   dangling 254
   modifiers of 251-253
   phrase 250, 254
   possessive case with 253
gone, went 137-141
good, well 118, 130
Grammatical order 36-40

H

half 185
hard, hardly 123, 132
have, with subjunctive 171-173

308

310

312

314

315

NOTES

NOTES

NOTES

NOTES

How to Order
Extra Copies of This Book

This book is one of a series of books which make up
the complete *Instant Reference Library*. Titles currently
included in the series are as follows. Other titles will
be added from time to time.

> Instant Spelling Dictionary
> Instant English Handbook
> Instant Quotation Dictionary
> Instant Synonyms and Antonyms
> Instant Medical Spelling Dictionary
> Instant World Atlas
> Instant Business Dictionary
> Instant Medical Adviser
> Instant Secretary's Handbook
> Instant Sewing Handbook
> Instant Home Repair Handbook

You may order any of the above books from your local
bookstore, or send your order directly to Career Institute,
Dept. 32151, 555 East Lange Street, Mundelein, Illinois
60060. Individuals, send check or money order. No COD's.
Business firms or other organizations with established credit
may send purchase order and be billed after delivery. The
books are available in either an attractive, colorful standard
edition at $2.65 or a deluxe leatherette, gold-stamped edition
at $3.45, less the following quantity discounts:

Quantity	Discount
1 to 5 books	None
6 to 15 books	15¢ per book
16 to 49 books	25¢ per book
50 to 149 books	35¢ per book

Orders for different titles may be combined to take ad-
vantage of the above quantity prices. On orders for three
or less, add 35 cents for postage and handling. Please speci-
fy whether you wish the "Standard" or "Deluxe" binding. Illinois residents add 5% Sales Tax.